Witchcraft, Oracles, and Magic
among the Azande

Witchcraft, Oracles, and Magic among the Azande

E. E. EVANS-PRITCHARD

ABRIDGED WITH AN INTRODUCTION
BY Eva Gillies

CLARENDON PRESS · OXFORD

OXFORD
UNIVERSITY PRESS

Great Clarendon Street, Oxford OX2 6DP

Oxford University Press is a department of the University of Oxford.
It furthers the University's objective of excellence in research, scholarship,
and education by publishing worldwide in

Oxford New York

Auckland Cape Town Dar es Salaam Hong Kong Karachi Kuala Lumpur
Madrid Melbourne Mexico City Nairobi New Delhi Shanghai Taipei Toronto

With offices in

Argentina Austria Brazil Chile Czech Republic France Greece
Guatemala Hungary Italy Japan Poland Portugal Singapore
South Korea Switzerland Thailand Turkey Ukraine Vietnam

Oxford is a registered trade mark of Oxford University Press
in the UK and in certain other countries

Published in the United States
by Oxford University Press Inc., New York

British Library Cataloguing in Publication Data
Data available

Library of Congress Cataloging in Publication Data
Data available

ISBN 978-0-19-874029-2

33

Printed in Great Britain
on acid-free paper by the
MPG Books Group, Bodmin and King's Lynn

Contents

Contents

Introduction

I

In presenting an abridged version of *Witchcraft, Oracles, and Magic among the Azande*, nearly forty years after its first publication, one cannot help feeling a trifle uncomfortable about the use of the ethnographic present. After all, the fieldwork this book refers to was done in the late 1920s: what is described here is a world long vanished. It will, I hope, presently appear that it is a world still fresh and relevant to the modern anthropologist, as well as to the philosopher and the historian of ideas. But for the Azande themselves, living as they do in turbulent Central Africa, in the watershed zone between the Nile and the Congo, time can hardly be said to have stood still meanwhile (nor, as we shall see, was it doing so at the period when Evans-Pritchard lived among them).

The traditional Zande homeland today lies across the frontiers of three modern African states: the Republic of the Sudan, Zaïre, and the République Centrafricaine. In Evans-Pritchard's day, all these territories were under colonial dominance: the Sudan was Anglo-Egyptian, Zaïre was the Belgian Congo, and the République Centrafricaine formed part of the vast expanse of French Equatorial Africa. Evans-Pritchard, engaged in ethnographic survey work for the Government of the Anglo-Egyptian Sudan, perforce concentrated his research on the Sudanese Azande, though he did, on his first two expeditions, also visit the Belgian Congo. Except where otherwise indicated, references to colonial Government, European influence, etc., therefore allude to the Government of the Anglo-Egyptian Sudan and its impact upon traditional Zande custom.

Evans-Pritchard found the Sudanese Azande living in sparsely wooded savannah country—a vast plain crossed by innumerable small tree-fringed streams. The structure of the countryside was, indeed, revealed only during the dry season—April to November—when the bush vegetation was fired; during the rains the whole land was covered with high, dense grass, so that in walking it was difficult to leave the man-made paths.

To the west, the Azande living under French administration occupied much the same vegetation-belt; those of the Belgian Congo on the other hand lived on the threshold of the tropical rain forest, which becomes denser as it nears the Equator.

The Azande at that time lived by cultivating the soil, by hunting, fishing, and collecting wild produce. They grew eleusine, corn, sweet potatoes, manioc, ground-nuts, bananas, and a variety of legumes and of oil-bearing plants. Evans-Pritchard speaks of the abundance of game, and of the annual swarmings of termites, which were eaten as a delicacy.

Azande also showed great technical ability as smiths, potters, carvers, basket-makers, and in a number of other crafts; but at the time of Evans-Pritchard's residence amongst them they had little opportunity to sell their labour, or incentive to grow marketable produce. Their culture was thus in important respects shielded from outside influences, though in other matters such influences were already substantially affecting traditional custom.

Azande also kept domestic fowls (which indeed played a central part, as we shall see, in their techniques for the control of hostile forces), but they did not use cattle. Nor could they in fact have kept them: their country was infested with tse-tse fly (*Glossina* spp.) conveying micro-organisms that cause trypanosomiasis in cattle as well as sleeping-sickness in man. In the 1920s the colonial Government was trying to control sleeping-sickness by concentrating the previously scattered population into large settlements along the new Government roads. Evans-Pritchard in fact did much of his work in such settlements and writes of the traditional pattern of residence in the past tense:

The whole countryside was dotted with homesteads, abodes of single families, often widely separated from each other by cultivations and stretches of forest. If we had taken a cross-section of a Zande district we would have found that a homestead comprised a man and his wife, or wives, and children, while his nearest neighbours were generally related to him by bonds of kinship or marriage.[1]

This traditional pattern of scattered residence had originally reflected a highly organized indigenous political system. The vast area here described as the Zande homeland in fact con-

[1] Evans-Pritchard 1937, p. 14.

sisted of a number of tribal kingdoms, separated from each other by wide fringes of unpopulated bush. Each kingdom was ruled by a different member of a single royal dynasty, the Avongara, under whose leadership the 'true' Azande (or, as they were also called, the Ambomu) had earlier conquered the land—displacing or, more frequently, absorbing a number of other peoples of the most varied ethnic and linguistic origins.

The number and size of these kingdoms varied in the course of time. The Avongara were an adventurous and warlike breed and, in the absence of a fixed rule of succession, many an ambitious prince had in pre-colonial days preferred to carve out a domain for himself rather than remain in feudal subjection to a father or brother. But the organization and lay-out of the kingdoms everywhere followed the same cultural pattern. Each was divided into provinces, administered by the king's younger brothers and sons and a few wealthy non-Avongara commoners appointed by him. The central province of each kingdom was under the monarch's personal administration: its people were his subjects in a much more immediate sense than those of the surrounding provinces, whose governors, though bound to pay tribute to the king and to obey his summons to war, enjoyed a large measure of autonomy. Particularly was this so in the case of princes. Commoner governors were rather more dependent on the king, who could and did displace them at pleasure, usually in favour of his own sons—though he seems in general to have felt it necessary to find some excuse for doing so. In speaking of the differences between the status of princely and commoner governors, Evans-Pritchard adds a cautionary gloss:

'Nevertheless when I speak of princes it must be understood that the commoner governors are included unless they are specifically excluded. Indeed, in a discussion of the organization and procedure of a ... court, king, prince and governor are all more or less interchangeable terms. A king's court was on a larger scale than a prince's but otherwise differed from it in no significant way, and he was governor in his province as they were in theirs. Likewise, a commoner governor's court does not seem to have differed in form and function from that of noble rulers.[2]

These courts were situated in each case at the centre of the province concerned, that of the king being therefore at the

[2] Evans-Pritchard 1971, p. 169.

centre both of his own province and of the whole kingdom. Broad paths struck out, starlike, from the royal court to the courts of the governors, and it was the responsibility of each governor to see that these paths were maintained in serviceable condition.

Each governor's court (and, in his capacity as governor of his own province, also the king's) was in turn the hub of a similar system, albeit on a smaller scale. At the centre was the court of the provincial ruler, from which lesser paths radiated to the hamlets where his principal deputies resided. Each deputy was responsible to his governor for summoning the people of his district for war and labour, and for collecting tribute when required; and it was his duty to maintain order in that district, to keep the all-important paths clear, to settle minor disputes on behalf of his master, and generally to keep him informed of all that went on in the district. (Military organization was separate from this, there being companies of warriors for each province.)

Each deputy usually chose for his homestead a site near one of the many small streams that traversed the country, and his relatives and clients settled, each in the midst of his own cultivations, more or less in the vicinity. In other words, the scattered residential pattern that had pre-existed colonial rule faithfully reflected a political system which, though highly organized, displayed throughout a hierarchical delegation of authority.

Now, the initial aim of the colonial administration was, in accordance with the then well-established principle of Indirect Rule, 'to rule the country through the media of the tribal "chiefs" and "sultans" subject to the right of appeal by the natives to a Government official'.[3] In one way this was a wise policy, since it was clearly impossible to rule the Azande otherwise than through the Avongara princes whose authority they recognized. At the same time some effort seems to have been made to preserve the Zande way of life from foreign influences, especially from the Arabic culture which could have been expected to infiltrate in the wake of colonial officials (Egyptian, it must be remembered, as well as British), their servants and the ubiquitous Egyptian and Sudanese traders. Evans-Pritchard speaks with obvious approval of the then District

[3] *Bahr El Ghazal Province Handbook* 1911, p. 37.

Commissioner, Major Larken, who 'has consistently spoken Zande and discouraged, I may even say fanatically discouraged, the use of Arabic and the borrowing of Islamic customs and beliefs'.[4]

But cultural conservatism is notoriously fraught with difficulties, and Indirect Rule, as indeed later experience has shown everywhere, necessarily a contradiction in terms. A ruling aristocracy like the Avongara cannot genuinely retain its traditional position when the real source of authority lies outside the system. In the early 1920s, new administrative measures had led to more direct control by government agencies, to the further detriment of traditional political organization.

First of all, the central feature of that organization had quite simply vanished when the king was replaced by a District Commissioner, however conscientious and enlightened. The Azande themselves seem to have felt this acutely. The part of their country in which Evans-Pritchard principally worked had been the domain of one King Gbudwe, a highly astute and successful monarch after the traditional model. Gbudwe had been killed in an affray with British forces in 1905, but his memory was still revered by his people. Evans-Pritchard writes:

> To Azande his death was not simply the death of a king but ... the end of an epoch, nay more, it was a catastrophe that changed the whole order of things. When older men talk about their customs they contrast what happens today with what happened 'when Gbudwe was alive', and in their opinion what happened in the days of Gbudwe is what ought to happen. Although Gbudwe died only twenty-one years before I commenced my work in his kingdom, his reign was already being looked back to with regrets by those who had experienced his rule. To them it was the Golden Age of law and custom.[5]

In the late 1920s Gbudwe's sons and other provincial governors still retained courts; but the courts themselves had been much reduced in size and importance, shorn of their glamour, no longer founts of patronage or power. War, the mainstay of the Zande political system, was no longer a possibility; the companies of warriors and pages had gone, and men no longer

---

[4] Evans-Pritchard 1937, p. 18.
[5] Ibid., p. 19

flocked to court for spears or other gifts or favours—indeed, there were seldom more than a few men there at any one time. Nor, when they did come, did they find the old lavish hospitality; for the princes now received from their subjects but little tribute, or help in planting and harvesting their crops. Even that little was given almost secretly, and could under no circumstances be enforced as it had been in former days: colonial administration had replaced labour in a prince's cultivations by labour on government roads, and held moreover that a prince had no right to exact service from his subjects

The princes still had a number of wives, but they no longer had the same control over them, for if they ran away it was not easy to get them back. If an outraged princely husband tried to do so, the wives could complain of ill-treatment at an administrative centre; and princes, understandably, were anxious to avoid having to answer to the Government in matters of this kind. Indeed, in Evans-Pritchard's day the general authority of men over women, as of elders over young men, was being undermined throughout Zandeland; here, too, old men would speak with longing of good King Gbudwe's golden days, when young men knew their place and wives were properly submissive. But even in the 1920s family life, based as it was on polygynous marriage and patrilocal residence, was still 'characterized by the inferiority of women and the authority of elders'.[6]

To return to the surviving princely courts, perhaps the most insidious change of all was that they were no longer, as they had been in the past, the ultimate tribunals of justice. In pre-colonial days, as we have seen, minor disputes were settled by a governor's deputy, who simply informed his master; more serious cases, however (typically witchcraft and adultery), were taken up to the provincial court, there to be settled by the prince—or, strictly speaking, by his poison oracle, which, as Evans-Pritchard says, was 'in the old days ... in itself the greater part of what we know as rules of evidence, judge, jury and witnesses'.[7]

The poison oracle is described in detail in Chapter VIII. Essentially it is a method for obtaining answers to obscure or difficult questions by administering poison to fowls; the verdict

---

[6] Evans-Pritchard 1937, p. 16.   [7] Ibid., p. 267.

of the oracle is expressed by whether or not the fowl survives the ordeal. The poison used by the Azande was a red powder extracted from a particular forest creeper; this was mixed with water to a paste, from which the liquid was then squeezed out into the beaks of small domestic fowls, which were compelled to swallow it. The dose was generally followed by violent convulsions; sometimes these proved fatal, but just as often the fowls recovered. Some, indeed, seemed unaffected by the poison. Evans-Pritchard took a sample of the powder back to England for chemical analysis; it proved to be analogous in many of its properties to strychnine.

The point here, obviously, is the unpredictability of the chicken's reaction: it is the fowl's behaviour under the ordeal, and more especially its death or survival, that answers the question put to the oracle, and unpredictability seems a guarantee of truth (much as we might distinguish between a 'rigged' experiment and a 'genuine' one by the uncertainty of the outcome). Azande operated a number of other oracular devices, but the poison oracle was regarded as the most reliable of all, and was therefore the one used in administering justice.

The two most frequent categories of cases, as has been stated, concerned witchcraft and adultery. Witchcraft was in fact tantamount to murder, since all deaths were *ipso facto* attributed to the maleficent action of human witches. These were, after any death except that of an infant, identified in a preliminary manner by private consultation of poison oracles on behalf of a surviving kinsman or kinsmen; and the verdict was then, in Zande eyes, irrefutably confirmed if the prince's oracle assented to the names placed before it. The compensation payable by the witch was laid down by custom. In a case of adultery, circumstantial evidence might be adduced, but here again the only really certain proof was held to be the verdict of the poison oracle; indeed an accused man's best defence was himself to request an oracular consultation to vindicate his innocence.

To Azande, believing as they did implicitly in the oracle's impartiality and reliability, these judicial procedures were highly satisfactory. To the colonial Government, naturally enough, they were superstitious nonsense. The new legal codes refused to recognize the reality of witchcraft, they did not accept the evidence of oracles, nor did they admit either compensation paid by witches or magical vengeance wreaked upon them. Princes were not supposed to hear cases except in government courts and under government supervision; and, though people did still in fact ask for verdicts from provincial oracles, they saw little point in paying fees for consultations whose outcome no longer had any legal validity. For the princes had now no certain means of enforcing judgements given in their courts: the case could always be taken to a government court afterwards, not on appeal but as if no judgement had been given. This was perhaps the most far-reaching of all the subtle changes wrought by early colonial rule in the texture of Zande society and culture.

The Azande seem to have reacted to the disruption of their notions of law and order by importing from neighbouring peoples new ways of protecting themselves against unseen malice. These were the secret societies described in Chapter XII, which constitute perhaps one of the most intriguing phenomena recorded in this book. Evans-Pritchard states that information about these societies was, in the nature of things, hard to come by; and also that it was difficult for him to make sense of it and fit it in with the rest of his data. Indeed, as he himself clearly saw, his account of the new secret societies rather spoilt the neat symmetry of his witchcraft–oracles–magic triangle.

In borrowing this cultural device so readily from their neighbours the Azande were acting very much 'in character'. Evans-Pritchard describes them in general terms as follows:

... the Azande are so used to authority that they are docile; ... it is unusually easy for Europeans to establish contact with them; ... they are hospitable, good-natured, and almost always cheerful and sociable; ... they adapt themselves without undue difficulty to new conditions of life and are always ready to copy the behaviour of those they regard as their superiors in culture, and to borrow new modes of dress, new weapons and utensils, new words and even new ideas and habits ... they are unusually intelligent, sophisticated and progressive, offering little opposition to foreign administration, and displaying little scorn of foreigners.[8]

In thus characterizing the Azande, Evans-Pritchard is careful to point out that he is here speaking only of commoners—that is, of non-members of the Avongara ruling class, which functioned both as a dynasty in all Zande kingdoms, and as

[8] Evans-Pritchard 1937, p. 13.

an exclusive aristocracy. All other Azande were of commoner status; though within this latter category Evans-Pritchard found a degree of differentiation between the Ambomu (or 'true' Azande) conquerors of the land and the various tribes they had originally subdued, whose members were collectively known as Auro. He believed, however, that the Ambomu/Auro distinction—in any case less marked than that between Avongara and commoners—depended less on birth than on political interests, the Ambomu as a rule keeping in closer touch with court life, even in Evans-Pritchard's day, than did other people. They also tended to be rather richer.

But the real difference lay between Avongara and commoners. The Avongara still, in the 1920s, lived on the diminishing tribute of commoners; thus, they took no part whatsoever in food production, beyond the killing of an occasional beast. Unlike their subjects, whom they held in contempt, they were haughty, conservative in their ways, resenting change and the European conquerors who had brought it about. Evans-Pritchard has left us an unforgettable picture of this doomed and disdainful aristocracy:

They are often handsome, frequently talented, and can be charming hosts and companions, but generally they mask behind a cold politeness their dislike of the new order of things and of those who impose it, and I found that, with rare exceptions, they were useless as informants, since they firmly refused to discuss their customs and beliefs, always deflecting conversation into some other channel ... Englishmen in Zandeland will not often mistake a commoner for a nobleman or vice versa. There is an aristocratic touch about their dress, the way they do their hair, the way they hold their heads, the way they walk, and their manner of speech and their tone of voice, and politeness of conversation, in their hands unused to toil, and in the expression of their faces, which show that they are men whose superiority is never challenged and whose commands receive immediate obedience.[9]

Such then, aristocrats and commoners, were the Azande as Evans-Pritchard knew them around the years 1926–9. He was, even then, consciously concerned to record what he knew to be a fast disappearing mode of life and belief; and since his day the constraints and influences then affecting Zande life have

[9] Evans-Pritchard 1937, pp. 13–14.

themselves shifted in a number of ways. In the early 1920s, as we have seen, the colonial Government had moved the people into settlements along the roads in order to control sleeping-sickness; by 1940 the number of cases of the disease had diminished appreciably, and the regulations were accordingly relaxed: people could once more live where they pleased. The Azande themselves seem to have interpreted this as an official order to leave the road settlements, to which they had by then become accustomed;[10] but worse was to follow. Up to 1940 the colonial Government's main concerns had been to keep the peace and protect the Zande population from outside influences; now, although these aims remained in force, they became overshadowed by another. The Government was now preoccupied with the long-term economic and social development of the southern Sudan, and indeed of the tropical African dependencies in general; and during the early 1940s Zande District was selected for the operation of a pilot scheme designed, ultimately, to fit this and other remote African peoples into the world economy.

The Zande Scheme, as the project came to be known, was essentially concerned with growing cotton for the world market. The aims were benevolently paternalistic:

to make these areas very nearly self-contained and to enable them to market sufficient ... products to enable them to obtain the small amount of ... funds for self-sufficiency ... [The scheme aimed] at nothing less than the complete social emergence and economic stability of the Zande people.[11]

For these laudable purposes, the Equatoria Projects Board was set up in 1946 by the Sudan Government, with a generous allocation of funds. And the Board was to do everything: supervise the growing of the cotton, buy it from the producers, organize its spinning and weaving at the new industrial centre of Nzara, export the production and, by setting up a network of shops 'protect the population from being exploited by commercial enterprise ... [and] teach it how to spend with wisdom the income from its cash crop'.[12]

[10] Reining 1966, pp. 101–2.
[11] H. Ferguson: 'The Zande Scheme'. _Empire Cotton-Growing Review_, April 1949, pp. 2–3; quoted in: De Schlippe 1956, p. 20.
[12] De Schlippe 1956, p. 21.

The growing of cotton, it was felt, would require particularly close supervision; not only because Azande had never grown it before, but in order to ensure a rational use of the land, soil conservation, and a proper rotation of crops. Accordingly, a resettlement plan was devised, whereby during the period 1945–50 between fifty and sixty thousand households were moved from the 1920s roadside settlements to areas of planned dispersal over the countryside.

On the basis of their national character and past history it was believed that the Azande as a whole would welcome such a move. They were regarded as docile, adaptable, above all obedient to their native rulers through whom it was intended to implement the new measures; moreover, a scattered settlement pattern had been traditional to them in pre-colonial days, and close spatial contiguity was associated with witchcraft fears. But the planners, and the resettlement officer himself (a well-intentioned and experienced former District Commissioner) had reckoned without the effects of time and change. Reining, an American anthropologist who visited the Azande in the 1950s, found them complaining bitterly of isolation—not only from the hospitals and other facilities to which they had, in the course of a generation, become accustomed, but also from each other. He comments:

The discomfort caused by isolation may seem strange when we recall that the traditional settlements were scattered through the forest. But the new type of settlement had no features that reminded the people of the older mode of residence, and furthermore they did not want to live in that manner. Almost without exception they yearned after the life on the roads. ... A very common Zande complaint was that they could no longer live *in the manner normal to them—that is, with their relatives.* Histories obtained from some families showed that in the roadside settlements sons often lived next to their fathers, and brothers lived adjacent or very near to each other. [Italics mine][13]

As we have seen,[14] it is true enough that in the pre-colonial dispersed pattern of residence a man's 'nearest neighbours were generally related to him by bonds of kinship or marriage'—bonds of which the new resettlement plan took no account. But at the same time, one cannot help suspecting that Zande ideas

---

[13] Reining op. cit., pp. 114–15.   [14] Cf. p. 2 above.

about the manner in which it was 'normal' for them to live had changed within a generation; though idealized accounts of pre-European days were still adduced as validation.[15]

Most interestingly of all, the renewed spacing out of homes seems to have done nothing to allay witchcraft fears. These were certainly still active at this period, and Azande still believed witchcraft to be most effective at close range. But their concern with such forces was, as always, triggered only by actual misfortune; then, indeed, they would consult diviners and oracles and, if it seemed advisable, move their homestead elsewhere. In the days of the roadside settlements, this had still been possible; now, with freedom of movement restricted by the resettlement plan, it seems likely that witchcraft fears had, if anything, increased.[16]

Reining is silent on the subject of the secret societies. Laynaud, a French anthropologist who visited the Azande under French colonial rule at about the same period, reports these associations as still active in that area.[17] The Avongara rulers, incidentally, were still objecting to them as strongly as they did in Evans-Pritchard's day.

On the whole, the ruling princes seem to have disliked the Zande Scheme less than most Azande. The resettlement plan, carried out through their authority, seemed to enhance it; and their subjects, once assigned to a particular plot of land and obliged to stay there, were likely to be easier to control. The princes also benefited from a small cotton bonus. But the long-term price was heavy: the rulers became more and more identified, in the eyes of their subjects, with an increasingly unpopular policy and, inevitably, the commoners became more and more disaffected.[18]

At the same time, new leaders were emerging. Western education was slow to develop in Zandeland, but there had

[15] Reining, op. cit., pp. 99, 114.

[16] Op. cit., pp. 125–6.

[17] Laynaud 1963, p. 346. The Azande on that side of the border had also been moved into roadside settlements during the inter-war years, but had been left pretty much undisturbed thereafter; Laynaud speaks of them as being (in 1955) in demographic decline, but retaining much of their traditional culture. The Congolese Azande on the other hand had been set to cotton-planting as early as the 1930s; this venture was economically more successful than the Sudanese one, and Sudanese Azande in the 1950s spoke enviously of Congolese wages and prices (Reining, op. cit., pp. 184–6).

[18] Reining, op. cit., pp. 27–38, 117–18.

been mission schools of a kind since 1916, and in 1927 the Government instituted a system of 'elementary vernacular schools'. These, as elsewhere in British colonial Africa, trained essentially village teachers and clerks: people who promptly and vocally resented both the arbitrary workings of the Zande Scheme and what they perceived as the despotism and greed of the traditional rulers. A traditionalist/modern cleavage began to overlay the old Avongara/commoner distinctions; in 1954, when the first parliamentary elections were held in the district, educated commoners successfully pitted their own candidate against the son of the ruling prince.[19]

These parliamentary elections took place during the period of internal self-government that was scheduled to precede full independence for the Republic of the Sudan. Other changes were afoot also: British officials were increasingly replaced by Sudanese, which in this historical context meant northern Sudanese. In 1955, conflict between Zande workers and the new northern Sudanese manager of the industrial centre at Nzara sparked off a riot which led to the establishment of martial law in the area, and was a factor contributing later on to a much more serious mutiny of the southern Sudanese troops against their new northern officers.[20] 1956 brought full independence, 1958 a military *coup d'état* in Khartoum; since 1962 the history of the southern Sudan has been, for much of the time, both bloodstained and confused. In the course of a civil war lasting, all in all, for some seventeen years, large numbers of Azande are said to have seeped across the border into what is now Zaïre.[21] For those who remain, things may be settling down again after the 1972 Addis Ababa Agreement; the hated northern officers have been replaced by southerners, and some of the bitterness of 1955 seems to have died down.[22] It remains to be seen how the remaining Azande will fare under this newest régime; but in any case, life must have changed for them beyond all recognition.

II

Fortunately, however, anthropological monographs are not meant to have 'news value' in the same sense as a factual *exposé*,

[19] Op. cit., pp. 9, 29, 118–19.   [20] Op. cit., pp. 215–16.
[21] A. Singer, personal communication.   [22] C. A. Bilal, personal communication.

but to contribute to a developing corpus of solidly based reasoning upon the principles governing human interaction at different times and in different places. Data must obviously be
reliable at the time and place of their collection; but in the
last resort data are raw material for theory, and theory is, or
should be, an ongoing process. Thus each original work,
fathered so to speak by theory upon raw data, can itself
be seen as a link in the lengthening genealogy of the
subject, with traceable ancestors and acknowledged descendants.

This can be seen particularly clearly with a book like *Witchcraft, Oracles, and Magic among the Azande.* First published in 1937,
when anthropological modes of approach to the study of human
societies were already well-established, it has, in the time that
has elapsed since then, fathered a number of quite distinguish-
able lines of descent. And, in the best tradition of genealogical
charters, the apical ancestor is frequently cited as validation:
even today it is quite difficult to write about witchcraft, magic,
beliefs concerning causation, the expression of social conflicts
and tensions in mystical idiom, or indeed the general sociology
of knowledge, without mentioning the name of Evans-
Pritchard.

Above the apical ancestor, the genealogy, though inevitably
foreshortened, is still clear enough. From Evans-Pritchard the
line goes directly back to the great Frenchman, Lévy-Bruhl, and
beyond him to Durkheim and others of the *Année Sociologique*
group, with Marx standing as a less overtly acknowledged
ancestor in the dimmer background. Lévy-Bruhl's reputation
seems now to be recovering from a temporary eclipse; Evans-
Pritchard himself certainly acknowledged his debt to him, and
indeed paid tribute to the 'exceptional brilliance and ori-
ginality' which triumphantly outweighed the elder author's
theoretical flaws.[23] What he was querying was Lévy-Bruhl's
postulate of a special 'primitive' cast of mind to explain
apparently irrational beliefs; but he fastened eagerly upon the
French writer's insights into the nature of 'collective representations': that is, of those beliefs which, after eliminating all individual variation, are the same for all members of a particular
society or social segment—the unquestioned basic assumptions

[23] Evans-Pritchard 1934, p. 9.

upon which, in that society or segment, all other reasoning must perforce be based. These are beliefs and assumptions collectively held, which every individual unconsciously accepts as a result of the pervasive influences exercised by society; and Lévy-Bruhl (though he owed the concept itself of 'collective representations' to Durkheim) had explored their nature much further than anyone else before him.

Marx, Durkheim, and Lévy-Bruhl had shared a concern to explain the tenacity of what seemed to them irrational religious beliefs; but Evans-Pritchard took the problem well beyond the sphere of religion. Taking as his starting-point the unquestioning belief of his highly intelligent, sophisticated, often sceptical Zande informants in the evil powers of witches and the reliability of the poison oracle, he asks why men anywhere should entertain any metaphysical assumptions at all. As Mary Douglas has recently pointed out, witchcraft as a system for explaining events does not in fact postulate any mysterious spiritual beings—only the mysterious powers of humans. And she adds:

> The belief is on the same footing as belief in the conspiracy theory of history, in the baneful effects of fluoridation or the curative value of psychoanalysis—or any belief that can be presented in an unverifiable form. The question then becomes one about rationality.[24]

For a decade or so after its publication—the Second World War intervening—Evans-Pritchard's book had no direct descendants (Kluckhon's *Navaho Witchcraft*, published in 1944, was clearly conceived quite independently). But when postwar research really began to get under way, *Witchcraft, Oracles, and Magic among the Azande* began to affect later writings in a very remarkable way.

First and most obviously, a number of studies directly concerned with witchcraft and sorcery beliefs acknowledge its influence. Some of these, indeed, seemed more concerned with the sociological distribution of witchcraft and sorcery accusations in a given society than with the nature of the beliefs themselves, which were treated simply as an idiom for the expression of latent tensions. To quote Mary Douglas again:

> [Evans-Pritchard's work] might have been expected to stimulate

[24] Douglas 1970 (b), p. xvi.

more studies of the social restraints upon perception. Instead, it fathered studies of micropolitics. The relation between belief and society, instead of appearing as infinitely complex, subtle and fluid, was presented as a control system with a negative feedback.[25]

But even for this limited use the conceptual tools forged among the Azande proved their worth: the 'studies in micropolitics' conducted in terms of witchcraft and sorcery did in fact illuminate, more clearly than had hitherto been possible, the realities of power and conflict in small face-to-face societies. Indeed, some of the understanding there gained might usefully be brought to bear on more complex political situations: the postwar journalistic use of the term 'witch-hunt' may well have embodied a genuine folk-sociological insight.

To say, however, that mutual accusations of possessing and exercising intangible harmful powers express social and political conflicts is not in itself either very startling or very useful. The question is, what conflicts? between whom? and in what circumstances? Is it possible, in other words, to predict that, at a particular moment in a given society, witchcraft and sorcery accusations will proliferate, only to die down again when conditions change? And can the ebb and flow in such tides of suspicion be correlated with observable changes in other, independent variables?

It must be admitted at once that Evans-Pritchard himself is not very helpful on these questions. In some ways he presents Zande witchcraft beliefs, in the classic functionalist style of his period, as a stabilizing influence on the social and moral system. He shows satisfactorily enough how the beliefs themselves were insulated from any situation where they might have come into conflict with the central norms governing Zande society. Thus, the belief that only commoners could be witches automatically precluded the levelling of accusations by commoners against any member of the Avongara aristocracy, where such accusations might have been detrimental to their authority and prestige. Similarly, the belief system rendered it impossible for women to accuse their husbands. Nor (since within the class of commoners witchcraft was held to be hereditary) could a son accuse his father without in the same breath branding himself as heir to a tainted line of descent. Thus the authority of

[25] Op. cit., p. xiv.

fathers over sons, husbands over wives, princes over commoners remained unchallenged. Witchcraft accusations, expressing as they did only tensions between unrelated equals and rivals, are presented as a sort of all-purpose social device, at one and the same time restraining uncharitable behaviour (which might give rise to accusations) and—in apparent contradiction— bringing grudges harmlessly out into the open. A control system, in fact, with a negative feedback.

Yet on Evans-Pritchard's own showing Zande society hardly displayed homeostasis at the time he was studying it. On the contrary, it was very much in the throes of change—not, indeed, at that time violent, but radical none the less, since the colonial administration was undermining that very authority structure which the witchcraft beliefs seemed so well adapted to protect. It is quite possible that, in these circumstances, the beliefs themselves and the practices surrounding them may have had not so much a homeostatic effect as an unambiguously conservative one, restraining and limiting the effects of change in a particular direction. It is possible also that there had actually been an increase in the number of accusations since the days of King Gbudwe. One would give a great deal to know; but on this point—and in the absence of any quantifiable data on the state of affairs in King Gbudwe's time—Evans-Pritchard cannot enlighten us. The one indication he gives of an indigenous response to change in terms of belief and ritual is, as has already been noted, his account of the new secret societies for the practice of magic. These must have represented a genuine innovation: it is significant that they were not merely banned by the Government but also cordially disliked by the conservative princes. The associations may well have channelled discontents that later found more overtly political expression.

The witchcraft and sorcery studies undertaken during the decade 1950–60 by a group of Manchester-trained anthropologists still followed functionalist tradition in allocating to beliefs of this kind an essentially sustaining role in societies themselves seen as being in long-term equilibrium. But they did in one sense pave the way for later historical studies by introducing a time dimension, albeit a short and cyclical one. Turner,[26]

[26] Turner 1954.

Mitchell,[27] and Marwick[28] published monographs in which witchcraft belief is no longer seen as a simple social and moral regulator in an immobile society, but as a political dynamic, mobilized for the cyclic changes periodically undergone by the system. When a small village reached, by natural population increase, a certain critical size (beyond the numbers its frail authority structure could encompass), mutual witchcraft accusations began to be flung about by rivals for dominance within it. When accusations and counter-accusations had thoroughly poisoned the atmosphere, a point of fission would be reached: a part of the village would hive off some distance away, under the leadership of one of the rival claimants; and the remainder, once again reduced to manageable size, would settle down again in a climate lightened (for the time being) of suspicion. More recently, Ardener[29] has applied a more sophisticated form of similar reasoning to the periodic quiescence and resurgence of witchcraft beliefs in relation to cycles of economic prosperity and depression.

The point here is that, in the societies described, witchcraft beliefs are present all the time, but remain as it were latent during periods of minimal social tension. Where the general situation deteriorates and powerful rivalries make their appearance—and especially where, as is often the case in pre-industrial societies, traditional ethical norms inhibit overt acknowledgement of such rivalries—the same witchcraft beliefs flare up into actual accusations, only to subside once more when tensions ease. From such analyses it was only a small step, though perhaps an ill-advised one, to see an increase in witchcraft accusations as a symptom of a 'sick' society;[30] and a sick society was defined, apparently by tacit consent, as one undergoing rapid and far-reaching change, such as was produced for instance by the colonial situation in Africa or the Industrial Revolution in Europe.[31] In such a society—so ran the theory—witchcraft beliefs ran wild and could cause damage; whereas in a society enjoying some pre-existing Edenic immobility they were controlled, socially useful, a 'fully domesticated species'.[32]

Leaving quite aside the unacknowledged and half-formed

---

[27] Mitchell 1956.   [28] Marwick 1952, 1965.
[29] Ardener 1970.   [30] Mayer 1954, p. 15.
[31] Ibid.   [32] Douglas, op. cit., p. 19.

moral judgements implicit in phrases like 'a sick society', such an hypothesis is completely unverifiable. Not only because of the almost insuperable difficulties of quantification (Marwick[33] did make a gallant effort with his Cewa material, but how does one measure the degree of inter-personal tension that shall be held to constitute social dysfunction?); but also because of the impossibility of anything like an adequate time-scale. Anthropologists visit the societies they study (as Evans-Pritchard visited the Azande) as a particular point in time; and, what with one thing and another, not many of them seem to return to the same societies later. With luck they may stay long enough, or return often enough, to witness fairly short-term cyclical changes such as those described by Turner, Mitchell, and Marwick; or they may be, as Ardener was, both fortunate and skilful in their use of earlier documents where these exist, or of elderly informants who have themselves witnessed change. But the term over which an anthropologist can extend his observations must always, in the nature of things, be painfully short; and for certain purposes this inadequacy cannot be offset by even the richest and minutest detail of observation.

Nor—working as he does in a pre-literate society lacking systematic documents and records—can the anthropologist usually derive much help from historical sources. Historians working, say, in Africa on even the recent pre-literate past must have recourse, as much as any ethnographer, to the statements of living informants; where such oral tradition breaks down their main reliance—apart from the scattered and often untrustworthy accounts of early travellers—must be on the findings of archaeology. None of these sources can, for various reasons, be relied upon for quantitative data on the rise and fall of witchcraft accusations over long but well-defined stretches of time— let alone for the chance to correlate such phenomena with other strands in the process of social change.

The situation is quite different, however, for the more traditional breed of historian, working on the written documents produced by a literate society, with access perhaps to such materials as parish registers, judicial records and the like, as well as to the comments of articulate contemporary witnesses. He, indeed, is deprived of the opportunity for direct observation

[33] Marwick 1965, *passim*.

and the questioning of informants; but on the other hand he
can, as Macfarlane[34] recently did for Tudor and Stuart Essex,
comb the records and other written sources for a given area over
a period of more than a century, and thus gain some idea of
the rise and fall of witchcraft accusations over long stretches of
time—stretches of time which are, moreover, well documented
as regards economic, political, religious and other possibly relevant factors. The material is poorer, but it is far more extensive.
It is as if Evans-Pritchard had enjoyed access to written records
of all cases brought before princely oracles from well before
King Gbudwe's time to our own day—but had been unable to
witness a single oracular seance or speak with a single informant.

   In recent years English historians of a sociological cast of
mind[35] have in fact been turning their attention to the evolution
of beliefs about, and more especially action taken against,
witches and other practitioners of occult evil in the English and
continental European past, and attempting to correlate variations in intensity with other historical phenomena. The results
are, so far, rather puzzling in terms of anthropological theory,
but may in the last resort be enlightening. It would appear that
in a European context the era of truly vigorous witch 'activity'
had a definite beginning and a definite end. From what seems
to have been a fairly modest and 'domesticated' previous level,
it came to flourish exceedingly during the sixteenth and seventeenth centuries, beginning to decline as the eighteenth wore
on and the Industrial Revolution began to get under way—
in direct contradiction of the hypothesis that saw witchcraft as
a 'symptom' of rapid social change. Not, of course, that European society was exactly static during the centuries that witnessed the Renaissance, Reformation, and Counter-Reforma-
tion; but it can clearly no longer be held that 'witchcraft fever',
even among the scientifically unsophisticated, accompanies any
and every social upheaval. (Some of the African evidence, indeed, had all along pointed in this direction.[36])

   Although much of the European material still awaits analysis, and the field remains wide open for speculation, two further

---

[34] Macfarlane 1970 (a) and (b).

[35] Trevor-Roper 1967; Cohn 1967 and 1970; Macfarlane op. cit.; Thomas 1970 and
1971.

[36] Wilson, 1945, p. 154; Mitchell 1965.

points seem clear. The historians have established beyond reasonable doubt the futility of simplistic, one-to-one sociological explanations of the spread and incidence of witchcraft accusations. And, on the other hand, as the same historians themselves unstintingly acknowledge, their approach to witchcraft phenomena has been substantially enriched and deepened by the insights of anthropology; most of which insights trace their descent back quite unambiguously to *Witchcraft, Oracles, and Magic among the Azande.*

So much, then, for the line that goes through 'studies in micropolitics' to theories about the symptomatology of social change and thence to the re-interpretation of certain aspects of the European past. But this is far from being the only line of descent traceable to Evans-Pritchard's study. Over the years, interest in the sociological restraints upon knowledge and perception has increased steadily; nor has it been confined to anthropologists. Within the discipline itself, Turner, having started with a classic functionalist study of the socio-political implications of causal beliefs,[37] went on to focus his analysis, most illuminatingly, upon the symbolic language in which the beliefs themselves are couched, giving us for the Ndembu a complete indigenous chart of society and the cosmos—a chart drawn in colours and textures and the natural properties of the plants and trees and stones used in ritual.[38] 'Cognitive maps' have become the fashion since then, but few can have been so carefully and lovingly drawn. In West Africa Horton, himself trained in the exact sciences, has explored the theoretical status of indigenous models of causation, finding in them both significant resemblances to, and significant differences from, the explanatory constructs of western science.[39] And these are only two among many. A few years ago, the Association of Social Anthropologists of Great Britain and the Commonwealth held a conference on the theme of 'Anthropology and Medicine', at which the social determinants acting upon notions of health, disease, and cure were discussed, not only in the context of pre-literate cultures but in that of advanced industrial ones as well. It is important that this conference was attended by medical practitioners as well as anthropologists; the medical profession

---

[37] Turner, op. cit. [38] Turner 1961, 1967, 1968, 1969.
[39] Horton 1967.

has traditionally been somewhat slow to interest itself in 'native' ideas on aetiology, though there have always been honourable exceptions.[40]

None the less, the 'sociology of knowledge' remains at bottom an epistemological problem; and, appropriately, philosophers concerned with it have made use of Evans-Pritchard's rich material and paid tribute to the accuracy of his observation and the depth of his understanding. Collingwood used his work in discussing the nature of aesthetic perception,[41] Polanyi in speculating about the very possibility of genuine personal knowledge.[42] In our own day, Gellner, Macintyre and Winch among others continue a discussion steadily enriched by data deriving, at a greater or lesser remove, from *Witchcraft, Oracles, and Magic among the Azande*.

Yet, whatever interest there may be in reconstructing the intellectual genealogy, in the last resort Evans-Pritchard is, for the anthropologist of the 1970s, something much more important than a revered ancestor: he is a colleague. Miraculously, he has made the Azande of half a century ago our own contemporaries as well as his; so that the use of the ethnographic present in this abridged version, at first sight so absurd, comes in the end to have a queer appropriateness of its own. In any case it has seemed best to retain it in the body of the text and allow Evans-Pritchard to speak in his own inimitable voice.

Despite every care, an abridgement of this nature must always have in it something of desecration. Long-loved passages—sometimes whole chapters—have perforce been chopped out; definitions and data relegated to a footnote or an appendix. Worst of all, most of the copious and detailed case-histories and recorded texts, which made up so much of the richness and flavour of the original work, have had to be sacrificed in the interests of brevity. In at least partial reparation, the best advice I can offer any reader of this abridged edition is, paradoxically, to regard it as preliminary reading only. As an introduction to one of the great classics of the subject, it may serve; but ideally it should induce the reader to go forth and

[40] Ackerknecht 1942 (a) and (b), 1946.
[41] Collingwood 1938.
[42] Polanyi 1958.

buy, beg, steal (or even borrow from the library) a complete edition of *Witchcraft, Oracles, and Magic among the Azande* and read the whole thing from start to finish.

EVA GILLIES

References

ACKERKNECHT E. H. 1942 (a): Problems of primitive medicine. *Bulletin of the History of Medicine*, XI, pp. 501–21.

ACKERKNECHT E. H. 1942 (b): Primitive medicine and culture pattern. *Bulletin of the History of Medicine*, XII, pp. 545—74.

ACKERKNECHT E. H. 1946: Natural diseases and rational treatment in primitive medicine. *Bulletin of the History of Medicine*, XIX, pp. 467–97.

ARDENER Edwin 1970: Witchcraft, economics and the continuity of belief. In: DOUGLAS 1970 (a), pp. 141–60.

Bahr-el-Ghazal Province Handbook 1911. Anglo-Egyptian Handbook Series. London: H.M.S.O.

COHN Norman 1967: *Warrant for genocide. The myth of the Jewish world conspiracy and the Protocols of the Elders of Zion.* London: Eyre and Spottiswoode.

COHN Norman 1970: The myth of Satan and his human servants. In: DOUGLAS 1970 (a), pp. 3–16.

COLLINGWOOD R. G. 1938: *The principles of art.* Oxford: Clarendon Press.

DE SCHLIPPE P. 1956: *Shifting cultivation in Africa: the Zande system of agriculture.* London: Routledge and Kegan Paul.

DOUGLAS Mary (ed.) 1970 (a): *Witchcraft confessions and accusations.* A.S.A. Monographs 9. Tavistock Publications.

DOUGLAS Mary 1970 (b): Introduction: Thirty years after *Witchcraft, oracles and magic.* In: DOUGLAS 1970 (a), pp. xiii–xxxviii.

EVANS-PRITCHARD E. E. 1934: Lévy-Bruhl's theory of primitive mentality. *Bulletin of the Faculty of Arts*, II (1), Egyptian University, Cairo.

EVANS-PRITCHARD E. E. 1937: *Witchcraft, oracles and magic among the Azande.* Oxford: Clarendon Press.

EVANS-PRITCHARD E. E. 1971: *The Azande: history and political institutions.* Oxford: Clarendon Press.

HORTON Robin 1967: African traditional thought and Western science. I: *Africa* XXXVII (1), pp. 50–71; II: *Africa* XXXVII (2), pp. 155–87.

LEYNAUD Émile 1963: Ligwa: un village zande de la R.C.A. *Cahiers d'études africaines* (École pratique des hautes etudes—Sorbonne—

6e section: Sciences économiques et sociales), vol. III, 3*e* cahier, num. 11, pp. 318–412.

MACFARLANE Alan 1970 (a): *Witchcraft in Tudor and Stuart England: a regional and comparative study.* London: Routledge and Kegan Paul.

MACFARLANE Alan 1970 (b): Witchcraft in Tudor and Stuart Essex. In: DOUGLAS 1970 (a), pp. 81–99.

MARWICK M. G. 1952: The social context of Ceŵa witch beliefs. I: *Africa* XXII (2), pp. 120–35; II; *Africa* XXII (3), pp. 215–233.

MARWICK M. G. 1965: *Sorcery in its social setting: a study of the Northern Rhodesian Ceŵa.* Manchester: Manchester University Press.

MAYER P. 1954: Witches. Inaugural Lecture. Rhodes University, Grahamstown.

MITCHELL Clyde 1956: *The Yao village: a study in the social structure of a Nyasaland tribe.* Manchester: Manchester University Press for Rhodes-Livingstone Institute.

MITCHELL Clyde 1965: The meaning of misfortune for urban Africans. In: FORTES M. and DIETERLEN G. (eds.): *African Systems of Thought.* London: O.U.P. for International African Institute, pp. 192–202.

POLANYI Michael 1958: *Personal knowledge.* London: Routledge and Kegan Paul.

REINING Conrad C. 1966: *The Zande Scheme: an anthropological case study of economic development in Africa.* Evanston, Illinois: Northwestern University Press.

THOMAS Keith 1963: History and anthropology. *Past and Present,* 24, pp. 3–24.

THOMAS Keith 1970: Anthropology and the study of English witchcraft. In: DOUGLAS 1970 (a), pp. 47–79.

THOMAS Keith 1971: *Religion and the decline of magic: studies in popular beliefs in sixteenth and seventeenth century England.* London: Weidenfeld and Nicolson.

TREVOR-ROPER H. 1967: *Religion, the Reformation and social change.* London: Macmillan.

TURNER V. W. 1957: *Schism and continuity in an African society: a study of Ndembu village life.* Manchester: Manchester University Press for Rhodes-Livingstone Institute.

TURNER V. W. 1961: *Ndembu divination: its symbolism and techniques.* Rhodes-Livingstone Paper No 31. Manchester: Manchester University Press.

TURNER V. W. 1967: *The forest of symbols.* Ithaca, New York: Cornell University Press.

TURNER V. W. 1968: *The drums of affliction.* Oxford: Clarendon Press.

TURNER V. W. 1969: *The ritual process: structure and anti-structure.* London: Routledge and Kegan Paul.

WILSON G. and M. 1945: *The analysis of social change: based on observations in Central Africa.* Cambridge: C.U.P.

CHAPTER I

Witchcraft is an Organic and Hereditary Phenomenon

I

AZANDE believe that some people are witches and can injure them in virtue of an inherent quality. A witch performs no rite, utters no spell, and possesses no medicines. An act of witchcraft is a psychic act. They believe also that sorcerers may do them ill by performing magic rites with bad medicines. Azande distinguish clearly between witches and sorcerers. Against both they employ diviners, oracles, and medicines. The relations between these beliefs and rites are the subject of this book.

I describe witchcraft first because it is an indispensable background to the other beliefs. When Azande consult oracles they consult them mainly about witches. When they employ diviners it is for the same purpose. Their leechcraft and closed associations are directed against the same foe.

I had no difficulty in discovering what Azande think about witchcraft, nor in observing what they do to combat it. These ideas and actions are on the surface of their life and are accessible to anyone who lives for a few weeks in their homesteads. Every Zande is an authority on witchcraft. There is no need to consult specialists. There is not even need to question Azande about it, for information flows freely from recurrent situations in their social life, and one has only to watch and listen. *Mangu*, witchcraft, was one of the first words I heard in Zandeland, and I heard it uttered day by day throughout the months.

Azande believe that witchcraft is a substance in the bodies of witches, a belief which is found among many peoples in Central and West Africa. Zandeland is the north-eastern limit of its distribution. It is difficult to say with what organ Azande associate witchcraft. I have never seen human witchcraft-substance, but it has been described to me as an oval blackish swelling or bag in which various small objects are sometimes found.

When Azande describe its shape they often point to the elbow of their bent arm, and when they describe its location they point to just beneath the xiphoid cartilage which is said to 'cover witchcraft-substance'. They say:

> It is attached to the edge of the liver. When people cut open the belly they have only to pierce it and witchcraft-substance bursts through with a pop.

I have heard people say that it is of a reddish colour and contains seeds of pumpkins and sesame and other food-plants which have been devoured by a witch in the cultivations of his neighbours. Azande know the position of witchcraft-substance because in the past it was sometimes extracted by autopsy. I believe it to be the small intestine in certain digestive periods. This organ is suggested by Zande descriptions of autopsies and was that shown to me as containing witchcraft-substance in the belly of one of my goats.

A witch shows no certain external symptoms of his condition though people say: 'One knows a witch by his red eyes.'

II

Witchcraft is not only a physical trait but is also inherited. It is transmitted by unilinear descent from parent to child. The sons of a male witch are all witches but his daughters are not, while the daughters of a female witch are all witches but her sons are not. Biological transmission of witchcraft from one parent to all children of the same sex is complementary to Zande opinions about procreation and to their eschatological beliefs. Conception is thought to be due to a unison of psychical properties in man and woman. When the soul of the man is stronger a boy will be born; when the soul of the woman is stronger a girl will be born. Thus a child partakes of the psychical qualities of both parents, though a girl is thought to partake more of the soul of her mother and a boy of the soul of his father. Nevertheless in certain respects a child takes after one or other parent according to its sex, namely, in the inheritance of sexual characters, of a body-soul, and of witchcraft-substance. There is a vague belief, hardly precise enough to be described as a doctrine, that man possesses two souls, a body-soul and a spirit-soul. At death the body-soul becomes a totem animal of the clan while its fellow soul becomes a ghost and leads a shadowy existence at the heads of streams. Many people say that the body-soul of a man becomes the totem animal of his father's clan while the body-soul of a woman becomes the totem animal of her mother's clan.

At first sight it seems strange to find a mode of matrilineal transmission in a society which is characterized by its strong patrilineal bias, but witchcraft like the body-soul is part of the body and might be expected to accompany inheritance of male or female characters from father or mother.

To our minds it appears evident that if a man is proven a witch the whole of his clan are *ipso facto* witches, since the Zande clan is a group of persons related biologically to one another through the male line. Azande see the sense of this argument but they do not accept its conclusions, and it would involve the whole notion of witchcraft in contradiction were they to do so. In practice they regard only close paternal kinsmen of a known witch as witches. It is only in theory that they extend the imputation to all a witch's clansmen. If in the eyes of the world payment for homicide by witchcraft stamps the kin of a guilty man as witches, a post-mortem in which no witchcraft-substance is discovered in a man clears his paternal kin of suspicion. Here again we might reason that if a man be found by post-mortem immune from witchcraft-substance all his clan must also be immune, but Azande do not act as though they were of this opinion.

Further elaborations of belief free Azande from having to admit what appear to us to be the logical consequences of belief in biological transmission of witchcraft. If a man is proven a witch beyond all doubt his kin, to establish their innocence, may use the very biological principle which would seem to involve them in disrepute. They admit that the man is a witch but deny that he is a member of their clan. They say he was a bastard, for among Azande a man is always of the clan of his *genitor* and not of his *pater*, and I was told that they may compel his mother if she is still alive to say who was her lover, beating her and asking her, 'What do you mean by going to the bush to get witchcraft in adultery?' More often they simply make the declaration that the witch must have been a bastard since they have no witchcraft in their bodies and that he could not therefore be one of their kinsmen, and they may support this contention by quoting cases where members of their kin have been shown by autopsy to have been free from witchcraft. It is unlikely that other people will accept this plea, but they are not asked either to accept it or reject it.

Also Zande doctrine includes the notion that even if a man is the son of a witch and has witchcraft-substance in his body he may not use it. It may remain inoperative, 'cool' as the Azande say, throughout his lifetime, and a man can hardly be classed as a witch if his witchcraft never functions. In point of fact, therefore, Azande generally regard witchcraft as an individual trait and it is treated as such in spite of its association with kinship. At the same time certain clans had a reputation for witchcraft in the reign of King Gbudwe. No one thinks any worse of a man if he is a member of one of these clans.

Azande do not perceive the contradiction as we perceive it because they have no theoretical interest in the subject, and those situations in which they express their beliefs in witchcraft do not force the problem upon them. A man never asks the oracles, which alone are capable of disclosing the location of witchcraft-substance in the living, whether a certain man is a witch. He asks whether at the moment this man is bewitching him. One attempts to discover whether a man is bewitching someone in particular circumstances and not whether he is born a witch. If the oracles say that a certain man is injuring you at the moment you then know that he is a witch, whereas if they say that at the moment he is not injuring you you do not know whether he is a witch or not and have no interest to inquire into the matter. If he is a witch it is of no significance to you so long as you are not his victim. A Zande is interested in witchcraft only as an agent on definite occasions and in relation to his own interests, and not as a permanent condition of individuals. When he is sick he does not normally say: 'Now let us consider who are well-known witches of the neighbourhood and place their names before the poison oracle.' He does not consider the question in this light but asks himself who among his neighbours have grudges against him and then seeks to know from the poison oracle whether one of them is on this particular occasion bewitching him. Azande are interested solely in the dynamics of witchcraft in particular situations.

Lesser misfortunes are soon forgotten and those who caused them are looked upon by the sufferer and his kin as having bewitched someone on this occasion rather than as confirmed witches, for only persons who are constantly exposed by the oracles as responsible for sickness or loss are regarded as confirmed witches, and in the old days it was only when a witch had killed someone that he became a marked man in the community.

III

Death is due to witchcraft and must be avenged. All other practices connected with witchcraft are epitomized in the action of vengeance. In our present context it will be sufficient to point out that in pre-European days vengeance was either executed directly, sometimes by the slaughter of a witch, and sometimes by acceptance of compensation, or by means of lethal magic. Witches were very seldom slain, for it was only when a man committed a second or third murder, or murdered an important person, that a prince permitted his execution. Under British rule the magical method alone is employed.

Vengeance seems to have been less a result of anger and hatred than the fulfilment of a pious duty and a source of profit. I have never heard that today the kin of a dead man, once they have exacted vengeance, show any rancour towards the family of the man whom their magic has struck down, nor that in the past there was any prolonged hostility between the kin of the dead and the kin of the witch who had paid compensation for his murder. Today if a man kills a person by witchcraft the crime is his sole responsibility and his kin are not associated with his guilt. In the past they assisted him to pay compensation, not in virtue of collective responsibility, but in virtue of social obligations to a kinsman. His relatives-in-law and his blood-brothers also contributed towards the payment. As soon as a witch is today slain by magic, or in the past had been speared to death or had paid compensation, the affair is closed. Moreover, it is an issue between the kin of the dead and the kin of the witch and other people are not concerned with it. They have the same social links with both parties.

It is extremely difficult today to obtain information about victims of vengeance-magic. Azande themselves do not know about them unless they are members of a murdered man's closest kin. One notices that his kinsmen are no longer observing taboos of mourning and one knows by this that their magic has performed its task, but it is useless to inquire from them who was its victim because they will not tell you. It is their private affair and is a secret between them and their prince who must be informed of the action of their magic since it is necessary for his poison oracle to confirm their poison oracle before they are permitted to end their mourning. Besides, it is a verdict of the poison oracle and one must not disclose its revelations about such matters.

If other people were acquainted with the names of those who have fallen victims to avenging magic the whole procedure of vengeance would be exposed as futile. If it were known that the death of a man X had been avenged upon a witch Y then the whole procedure would be reduced to an absurdity because the death of Y is also avenged by his kinsmen upon a witch Z. Some Azande have indeed explained to me their doubts about the honesty of the princes who control the oracles, and a few have seen that the present-day system is fallacious. At any rate, its fallaciousness is veiled so long as everybody concerned keeps silence about the victims of their vengeance-magic. In the past things were different, for then a person accused by the prince's oracles of having killed another by witchcraft either paid immediate compensation or was killed. In either case the matter was closed because the man who had paid compensation had no means of proving that he was not a witch, and if he were killed at the prince's orders his death could not be avenged. Nor was an autopsy permitted on his corpse to discover whether it contained witchcraft-substance.

When I have challenged Azande to defend their system of vengeance they have generally said that a prince whose oracles declare that Y has died from the magic of X's kinsmen will not place the name of Z before his oracles to discover whether he died from the magic of Y's kinsmen. When Y's kinsmen ask their prince to place Z's name before his poison oracle he will decline to do so and will tell them that he knows Y to have died in expiation of a crime and that his death cannot therefore be avenged. A few Azande explained the present system by saying that perhaps vengeance-magic and witchcraft participate in causing death. The part of the vengeance-magic explains the termination of mourning of one family and the part of witchcraft explains the initiation of vengeance by another family, i.e. they seek to explain a contradiction in their beliefs in the mystical idiom of the beliefs themselves. But I have only been offered this explanation as a general and theoretical possibility in reply to my objections. Since the names of victims of vengeance are kept secret the contradiction is not apparent, for it would only be evident if all deaths were taken into consideration and not any one particular death. So long therefore as they are able to conform to custom and maintain family honour Azande are not interested in the broader aspects of vengeance in general. They saw the objection when I raised it but they were not incommoded by it.

Princes must be aware of the contradiction because they know the outcome of every death in their provinces. When I asked Prince Gangura how he accepted the death of a man both as the action of vengeance-magic and of witchcraft he smiled and admitted that all was not well with the present-day system. Some princes said that they did not allow a man to be avenged if they knew he had died from vengeance-magic, but I think they were lying. One cannot know for certain, for even if a prince were to tell the kin of a dead man that he had died from vengeance-magic and might not be avenged he would tell them in secret and they would keep his words a secret. They would pretend to their neighbours that they were avenging their kinsmen and after some months would hang up the barkcloth of mourning as a sign that vengeance was accomplished, for they would not wish people to know that their kinsman was a witch.

Consequently if the kinsmen of A avenge his death by magic on B and then learn that B's kinsmen have ceased mourning in sign of having accomplished vengeance also, they believe that this second vengeance is a pretence. Contradiction is thereby avoided.

IV

Being part of the body, witchcraft-substance grows as the body grows. The older a witch the more potent his witchcraft and the more unscrupulous its use. This is one of the reasons why

Azande often express apprehension of old persons. The witch-craft-substance of a child is so small that it can do little injury to others. Therefore a child is never accused of murder, and even grown boys and girls are not suspected of serious witchcraft though they may cause minor misfortunes to persons of their own age. We shall see later how witchcraft operates when there is ill-feeling between witch and victim, and ill-feeling is unlikely to arise frequently between children and adults. Only adults can consult the poison oracle and they do not normally put the names of children before it when asking it about witchcraft. Children cannot express their enmities and minor misfortunes in terms of oracular revelations about witchcraft because they cannot consult the poison oracle.

Nevertheless, rare cases have been known in which, after asking the oracle in vain about all suspected adults, a child's name has been put before it and he has been declared a witch. But I was told that if this happens an old man will point out that there must be an error. He will say: 'A witch has taken the child and placed him in front of himself as a screen to protect himself.'

Children soon know about witchcraft, and I have found in talking to little boys and girls, even as young as six years of age, that they apprehend what is meant when their elders speak of it. I was told that in a quarrel one child may bring up the bad reputation of the father of another. However, people do not comprehend the nature of witchcraft till they are used to operating oracles, to acting in situations of misfortune in ac-cordance with oracular revelations, and to making magic. The concept grows with the social experience of each individual.

Men and women are equally witches. Men may be bewitched by other men or by women, but women are generally bewitched only by members of their own sex. A sick man usually asks the oracles about his male neighbours, while if he is consulting them about a sick wife or kinswoman he normally asks about other women. This is because ill-feeling is more likely to arise between man and man and between woman and woman than between man and woman. A man comes in contact only with his wives and kinswomen and has therefore little opportunity to incur the hatred of other women. It would, in fact, be suspicious if he consulted the oracles about another man's wife on his own behalf, and her husband might surmise adultery. He would wonder what contact his wife had had with her accuser that had led to disagreement between them. Nevertheless, a man frequently consults the oracles about his own wives, because he is sure to displease them from time to time, and often they hate him. I have never heard of cases in which a man has been accused of bewitching his wife. Azande say that no man would do such a thing as no one wishes to kill his wife or cause her sickness since he would himself be the chief loser. Kuagbiaru told me that he had never known a man to pay compensation for the death of his wife. Another reason why one does not hear of fowls' wings being presented to husbands in accusation of witchcraft[1] on account of the illnesses of their wives is that a woman cannot herself consult the poison oracle and usually entrusts this task to her husband. She may ask her brother to consult the oracle on her behalf, but he is not likely to place his brother-in-law's name before it because a husband does not desire the death of his wife.

I have never known a case in which a man has been bewitched by a kinswoman or in which a woman has been bewitched by a kinsman. Moreover, I have heard of only one case in which a man was bewitched by a kinsman. A kinsman may do a man wrong in other ways but he would not bewitch him. It is evident that a sick man would not care to ask the oracles about his brothers and paternal cousins, because if the poison oracle declared them to have bewitched him, by the same declaration he would himself be a witch, since witchcraft is inherited in the male line.

Members of the princely class, the Avongara, are not accused of witchcraft, for if a man were to say that the oracles had declared the son of a prince to have bewitched him he would be asserting that the king and princes were also witches. However much a prince may detest members of his lineage he never allows them to be brought into disrepute by a commoner. Hence, although Azande will tell one privately that they believe some members of the noble class may be witches, they seldom consult

[1] It is customary, when witchcraft is suspected, to ask the local prince, or more often his deputy, to send a fowl's wing to the presumed witch, courteously requesting him to blow water upon it from his mouth in token of goodwill towards the injured person; cf. pp. 40–42. Sending a fowl's wing to someone is therefore tantamount to an accusation of witchcraft.

the oracles about them, so that they are not accused of witch-craft. In the past they never consulted the oracles about them. There is an established fiction that Avongara are not witches, and it is maintained by the overwhelming power and prestige of the ruling princes.

Governors of provinces, deputies of districts, men of the court, leaders of military companies, and other commoners of position and wealth are not likely to be accused of witchcraft unless by a prince himself on account of his own hunting or on account of the death of some equally influential commoner. Generally lesser people do not dare to consult the oracles about influential persons because their lives would be a misery if they insulted the most important men in their neighbourhood. So we may say that the incidence of witchcraft in a Zande com-munity falls equally upon both sexes in the commoner class while nobles are entirely, and powerful commoners largely, im-mune from accusations. All children are normally free from suspicion.

The relations of ruling princes to witchcraft are peculiar. Though immune from accusations they believe in witches as firmly as other people, and they constantly consult the poison oracle to find out who is bewitching them. They especially con-sult it about their wives. A prince's oracle is also the final auth-ority which decides on all witchcraft cases involving homicide, and in the past it was also used to protect his subjects from witchcraft during warfare. When a lesser noble dies his death is attributed to a witch and is avenged in the same way as deaths of commoners, but the death of a king or ruling prince is not so avenged and is generally attributed to sorcery or other evil agents of a mystical nature.

v

While witchcraft itself is part of the human organism its action is psychic. What Azande call *mbisimo mangu*, the soul of witch-craft, is a concept that bridges over the distance between the person of the witch and the person of his victim. Some such explanation is necessary to account for the fact that a witch was in his hut at the time when he is supposed to have injured someone. The soul of witchcraft may leave its corporeal home at any time during the day or night, but Azande generally think of a witch sending his soul on errands by night when his victim is asleep. It sails through the air emitting a bright light. During the daytime this light can only be seen by witches, and by witch-doctors when they are primed with medicines, but anyone may have the rare misfortune to observe it at night. Azande say that the light of witchcraft is like the gleam of fire-fly beetles, only it is ever so much larger and brighter than they. They also say that a man may see witchcraft as it goes to rest on branches for 'Witchcraft is like fire, it lights a light'. If a man sees the light of witchcraft he picks up a piece of charcoal and throws it under his bed so that he may not suffer misfortune from the sight.

I have only once seen witchcraft on its path. I had been sitting late in my hut writing notes. About midnight, before retiring, I took a spear and went for my usual nocturnal stroll. I was walking in the garden at the back of my hut, amongst banana trees, when I noticed a bright light passing at the back of my servants' huts towards the homestead of a man called Tupoi. As this seemed worth investigation I followed its passage until a grass screen obscured the view. I ran quickly through my hut to the other side in order to see where the light was going to, but did not regain sight of it. I knew that only one man, a member of my household, had a lamp that might have given off so bright a light, but next morning he told me that he had neither been out late at night nor had he used his lamp. There did not lack ready informants to tell me that what I had seen was witchcraft. Shortly afterwards, on the same morning, an old relative of Tupoi and an inmate of his homestead died. This event fully explained the light I had seen. I never discovered its real origin, which was possibly a handful of grass lit by someone on his way to defecate, but the coincidence of the direction along which the light moved and the subsequent death accorded well with Zande ideas.

This light is not the witch in person stalking his prey but is an emanation from his body. On this point Zande opinion is quite decided. The witch is on his bed, but he has dispatched the soul of his witchcraft to remove the psychical part of his victim's organs, his *mbisimo pasio*, the soul of his flesh, which he and his fellow witches will devour. The whole act of vampirism is an incorporeal one: the soul of witchcraft removes the soul of the organ. I have not been able to obtain a precise explanation of what is meant by the soul of witchcraft and the soul of an organ. Azande know that people are killed in this way, but only a witch himself could give an exact account of what happens in the process.

Azande use the same word in describing the psychical parts of witchcraft-substance and other organs as they use for what we call the soul of a man. Anything the action of which is not subject to the senses may likewise be explained by the existence of a soul. Medicines act by means of their soul, an explanation which covers the void between a magical rite and the achievement of its purpose. The poison oracle also has a soul, which accounts for its power to see what a man cannot see.

The action of witchcraft is therefore not subject to the ordinary conditions which limit most objects of daily use, but its activity is thought to be limited to some extent by conditions of space. Witchcraft does not strike a man at a great distance, but only injures people in the vicinity. If a man leaves the district in which he is living when attacked by witchcraft it will not follow him far. Witchcraft needs, moreover, conscious direction. The witch cannot send out his witchcraft and leave it to find its victim for itself, but he must define its objective and determine its route. Hence a sick man can often elude its further ravages by withdrawing to the shelter of a grass hut in the bush unknown to all but his wife and children. The witch will dispatch his witchcraft after his victim and it will search his homestead in vain and return to its owner.

Likewise, a man will leave a homestead before dawn in order to escape witchcraft, because then witches are asleep and will not observe his departure. When they become aware that he has left he will already be out of range of their witchcraft. If, on the other hand, they see him starting they may bewitch him and some misfortune will befall him on his journey or after his return home. It is because witchcraft is believed to act only at a short range that if a wife falls sick on a visit to her parents' home they search for the responsible witch there and not at her husband's home, and if she dies in her parents' home her husband may hold them responsible because they have not protected her by consulting the oracles about her welfare.

The farther removed a man's homestead from his neighbours the safer he is from witchcraft. When Azande of the Anglo-

Egyptian Sudan were compelled to live in roadside settlements they did so with profound misgivings, and many fled to the Belgian Congo rather than face close contact with their neighbours. Azande say that their dislike of living in close proximity to others is partly due to a desire to place a stretch of country between their wives and possible lovers and partly to their belief that a witch can injure the more severely the nearer he is to his victim.

The Zande verb 'to bewitch' is *no*, and in its only other uses we translate this word 'to shoot'. It is used for shooting with bow and arrow or with a gun. By a jerk of a leg witch-doctors will shoot (*no*) pieces of bone into one another at a distance. We may notice the analogy between these different shootings and their common factor, the act of causing injury at a distance.

VI

In speaking of witches and witchcraft it is necessary to explain that Azande normally think of witchcraft quite impersonally and apart from any particular witch or witches. When a man says he cannot live in a certain place because of witchcraft he means that he has been warned against this spot by the oracles. The oracles have told him that if he lives there he will be attacked by witches, and he thinks of this danger as a general danger from witchcraft. Hence he speaks always of *mangu*, witchcraft. This force does not exist outside individuals; it is, in fact, an organic part of them, but when particular individuals are not specified and no effort is made to identify them, then it must be thought of as a generalized force. Witchcraft means, therefore, some or any witches. When a Zande says about a mishap, 'It is witchcraft', he means that it is due to a witch but he does not know to which particular one. In the same way he will say in a magic spell, 'Let witchcraft die', meaning whoever may attempt to bewitch him. The concept of witchcraft is not that of an impersonal force that may become attached to persons but of a personal force that is generalized in speech, for if Azande do not particularize they are bound to generalize.

VII

A witch does not immediately destroy his victim. On the contrary, if a man becomes suddenly and acutely ill he may be sure that he is a victim of sorcery and not of witchcraft. The effects of witchcraft lead to death by slow stages, for it is only when a witch has eaten all the soul of a vital organ that death ensues. This takes time, because he makes frequent visits over a long period and consumes only a little of the soul of the organ on each visit, or, if he removes a large portion, he hides it in the thatch of his hut or in a hole of a tree and eats it bit by bit. A slow wasting disease is the type of sickness caused by witchcraft. It may be asked whether Azande consider the consumption of the soul of an organ leads at the same time to its physical deterioration. They are certainly sometimes of this opinion. Witches also shoot objects, called *ahu mangu*, things of witchcraft, into the bodies of those whom they wish to injure. This leads to pain in the place where the missile is lodged, and a witch-doctor, in his role of leech, will be summoned to extract the offending objects, which may be material objects or worms and grubs.

Witches usually combine in their destructive activities and subsequent ghoulish feasts. They assist each other in their crimes and arrange their nefarious schemes in concert. They possess a special kind of ointment, which, rubbed into their skins, renders them invisible on nocturnal expeditions, a statement which suggests that witches are sometimes thought to move in the body to attack their enemies. They also possess small drums which are beaten to summon them to congress where their discussions are presided over by old and experienced members of the brotherhood, for there are status and leadership among witches. Experience must be obtained under tuition of elder witches before a man is qualified to kill his neighbours. Growth in experience goes hand in hand with growth of witchcraft-substance. It is also said that a witch may not kill a man entirely on his own initiative but must present his proposals to a meeting of his fellows presided over by a witch-leader. The question is thrashed out among them.

Sooner or later a witch falls a victim to vengeance or, if he is clever enough to avoid retribution, is killed by another witch or by a sorcerer. We may ask whether the distinction between witches, *aboro mangu*, and those who are not witches, *amokundu*, is maintained beyond the grave? I have never been given a spontaneous statement to this effect, but in answer to direct and leading questions I have on one or two occasions been told that when witches die they become evil ghosts (*agirisa*). *Atoro*, the ordinary ghosts, are benevolent beings, at least as benevolent as a Zande father of a family, and their occasional participation in the world they have left behind them is on the whole orderly and conducive to the welfare of their children. The *agirisa*, on the other hand, show a venomous hatred of humanity. They bedevil travellers in the bush and cause passing states of dissociation.

VIII

The existence of witchcraft-substance in a living person is known by oracular verdicts. In the dead it is discovered by opening up the belly, and it is this second method of identification that interests us in our account of the physical basis of witchcraft. I have already suggested that the organ in which witchcraft-substance is found is the small intestine.

The conditions in which an autopsy took place in pre-European days are obscure. According to one informant, Gbaru, autopsies were an ancient Mbomu custom, and difficulties only began to arise in Gbudwe's time. Possibly the practice was an old one which disappeared as political control of the Avongara increased and reappeared with its old vigour after European conquest. King Gbudwe, as I have been told by all informants, discouraged the practice.

However, autopsies were sometimes made when a witch was executed without royal authority. Occasionally kinsmen of a dead man acted on the verdict of their own poison oracle and avenged themselves on a witch without waiting for confirmation from the king's poison oracle. In such a case their action was *ultra vires*, and if the relatives of the victim of vengeance could show that there was no witchcraft-substance in his belly they could claim compensation in the king's court from the kin who had taken the law into their own hands. On the other hand, autopsies to clear the good name of a lineage, a member of which had been accused of minor acts of witchcraft not involving payment of damages, may have been fairly frequent even before European conquest, and they were certainly common after it.

A man who had frequently been accused of witchcraft, even

though he were never accused of homicide, would feel that he had been insulted without cause and that the name of his kin had been brought into ill repute. He would therefore sometimes instruct his sons to open his abdomen before burial to ascertain whether these reflections on the honour of his lineage were justified, or he might have the operation performed on a son who had died prematurely. For the Zande mind is logical and inquiring within the framework of its culture and insists on the coherence of its own idiom. If witchcraft is an organic substance its presence can be ascertained by post-mortem search. If it is hereditary it can be discovered in the belly of a close male kinsman of a witch as surely as in the belly of the witch himself. An autopsy is performed in public at the edge of the grave. Those who attend are relatives of the dead, his relatives-in-law, his friends, his blood-brothers, and old men of standing in the neighbourhood who commonly attend funerals and sit watching the grave-diggers at their labour and other preparations for burial. Many of these old men have been present on similar occasions in the past, and it is they who will decide upon the presence or absence of witchcraft-substance. They can tell its presence by the way the intestines come out of the belly.

Two lateral gashes are made in the belly and one end of the intestines is placed in a cleft branch and they are wound round it. After the other end has been severed from the body another man takes it and unwinds the intestines as he walks away from the man holding the cleft branch. The old men walk alongside the entrails as they are stretched in the air and examine them for witchcraft-substance. The intestines are usually replaced in the belly when the examination is finished and the corpse is buried. I have been told that if no witchcraft-substance were discovered in a man's belly his kinsmen might strike his accusers in the face with his intestines or might dry them in the sun and afterwards take them to court and there boast of their victory. I have also heard that if witchcraft-substance were discovered the accusers might take the entrails and hang them on a tree bordering one of the main paths leading to a prince's court.

The cutting and the burial must be performed by a blood-brother, for this is one of the duties of blood-brotherhood. One informant told me that if a man who had not made blood-brotherhood with the kin of the dead person performed the ceremony he would by so doing become their blood-brother. If witchcraft-substance is found the cutter will have to be paid heavily for his services. Whether there is witchcraft-substance or not he must be ritually cleansed after the operation. He is carried round on the shoulders of a relative of the dead and greeted with ceremonial cries and pelted with earth and red ground-fruits of the *nonga* plant (*Amomum korarima*) 'to take coldness from him'. He is carried to a stream and the relatives of the dead wash his hands and give him an infusion, made from various trees, to drink. Before he has been cleansed he may neither eat nor drink, for he is polluted like a woman whose husband has died. Finally, if there was no witchcraft-substance, a feast is prepared at which the cutter and a kinsman of the dead pull a gourd containing beer into halves and the kinsmen of the dead and the kinsmen of the cutter exchange gifts, a man from each party advancing in turn to the other party and throwing his gift on the ground before them.

CHAPTER II

The Notion of Witchcraft explains Unfortunate Events

I

WITCHES, as the Azande conceive them, clearly cannot exist. None the less, the concept of witchcraft provides them with a natural philosophy by which the relations between men and unfortunate events are explained and a ready and stereotyped means of reacting to such events. Witchcraft beliefs also embrace a system of values which regulate human conduct.

Witchcraft is ubiquitous. It plays its part in every activity of Zande life; in agricultural, fishing, and hunting pursuits; in domestic life of homesteads as well as in communal life of district and court; it is an important theme of mental life in which it forms the background of a vast panorama of oracles and magic; its influence is plainly stamped on law and morals, etiquette and religion; it is prominent in technology and language; there is no niche or corner of Zande culture into which it does not twist itself. If blight seizes the ground-nut crop it is witchcraft; if the bush is vainly scoured for game it is witchcraft; if women laboriously bale water out of a pool and are rewarded by but a few small fish it is witchcraft; if termites do not rise when their swarming is due and a cold useless night is spent in waiting for their flight it is witchcraft; if a wife is sulky and unresponsive to her husband it is witchcraft; if a prince is cold and distant with his subject it is witchcraft; if a magical rite fails to achieve its purpose it is witchcraft; if, in fact, any failure or misfortune falls upon anyone at any time and in relation to any of the manifold activities of his life it may be due to witchcraft. The Zande attributes all these misfortunes to witchcraft unless there is strong evidence, and subsequent oracular confirmation, that sorcery or some other evil agent has been at work, or unless they are clearly to be attributed to incompetence, breach of a taboo, or failure to observe a moral rule.

To say that witchcraft has blighted the ground-nut crop, that witchcraft has scared away game, and that witchcraft has made so-and-so ill is equivalent to saying in terms of our own culture that the ground-nut crop has failed owing to blight, that game is scarce this season, and that so-and-so has caught influenza. Witchcraft participates in all misfortunes and is the idiom in which Azande speak about them and in which they explain them. To us witchcraft is something which haunted and disgusted our credulous forefathers. But the Zande expects to come across witchcraft at any time of the day or night. He would be just as surprised if he were not brought into daily contact with it as we would be if confronted by its appearance. To him there is nothing miraculous about it. It is expected that a man's hunting will be injured by witches, and he has at his disposal means of dealing with them. When misfortunes occur he does not become awestruck at the play of supernatural forces. He is not terrified at the presence of an occult enemy. He is, on the other hand, extremely annoyed. Someone, out of spite, has ruined his ground-nuts or spoilt his hunting or given his wife a chill, and surely this is cause for anger! He has done no one harm, so what right has anyone to interfere in his affairs? It is an impertinence, an insult, a dirty, offensive trick! It is the aggressiveness and not the eerieness of these actions which Azande emphasize when speaking of them, and it is anger and not awe which we observe in their response to them.

Witchcraft is not less anticipated than adultery. It is so intertwined with everyday happenings that it is part of a Zande's ordinary world. There is nothing remarkable about a witch—you may be one yourself, and certainly many of your closest neighbours are witches. Nor is there anything awe-inspiring about witchcraft. We do not become psychologically transformed when we hear that someone is ill—we expect people to be ill—and it is the same with Zande. They expect people to be ill, i.e. to be bewitched, and it is not a matter for surprise or wonderment.

I found it strange at first to live among Azande and listen to naïve explanations of misfortunes which, to our minds, have apparent causes, but after a while I learnt the idiom of their thought and applied notions of witchcraft as spontaneously as themselves in situations where the concept was relevant. A boy knocked his foot against a small stump of wood in the centre of a bush path, a frequent happening in Africa, and suffered pain and inconvenience in consequence. Owing to its position on his toe it was impossible to keep the cut free from dirt and it began to fester. He declared that witchcraft had made him knock his foot against the stump. I always argued with Azande and criticized their statements, and I did so on this occasion. I told the boy that he had knocked his foot against the stump of wood because he had been careless, and that witchcraft had not placed it in the path, for it had grown there naturally. He agreed that witchcraft had nothing to do with the stump of wood being in his path but added that he had kept his eyes open for stumps, as indeed every Zande does most carefully, and that if he had not been bewitched he would have seen the stump. As a conclusive argument for his view he remarked that all cuts do not take days to heal but, on the contrary, close quickly, for that is the nature of cuts. Why, then, had his sore festered and remained open if there were no witchcraft behind it? This, as I discovered before long, was to be regarded as the Zande explanation of sickness.

Shortly after my arrival in Zandeland we were passing through a government settlement and noticed that a hut had been burnt to the ground on the previous night. Its owner was overcome with grief as it had contained the beer he was preparing for a mortuary feast. He told us that he had gone the previous night to examine his beer. He had lit a handful of straw and raised it above his head so that light would be cast on the pots, and in so doing he had ignited the thatch. He, and my companions also, were convinced that the disaster was caused by witchcraft.

One of my chief informants, Kisanga, was a skilled wood-carver, one of the finest carvers in the whole kingdom of Gbudwe. Occasionally the bowls and stools which he carved split during the work, as one may well imagine in such a climate. Though the hardest woods be selected they sometimes split in process of carving or on completion of the utensil even if the craftsman is careful and well acquainted with the technical rules of his craft. When this happened to the bowls and stools of this particular craftsman he attributed the misfortune to witchcraft and used to harangue me about the spite and jealousy of his neighbours. When I used to reply that I thought he was mistaken and that people were well disposed towards him he used to hold the split bowl or stool towards me as concrete evidence of his assertions. If people were not bewitching his work, how would I account for that? Likewise a potter will attribute the cracking of his pots during firing to witchcraft. An experienced potter need have no fear that his pots will crack as a result of error. He selects the proper clay, kneads it thoroughly till he has extracted all grit and pebbles, and builds it up slowly and carefully. On the night before digging out his clay he abstains from sexual intercourse. So he should have nothing to fear. Yet pots sometimes break, even when they are the handiwork of expert potters, and this can only be accounted for by witchcraft. 'It is broken—there is witchcraft,' says the potter simply. Many similar situations in which witchcraft is cited as an agent are instanced throughout this and following chapters.

II

In speaking to Azande about witchcraft and in observing their reactions to situations of misfortune it was obvious that they did not attempt to account for the existence of phenomena, or even the action of phenomena, by mystical causation alone. What they explained by witchcraft were the particular conditions in a chain of causation which related an individual to natural happenings in such a way that he sustained injury. The boy who knocked his foot against a stump of wood did not account for the stump by reference to witchcraft, nor did he suggest that whenever anybody knocks his foot against a stump it is necessarily due to witchcraft, nor yet again did he account for the cut by saying that it was caused by witchcraft, for he knew quite well that it was caused by the stump of wood. What he attributed to witchcraft was that on this particular occasion, when exercising his usual care, he struck his foot against a stump of wood, whereas on a hundred other occasions he did not do so, and that on this particular occasion the cut, which he expected to result from the knock, festered whereas he had had dozens of cuts which had not festered. Surely these peculiar conditions demand an explanation. Again, every year hundreds of Azande go and inspect their beer by night and they always take with them a handful of straw in order to illuminate the hut in which it is fermenting. Why then should this particular man on this single occasion have ignited the thatch of his hut? Again, my friend the wood-carver had made scores of bowls and stools without mishap and he knew all there was to know about the selection of wood, use of tools, and conditions of carving. His bowls and stools did not split like the products of craftsmen who were unskilled in their work, so why on rare occasions should his bowls and stools split when they did not split usually and when he had exercised all his usual knowledge and care? He knew the answer well enough and so, in his opinion, did his envious, back-biting neighbours. In the same way, a potter wants to know why his pots should break on an occasion when he uses the same material and technique as on other occasions; or rather he already knows, for the reason is known in advance, as it were. If the pots break it is due to witchcraft.

We shall give a false account of Zande philosophy if we say that they believe witchcraft to be the sole cause of phenomena. This proposition is not contained in Zande patterns of thought, which only assert that witchcraft brings a man into relation with events in such a way that he sustains injury.

In Zandeland sometimes an old granary collapses. There is nothing remarkable in this. Every Zande knows that termites eat the supports in course of time and that even the hardest woods decay after years of service. Now a granary is the summerhouse of a Zande homestead and people sit beneath it in the heat of the day and chat or play the African hole-game or work at some craft. Consequently it may happen that there are people sitting beneath the granary when it collapses and they are injured, for it is a heavy structure made of beams and clay and may be stored with eleusine as well. Now why should these particular people have been sitting under this particular granary at the particular moment when it collapsed? That it should collapse is easily intelligible, but why should it have collapsed at the particular moment when these particular people were sitting beneath it? Through years it might have collapsed, so why should it fall just when certain people sought its kindly shelter? We say that the granary collapsed because its supports were eaten away by termites; that is the cause that explains the collapse of the granary. We also say that people were sitting under it at the time because it was in the heat of the day and they thought that it would be a comfortable place to talk and work. This is the cause of people being under the granary at the time it collapsed. To our minds the only relationship between these two independently caused facts is their coincidence in time and space. We have no explanation of why the two chains of causation intersected at a certain time and in a certain place, for there is no interdependence between them. Zande philosophy can supply the missing link. The Zande knows that the supports were undermined by termites and that people were sitting beneath the granary in order to escape the heat and glare of the sun. But he knows besides why these two events occurred at a precisely similar moment in time and space. It was due to the action of witchcraft. If there had been no witchcraft people would have been sitting under the granary and it would not have fallen on them, or it would have collapsed but the people would not have been sheltering under it at the time. Witchcraft explains the coincidence of these two happenings.

III

I hope I am not expected to point out that the Zande cannot analyse his doctrines as I have done for him. It is no use saying to a Zande 'Now tell me what you Azande think about witchcraft' because the subject is too general and indeterminate, both too vague and too immense, to be described concisely. But it is possible to extract the principles of their thought from dozens of situations in which witchcraft is called upon to explain happenings and from dozens of other situations in which failure is attributed to some other cause. Their philosophy is explicit, but is not formally stated as a doctrine. A Zande would not say 'I believe in natural causation but I do not think that that fully explains coincidences, and it seems to me that the theory of witchcraft offers a satisfactory explanation of them', but he expresses his thought in terms of actual and particular situations. He says 'a buffalo charges', 'a tree falls', 'termites are not making their seasonal flight when they are expected to do so', and so on. Herein he is stating empirically ascertained facts. But he also says 'a buffalo charged and wounded so-and-so', 'a tree fell on so-and-so and killed him', 'my termites refuse to make their flight in numbers worth collecting but other people are collecting theirs all right', and so on. He tells you that these things are due to witchcraft, saying in each instance, 'So-and-so has been bewitched.' The facts do not explain themselves or only partly explain themselves. They can only be explained fully if one takes witchcraft into consideration.

One can only obtain the full range of a Zande's ideas about causation by allowing him to fill in the gaps himself, otherwise one will be led astray by linguistic conventions. He tells you 'So-and-so was bewitched and killed himself' or even simply that 'So-and-so was killed by witchcraft'. But he is telling you the ultimate cause of his death and not the secondary causes. You can ask him 'How did he kill himself?' and he will tell you that he committed suicide by hanging himself from the branch of a tree. You can also ask 'Why did he kill himself?' and he will tell you that it was because he was angry with his brothers. The cause of his death was hanging from a tree, and the cause of his hanging from a tree was his anger with his brothers. If you then ask a Zande why he should say that the man was bewitched if he committed suicide on account of his anger with his brothers, he will tell you that only crazy people commit suicide, and that if everyone who was angry with his brothers committed suicide there would soon be no people left in the world, and that if this man had not been bewitched he would not have done what he did do. If you persevere and ask why witchcraft caused the man to kill himself the Zande will reply that he supposes someone hated him, and if you ask him why someone hated him your informant will tell you that such is the nature of men.

For if Azande cannot enunciate a theory of causation in terms acceptable to us they describe happenings in an idiom that is explanatory. They are aware that it is particular circumstances of events in their relation to man, their harmfulness to a particular person, that constitutes evidence of witchcraft. Witchcraft explains *why* events are harmful to man and not *how* they happen. A Zande perceives how they happen just as we do. He does not see a witch charge a man, but an elephant. He does not see a witch push over a granary, but termites gnawing away its supports. He does not see a psychical flame igniting thatch, but an ordinary lighted bundle of straw. His perception of how events occur is as clear as our own.

IV

Zande belief in witchcraft in no way contradicts empirical knowledge of cause and effect. The world known to the senses is just as real to them as it is to us. We must not be deceived by their way of expressing causation and imagine that because they say a man was killed by witchcraft they entirely neglect the secondary causes that, as we judge them, were the true causes of his death. They are foreshortening the chain of events, and in a particular social situation are selecting the cause that is socially relevant and neglecting the rest. If a man is killed by a spear in war, or by a wild beast in hunting, or by the bite of a snake, or from sickness, witchcraft is the socially relevant cause, since it is the only one which allows intervention and determines social behaviour.

Belief in death from natural causes and belief in death from witchcraft are not mutually exclusive. On the contrary, they supplement one another, the one accounting for what the other does not account for. Besides, death is not only a natural fact but also a social fact. It is not simply that the heart ceases to beat and the lungs to pump air in an organism, but it is also the destruction of a member of a family and kin, of a community and tribe. Death leads to consultation of oracles, magic rites, and revenge. Among the causes of death witchcraft is the only one that has any significance for social behaviour. The attribution of misfortune to witchcraft does not exclude what we call its real causes but is superimposed on them and gives to social events their moral value.

Zande thought expresses the notion of natural and mystical causation quite clearly by using a hunting metaphor to define their relations. Azande always say of witchcraft that it is the *umbaga* or second spear. When Azande kill game there is a division of meat between the man who first speared the animal and the man who plunged a second spear into it. These two are considered to have killed the beast and the owner of the second spear is called the *umbaga*. Hence if a man is killed by an elephant Azande say that the elephant is the first spear and that witchcraft is the second spear and that together they killed the man. If a man spears another in war the slayer is the first spear and witchcraft is the second spear and together they killed him.

Since Azande recognize plurality of causes, and it is the social situation that indicates the relevant one, we can understand why the doctrine of witchcraft is not used to explain every failure and misfortune. It sometimes happens that the social situation demands a common-sense, and not a mystical, judgement of cause. Thus, if you tell a lie, or commit adultery, or steal, or deceive your prince, and are found out, you cannot elude punishment by saying that you were bewitched. Zande doctrine declares emphatically 'Witchcraft does not make a person tell lies'; 'Witchcraft does not make a person commit adultery'; 'Witchcraft does not put adultery into a man. "Witchcraft" is in yourself (you alone are responsible), that is, your penis becomes erect. It sees the hair of a man's wife and it rises and becomes erect because the only "witchcraft" is, itself' ("witchcraft" is here used metaphorically); 'Witchcraft does not make a person steal'; 'Witchcraft does not make a person disloyal.' Only on one occasion have I heard a Zande plead that he was bewitched when he had committed an offence and this was when he lied to me, and even on this occasion everybody present laughed at him and told him that witchcraft does not make people tell lies.

If a man murders another tribesman with knife or spear he is put to death. It is not necessary in such a case to seek a witch, for an objective towards which vengeance may be directed is already present. If, on the other hand, it is a member of another tribe who has speared a man his relatives, or his prince, will take steps to discover the witch responsible for the event.

It would be treason to say that a man put to death on the orders of his king for an offence against authority was killed by witchcraft. If a man were to consult the oracles to discover the witch responsible for the death of a relative who had been put to death at the orders of his king he would run the risk of being put to death himself. For here the social situation excludes the notion of witchcraft as on other occasions it pays no attention to natural agents and emphasizes only witchcraft. Also, if a man were killed in vengeance because the oracles said that he was a witch and had murdered another man with his witchcraft then his relatives could not say that he had been killed by witchcraft. Zande doctrine lays it down that he died at the hand of avengers because he was a homicide. If a man were to have expressed the view that his kinsman had been killed by witchcraft and to have acted upon his opinion by consulting the poison oracle, he might have been punished for ridiculing the king's poison oracle, for it was the poison oracle of the king that had given official confirmation of the man's guilt, and it was the king himself who had permitted vengeance to take its course.

In these situations witchcraft is irrelevant and, if not totally excluded, is not indicated as the principal factor in causation. As in our own society a scientific theory of causation, if not excluded, is deemed irrelevant in questions of moral and legal responsibility, so in Zande society the doctrine of witchcraft, if not excluded, is deemed irrelevant in the same situations. We accept scientific explanations of the causes of disease, and even of the causes of insanity, but we deny them in crime and sin because here they militate against law and morals which are axiomatic. The Zande accepts a mystical explanation of the causes of misfortune, sickness, and death, but he does not allow this explanation if it conflicts with social exigencies expressed in law and morals.

For witchcraft is not indicated as a cause for failure when a taboo has been broken. If a child becomes sick, and it is known that its father and mother have had sexual relations before it was weaned, the cause of death is already indicated by breach of a ritual prohibition and the question of witchcraft does not arise. If a man develops leprosy and there is a history of incest in his case then incest is the cause of leprosy and not witchcraft. In these cases, however, a curious situation arises because when the child or the leper dies it is necessary to avenge their deaths and the Zande sees no difficulty in explaining what appears to us to be most illogical behaviour. He does so on the same principles as when a man has been killed by a wild beast, and he invokes the same metaphor of 'second spear'. In the cases mentioned above there are really three causes of a person's death. There is the illness from which he dies, leprosy in the case of the man, perhaps some fever in the case of the child. These sicknesses are not in themselves products of witchcraft, for they exist in their own right just as a buffalo or a granary exist in their own right. Then there is the breach of a taboo, in the one case of weaning, in the other case of incest. The child, and the man, developed fever, and leprosy, because a taboo was broken. The breach of a taboo was the cause of their sickness, but the sickness would not have killed them it witchcraft had not also been operative. If witchcraft had not been present as 'second spear' they would have developed fever and leprosy just the same, but they would not have died from them. In these instances there are two socially significant causes, breach of taboo and witchcraft, both of which are relative to different social processes, and each is emphasized by different people.

But where there has been a breach of taboo and death is not involved witchcraft will not be evoked as a cause of failure. If a man eats a forbidden food after he has made powerful punitive magic he may die, and in this case the cause of his death is known beforehand, since it is contained in the conditions of the situation in which he died even if witchcraft was also operative. But it does not follow that he will die. What does inevitably follow is that the medicine he has made will cease to operate against the person for whom it is intended and will have to be destroyed lest it turn against the magician who sent it forth. The failure of the medicine to achieve its purpose is due to breach of a taboo and not to witchcraft. If a man has had sexual relations with his wife and on the next day approaches the poison oracle it will not reveal the truth and its oracular efficacy will be permanently undermined. If he had not broken a taboo it would have been said that witchcraft had caused the oracle, to lie, but the condition of the person who had attended the seance provides a reason for its failure to speak the truth without having to bring in the notion of witchcraft as an agent. No one will admit that he has broken a taboo before consulting the poison oracle, but when an oracle lies everyone is prepared to admit that a taboo may have been broken by someone.

Similarly, when a potter's creations break in firing witchcraft is not the only possible cause of the calamity. Inexperience and bad workmanship may also be reasons for failure, or the potter may himself have had sexual relations on the preceding night. The potter himself will attribute his failure to witchcraft, but others may not be of the same opinion.

Not even all deaths are invariably and unanimously attributed to witchcraft or to the breach of some taboo. The deaths of babies from certain diseases are attributed vaguely to the Supreme Being. Also, if a man falls suddenly and violently sick and dies, his relatives may be sure that a sorcerer has made magic against him and that it is not a witch who has killed him. A breach of the obligations of blood-brotherhood may sweep away whole groups of kin, and when one after another of brothers and cousins die it is the blood and not witchcraft to which their deaths are attributed by outsiders, though the relatives of the dead will seek to avenge them on witches. When a very old man dies unrelated people say that he has died of old age, but they do not say this in the presence of kinsmen, who declare that witchcraft is responsible for his death.

It is also thought that adultery may cause misfortune, though it is only one participating factor, and witchcraft is also believed to be present. Thus is it said that a man may be killed in warfare or in a hunting accident as a result of his wife's infidelities. Therefore, before going to war or on a large-scale hunting expedition a man might ask his wife to divulge the names of her lovers.

Even where breaches of law and morals do not occur witchcraft is not the only reason given for failure. Incompetence, laziness, and ignorance may be selected as causes. When a girl smashes her water-pot or a boy forgets to close the door of the hen-house at night they will be admonished severely by their parents for stupidity. The mistakes of children are due to carelessness or ignorance and they are taught to avoid them while they are still young. People do not say that they are effects of witchcraft, or if they are prepared to concede the possibility of witchcraft they consider stupidity the main cause. Moreover, the Zande is not so naïve that he holds witchcraft responsible for the cracking of a pot during firing if subsequent examination shows that a pebble was left in the clay, or for an animal escaping his net if someone frightened it away by a move or a sound. People do not blame witchcraft if a woman burns her porridge nor if she presents it undercooked to her husband. And when an inexperienced craftsman makes a stool which lacks polish or which splits, this is put down to his inexperience.

In all these cases the man who suffers the misfortune is likely to say that it is due to witchcraft, but others will not say so.

We must bear in mind nevertheless that a serious misfortune, especially if it results in death, is normally attributed by everyone to the action of witchcraft, especially by the sufferer and his kin, however much it may have been due to a man's incompetence or absence of self-control. If a man falls into a fire and is seriously burnt, or falls into a game-pit and breaks his neck or his leg, it would undoubtedly be attributed to witchcraft. Thus when six or seven of the sons of Prince Rikita were entrapped in a ring of fire and burnt to death when hunting cane-rats their death was undoubtedly due to witchcraft.

Hence we see that witchcraft has its own logic, its own rules of thought, and that these do not exclude natural causation. Belief in witchcraft is quite consistent with human responsibility and a rational appreciation of nature. First of all a man must carry out an activity according to traditional rules of technique, which consist of knowledge checked by trial and error in each generation. It is only if he fails in spite of adherence to these rules that people will impute his lack of success to witchcraft.

v

It is often asked whether primitive peoples distinguish between the natural and the supernatural, and the query may be here answered in a preliminary manner in respect to the Azande. The question as it stands may mean, do primitive peoples distinguish between the natural and the supernatural in the abstract? We have a notion of an ordered world conforming to what we call natural laws, but some people in our society believe that mysterious things can happen which cannot be accounted for by reference to natural laws and which therefore are held to transcend them, and we call these happenings supernatural. To us supernatural means very much the same as abnormal or extraordinary. Azande certainly have no such notions of reality. They have no conceptions of 'natural' as we understand it, and therefore neither of the 'supernatural' as we understand it. Witchcraft is to Azande an ordinary and not an extraordinary, even though it may in some circumstances be an infrequent, event. It is a normal, and not an abnormal, happening. But if they do not give to the natural and supernatural the meanings which educated Europeans give to them they nevertheless distinguish between them. For our question may be formulated, and should be formulated, in a different manner. We ought rather to ask whether primitive peoples perceive any difference between the happenings which we, the observers of their culture, class as natural and the happenings which we class as mystical. Azande undoubtedly perceive a difference between what we consider the workings of nature on the one hand and the workings of magic and ghosts and witchcraft on the other hand, though in the absence of a formulated doctrine of natural law they do not, and cannot, express the difference as we express it.

The Zande notion of witchcraft is incompatible with our ways of thought. But even to the Azande there is something peculiar about the action of witchcraft. Normally it can be perceived only in dreams. It is not an evident notion but transcends sensory experience. They do not profess to understand witchcraft entirely. They know that it exists and works evil, but they have to guess at the manner in which it works. Indeed, I have frequently been struck when discussing witchcraft with Azande by the doubt they express about the subject, not only in what they say, but even more in their manner of saying it, both of which contrast with their ready knowledge, fluently imparted, about social events and economic techniques. They feel out of their depth in trying to describe the way in which witchcraft accomplishes its ends. That it kills people is obvious, but how it kills them cannot be known precisely. They tell you that perhaps if you were to ask an older man or a witch-doctor he might give you more information. But the older men and the witch-doctors can tell you little more than youth and laymen. They only know what the others know: that the soul of witchcraft goes by night and devours the soul of its victim. Only witches themselves understand these matters fully. In truth Azande experience feelings about witchcraft rather than ideas, for their intellectual concepts of it are weak and they know better what to do when attacked by it than how to explain it. Their response is action and not analysis.

There is no elaborate and consistent representation of witchcraft that will account in detail for its workings, nor of nature which expounds its conformity to sequences and functional interrelations. The Zande actualizes these beliefs rather than intellectualizes them, and their tenets are expressed in socially

controlled behaviour rather than in doctrines. Hence the difficulty of discussing the subject of witchcraft with Azande, for
their ideas are imprisoned in action and cannot be cited to
explain and justify action.

CHAPTER III

Sufferers from Misfortune seek
for Witches among their Enemies

I

WE must now view witchcraft in a more objective manner, for it is a mode of behaviour as well as a mode of thought. The reader will rightly ask what a Zande does when he is bewitched, how he discovers who is bewitching him, how he expresses his resentment and ensures his protection, and what system of control inhibits violent retaliation.

Only when the misfortune is death can vengeance or compensation be exacted for injury from witchcraft. In a lesser loss all that can be done is to expose the witch responsible and to persuade him to withdraw his baneful influence. When a man suffers an irreparable loss it is therefore useless for him to pursue the matter further, since no compensation can be obtained for the loss, and a witch cannot undo what he has already done. In such circumstances a Zande laments his misfortune and blames witchcraft in general, but is unlikely to take steps to identify any particular witch since the man will either deny his responsibility or will say that he is not conscious of having caused anyone an injury, and that if he has done so unwittingly he is sorry, and in either case the sufferer will be no better off.

But if a misfortune is incipient there is sound reason for immediate identification of the witch responsible since he can be persuaded to withdraw his witchcraft before matters take a serious turn. If game is scarce at the end of the hunting season it is useless to seek out the witches who have scared it away, but at the height of the season discovery of the witches may result in a good bag. If a man is bitten by a poisonous snake he either gets well soon or he dies. Should he recover, no good can come of asking the oracles for the name of the witch responsible for the bite. But if a man falls sick and his sickness is likely to be serious and of some duration, then his relatives approach the witch responsible in order to turn the scales between recovery and death.

The manner in which oracles are operated will be explained later. Here we shall refer simply to their verdicts as part of the social mechanism for dealing with witchcraft. It is apparent that when a witch is exposed by the oracles a situation fraught with danger is created, since the injured man and his kinsmen are angry at an affront to their dignity and an attack on their welfare by a neighbour. No one accepts lightly that another shall ruin his hunting or undermine his health out of spite and jealousy, and Azande would certainly assault witches who are proved to be injuring them if their resentment were not directed into customary channels backed by political authority.

I must again stress that we are not here concerned with crime that can be brought before the courts and penalized, nor with civil offences for which compensation can be exacted by legal suits. Unless a witch actually kills a man it is impossible to take legal steps against him in a prince's court; and I have recorded no cases of witches being punished for causing other losses. Old men, however, have told me that very occasionally in the old days a man in favour at court persuaded a prince to grant him damages for loss of his entire eleusine crop by fire or disease.

Hence the procedure described in this chapter is customary procedure in which the question of retaliation does not arise. So long as injured party and witch observe the correct forms of behaviour the incident will be closed without any hard words, far less blows, passing between them, and even without relations becoming embittered. You have a right to ask a witch to leave you in peace, and you may even go so far as to warn him that if your kinsman dies he will be accused of murder, but you must not insult him or cause him an injury. For a witch is also a tribesman, and so long as he does not kill people he has a right to live his life free from molestation. However, a witch must adhere to custom by recalling his witchcraft when requested to do so by those whom it is injuring. If a man were to assault a witch he would lose prestige, he would render himself liable for damages at court, and he would only incur additional hatred of the witch, whereas the object of the whole procedure is to allay it and get him to withdraw his witchcraft by a polite request that he will cease from troubling his victim further. On the other hand, if a witch refuses to comply with a request couched in the usual form he will lose social prestige, he will have openly admitted his guilt, and he will be running a grave risk lest he bring death upon his victims and inevitable retribution on himself.

II

It must not be thought that Azande consult the poison oracle, or even cheaper and more easily obtainable oracles, about every doubt and misfortune. Life is too short to be always consulting oracles, and, moreover, to what purpose? There is always witchcraft about, and you cannot possibly eradicate it from your life. You are sure to make enemies, and you cannot always be exposing them for witchcraft. Some risk has to be taken. So when a Zande says that a loss is due to witchcraft he is merely expressing his disappointment in the usual phrases that such situations evoke, but we must not suppose that his emotions are deeply stirred, or that he immediately rushes off to discover who are the witches responsible for his misfortune. Nine times out of ten he does nothing. He is a philosopher and knows that in life the ill must be taken with the good.

It is only in matters affecting his health and in his more serious social and economic ventures that he consults oracles and witch-doctors about witchcraft. Generally he consults them about possible misfortunes in the future, for he is mainly worried to know whether undertakings may be commenced with confidence or whether there is already witchcraft hanging over them in advance, even before they have been begun and while still only propositions. For example: a man wishes to send his son to be brought up as a page at the king's court, or to make a journey to the Bongo people to the north of Gbudwe's kingdom to collect meat and butter-tree oil, and either of these undertakings may end in disaster if witchcraft interferes with them. He therefore consults the oracles about them, and if the oracles tell him that they are inauspicious, that witchcraft hangs over them, he gives up his plans. No one will blame him for not proceeding with his intentions, since it would be suicidal to do so if the poison oracle has given adverse verdicts. In these examples he either gives up his projects altogether or waits a month or two and then consults the oracles again, when perhaps they will give a different verdict, since witchcraft may then no longer threaten his ventures. Or a man wishes to change his homestead or to sow his staple crop of eleusine or to dig a game-pit and consults the oracles about suitable sites. He asks: Shall I build my homestead in this place? Shall I prepare this piece of ground for my eleusine crop? Shall I dig a game-pit in this spot? If the poison oracle decides against one site he can always ask it about other sites until it announces that one of them is auspicious and that there is no danger to the health of his family or to their economic success. For it is useless to perform the great labour of building a new homestead, of clearing bush for gardens, of digging a wide and deep elephant pit, if the undertaking is known to be unsuccessful before it is even started. If witchcraft has ensured failure in advance, why not choose another site where labour will reap its just reward? A man wishes to marry a girl and consults the poison oracle to find out if his marriage is going to be a success or if his wife will die in his homestead during the first few years of their married life. Here an inauspicious verdict of the oracles involves a more complicated procedure, since a girl is not like an eleusine plot or homestead site, for one cannot ask the oracles about a series of girls as one can about parts of the bush. The Zande must now find out what particular witches are threatening his future marriage and then try to persuade them to withdraw their ill-will. When he has approached the witches he will let things lie fallow for a while and will then consult the oracles a second time to find out if there is still danger ahead or if the road to marriage is now clear. For it is useless to marry a girl about whom it is known in advance that she will die if she marries you.

It is advisable to point out that when a Zande says a venture is bewitched he is occasionally lying. Since no one can be expected to fulfil an obligation if its fulfilment entails disaster, the easiest way of eluding an undertaking is to say that the oracles have informed you that if you were to embark upon it you would die. No one can expect you to court disaster. Good faith is therefore sometimes abused. If you merely do not wish to send your son to act as a page at the king's court, or to accompany your friend to Bongo country, or to give your daughter in marriage to the man to whom you have pledged her, or to allow your wife to visit her parents, you have only to plead that the oracles prophesy death as the outcome of these ventures. However, by these circumlocutions you may delay but not permanently avoid carrying out your obligations; for the persons to whom you are pledged, your king, your friend, your future son-in-law, your parents-in-law will also consult their oracles to check your oracles, and even if the declarations of their oracles agree with what you have untruthfully stated to be the declarations of your oracles they will only release you for a while from your obligations. Efforts will at once be made by those concerned to find the witch whose influence threatens your future, and when they have persuaded him to withdraw his influence you will have to think of a new excuse if you do not wish to carry out your obligations. Thus oracles are used as a means of compelling behaviour, and their authority may also be used improperly to avoid duties. Nevertheless, no Zande would state the declaration of an oracle other than it was given. If he wishes to lie he fakes an oracular declaration without consulting the oracles at all.

III

Generally it is about his health that a Zande consults oracles and approaches witches by traditional steps. The kinsmen or family of a sick man will find out who is bewitching him and will request the witch to desist from his actions. But many Azande who are in perfect health will consult one of the oracles at the commencement of each month about their health during the coming month, and I have noticed that at any consultation of the rubbing-board oracle a man will almost invariably ask the oracle whether he will die in the near future. Should the oracle inform such a man that someone is threatening his health, and that he will die in the near future, he will return home depressed, for Azande do not disguise their anxiety in these circumstances. The most cheerful of my Zande friends would be downcast until they had annulled the verdict of the oracle by getting the witch who threatened them to quiet his witchcraft. Nevertheless, I doubt whether any Zande ever died from, or was for long seriously discomforted by, knowledge that he was bewitched, and I have never come across a case of death from suggestion of this kind.

A Zande who is ill, or who has been informed by the oracles that he is about to fall sick, has always at his hand means of dealing with the situation. Let us consider the position of a man who is quite well but knows in advance that he will fall sick unless he counteracts witchcraft. He does not summon a leech or eat drugs, but otherwise his ritual behaviour is the same as if he were actually ill. He goes to a kinsman or friend who possesses some oracle poison and asks him to consult the poison oracle on his behalf. He obtains a few fowls, and he and his friend slip away in the early morning to a quiet spot in the bush where they conduct an oracular seance. The man whose health is being threatened brings with him a wing of the fowl that died in inauspicious prognosis for the coming month, and he places this wing on the ground in front of the poison oracle to show it concretely the nature of the questions they are about to put to it. They tell the poison oracle that they want a more detailed account of the future than it has already vouchsafed them, that they have come to put some names of persons before it, and that they wish to know who of these persons intends to injure the health of the inquirer. They take a chicken to the name of one person and pour poison down its throat, and ask the poison oracle whether this man is the witch or not. If the oracle says that this particular person has nothing to do with the health of the inquirer then they take another chicken to the name of a second person and repeat the test. When the oracle kills a fowl to a man's name, i.e. says that it is he who will cause the inquirer sickness during the coming month, they then ask it whether this is the only witch who threatens his welfare or whether there are also others in the offing. If the oracle says that there are others, then they must seek them out till the oracle says that there is no need to inquire further since they now possess the names of all the witches who will cause the inquirer ill-health. There may therefore be a whole series of consultations on several consecutive days, and they will take up hours of a man's time in preparation and performance, but a Zande does not consider time wasted when he is thwarting otherwise inevitable pain and misfortune, perhaps even death.

A man who is actually sick and not merely apprehensive of the future often retires to a grass hut in the bush where he can remain hidden from witchcraft, and from its secret shelter he organizes his defence. He asks a close kinsman or a son-in-law or some other person upon whom he can rely to consult the poison oracle on his behalf, and it will be asked the same questions as those I have recorded above, save that they now ask it who is actually injuring the sick man instead of who is about to injure him in the future.

I have said that they consult the poison oracle but they are more likely to commence inquiries with the rubbing-board oracle, which will select from a large number of names several witches who may be responsible for the sickness. If a man is poor he will then place the names selected by the rubbing-board oracle before the termites oracles, but if he is able to obtain oracle poison and chicken he will place them before the poison oracle.

I do not want to enter here into the complicated technicalities of oracles, but will suppose that the rubbing-board oracle has chosen the name of the responsible witch and that the poison oracle has confirmed its verdict, and that both have declared that this man alone is causing the sickness about which they have sought information. There are now two lines of action open to the sick man and his kinsmen, and I will describe the less usual course first. We must remember that they must avoid an open quarrel with the witch, since this will only aggravate him and perhaps cause him to kill his victim outright, and will in any case involve the aggressors in serious social, and possibly legal, difficulties.

They may *de kuba*, make a public oration, in which they declare that they know the name of the witch who is injuring their relative but that they do not wish to disclose it and thus shame him, and that since they are honouring him they expect him to return their courtesy by leaving their kinsman in peace. This procedure is especially suitable when the witch is a person of social standing whom they do not wish to affront, or someone enjoying the esteem and respect of his fellows whom they do not wish to humiliate. The witch will understand from the oration that they are speaking about him, while others will remain ignorant of his identity. The oration is made dramatically, shortly after sunset or at dawn. I have heard these orations on three occasions. The orator mounts a termite mound or stands on the branch of a tree and utters a shrill cry 'Hi! Hi! Hi! Hi!'

to attract the attention of his neighbours. All give immediate attention to this cry, for it is uttered when some animal is sighted or when an armed man is discovered lurking in the undergrowth. He repeats this cry several times and then tells his listeners that it is not an animal about which he is calling them, but that he wishes to speak to them about witchcraft. The following text tells what happens:

Hi! Hi! Hi! Hi! It is not an animal O! It is not an animal O! I went to-day to consult the rubbing-board oracle, and it said to me that those men who are killing my kinsman are not far off, that they are right here nearby, and that it is those neighbours of mine who are killing my kinsman. It is thus I honour you by telling you that I will not speak his name (the name of the witch). I will not choose him out by himself. If he has ears he will hear what I am saying. Were my kinsman to die I would make magic and then someone would die and my name would be tarnished because I have kept silence. This is why I am telling you that, if my kinsman continues to be sick unto death, I will surely reveal that man so that everyone will know him. Since I have been your neighbour I have not acted greedily in any man's homestead; against no man have I borne ill will; I have not committed adultery with any man's wife; no man's child have I killed; I have not stolen the goods of other men; I have done none of these things that a man should bear a grudge against me. O subjects of Gbudwe, indeed you are men of ill will! Why are you killing my kinsman? If he has done any evil you should have told me, saying, 'Your kinsman has brought vengeance on himself.' Do not slay my kinsman. It is thus that I have spoken. I have spoken much. That man that has ears, one speaks but a few words and he can hear them. After what I have spoken to you I will not burden my mouth again, but I will choose out the man by himself and expose him before his face. All of you hear well my words. It is finished.

If a witch is not persuaded to cease his activities by an oration of this kind the kinsmen of a sick man resort to procedure which is generally employed immediately after the poison oracle has identified him without being preceded by a public oration, for a public oration is not often made, and only if it appears more convenient and is authorized by the rubbing-board oracle. The normal procedure is to put the names of all suspects before the rubbing-board oracle and let it select those guilty of causing sickness. If a man is dangerously ill they at once make known the verdict of the rubbing-board oracle, but otherwise they place the names of witches it has chosen before the poison oracle, for the poison oracle is considered the more reliable, and usually exposure of witches should come from its declarations alone. The poison oracle finds perhaps several witches, perhaps only one, responsible for the sickness, but the procedure is the same for many as for one. They cut off a wing of the fowl that has died to the name of a witch and thrust it on the end of a small pointed stick, spreading out the feathers in the shape of a fan, and they take it home with them at the end of the seance. One of the sick man's kinsmen then takes it to a prince's deputy, since a prince is not always accessible and, in any case, does not wish to be troubled with every little affair of this kind. A deputy does not mind being troubled now and again with these requests. He receives no fee, but the requests are a tribute to his importance, so he is pleased to grant them.

The messenger lays the wing at the deputy's feet and squats down to inform him of its meaning. In the Zande way he begins at the beginning and tells the deputy how his kinsman fell sick, about the declarations of the rubbing-board oracle, and finally about the verdict of the poison oracle, and he requests the deputy to send someone with the wing to notify the witch that the poison oracle has denounced him and to ask him to desist from persecuting their kinsman. It is possible that they may approach the witch directly and not through the intermediary of a prince's deputy, but if they do this they will ask the rubbing-board oracle to choose a suitable messenger to send to the witch from among the names of several men presented to it; it is wiser to act through the prince's deputy, whose official position gives added support to their action. The deputy then sends a man to deliver the chicken's wing to the witch and to report the witch's behaviour when it is presented to him. But before taking this step the deputy probably consults the rubbing-board oracle to find out who is the most suitable man to send. It is well not to take any steps in such matters without a statement from an oracle that they will prove successful. When the deputy has been assured by the rubbing-board oracle that a certain man is an auspicious messenger, he dispatches him with the chicken's wing to the homestead of the witch. On his arrival the messenger lays the wing on the ground in front of the witch and says simply that the deputy has sent him with it on account of the illness of so-and-so. He treats the witch with respect, for such is the custom, and anyhow it is none of his business. Almost invariably the witch replies courteously that he is unconscious of injuring anyone, that if it is true that he has injured the man in question he is very sorry, and that if it is he alone who is troubling him then he will surely recover, because from the bottom of his heart he wishes him health and happiness, in sign of which he will blow out water. He calls for a gourdful of water, and when his wife brings it he takes a draught, swills it round in his mouth, and blows it out in a thin spray over the chicken's wing lying before him on the ground. He says aloud, so that the messenger may hear, and later report his words, that if he is a witch he is unaware of his state and that he is not causing the sick man injury with intent. He says that he addresses the witchcraft in his belly, beseeching it to become cool (inactive), and that he makes this appeal from his heart and not merely with his lips.

The messenger now returns to the deputy to report what he has done and what he has seen, and the deputy informs the kinsman of the sick man that he has carried out the task he undertook. A messenger does not receive a fee. His service is an act of courtesy to the deputy and to the kin of the sick man. The sick man and his friends wait anxiously for a few days to discover what is going to be the effect of having delivered the chicken's wing to the witch. If the sick man shows signs of re-covery they praise the poison oracle for having so quickly revealed the witch and thus opened up a road to recovery. On the other hand, if sickness continues, they start a fresh round of oracle consultations to discover whether the witch was only pretending repentance and was in reality as hostile as ever, or whether some new witch has meanwhile started to trouble their kinsman and to aggravate his sickness. In either case the formal presentation of chickens' wings is continued through the inter-mediary of a prince's deputy.

Though, in the past, princes may sometimes have taken more drastic steps to ensure their safety, the procedures described above are the everyday usages of every section of Zande society in situations of sickness. The chances of violent action on the part of relatives of the sick man and his kin are lessened by the routine character of the proceedings, for since they are established and normative modes of action people do not think, save in rare cases, of acting in any other way.

IV

Apart from the fact that good behaviour on both sides is habitual and has therefore all the compulsory nature of habitual action, other factors assist in eliminating friction: the great authority of the poison oracle, for it is useless to protest against its declarations; the employment of intermediaries between the parties which obviates the necessity of their meeting during the whole affair; the social standing of a prince's deputy, for an insult to his messenger is an insult to the prince himself; and Zande notions of witchcraft which make the procedure of advantage to both parties.

But if the verdict of the poison oracle by itself suffices to eliminate in advance all denial and opposition it is necessary to be able to produce a valid oracular declaration. If a man were to accuse another of witchcraft without basing his declaration on a verdict of the poison oracle, or at least the termites' oracle, he would be laughed at for his pains, if not beaten into the bargain. Therefore relatives of a sick man generally invite someone who is not of their kin to be present when they consult the poison oracle about the illness of their kinsman so that he can vouch that the oracle has really been consulted and has been consulted in the correct manner.

It is, moreover, to the interest of both parties that they should not become estranged through the incident. They have to live together as neighbours afterwards and to co-operate in the life of the community. It is also to their mutual advantage to avoid all appearance of anger or resentment for a more direct and immediate reason. The whole point of the procedure is to put the witch in a good temper by being polite to him. The witch on his part ought to feel grateful to the people who have warned him so politely of the danger in which he stands. We must remember that since witchcraft has no real existence a man does not know that he has bewitched another, even if he is aware that he bears him ill will. But, at the same time, he believes firmly in the existence of witchcraft and in the accuracy of the poison oracle, so that when the oracle says that he is killing a man by his witchcraft he is probably thankful for having been warned in time, for if he had been allowed to murder the man, all the while ignorant of his action, he would inevitably have fallen a victim to vengeance. By the polite indication of an oracular verdict from the relatives of a sick man to the witch who has made him sick both the life of the sick man and the life of the witch are saved. Hence the Zande aphorism, 'The blower of water does not die.'

By this maxim they refer to the action of a witch when he blows from his mouth a spray of water on the fowl's wing which has been placed at his feet by the messenger of a deputy. When the witch blows water on the wing he 'cools' his witchcraft. By performing this simple rite he ensures that the sick man will recover and also that he will himself escape vengeance. Nevertheless, Azande hold very decidedly that the mere action of blowing water is valueless in itself if the witch does not sincerely hope for the recovery of the sick man. They assert the moral and volitional character of witchcraft. They say 'A man must blow water from his heart and not merely from his lips,' and that 'The blowing of water from the mouth alone does not finish the matter; but the blowing of water from the belly cools the heart, it is that which is true blowing of water.'

The procedure to counteract witchcraft which I have described is normally utilized in situations of illness or when the oracles have predicted illness for a man who may be at the time in perfect health. It is also used when hunting, or some other economic activity, is unsuccessful; or when the oracles have predicted its failure, though it has not yet commenced, but is only anticipated. Beyond doubt the great majority of fowls' wings are presented to witches about sickness. So long as the sick man lives, every polite effort is made by his relatives to persuade the witches who are sapping his strength to desist from their nocturnal predations. So far no injury recognized in law has been committed. But once the sick man is dead the whole situation changes, for then his kinsmen are compelled to vengeance. All negotiations with the witch are broken off and steps are taken at once to execute vengeance.

v

I was aided in my understanding of the feelings of bewitched Azande by sharing, at least to some extent, like experiences.

I tried to adapt myself to their culture by living the life of my hosts, as far as convenient, and by sharing their hopes and joys, apathy and sorrows. In many respects my life was like theirs: I suffered their illnesses; exploited the same food supplies; and adopted as far as possible their own patterns of behaviour with resultant enmities as well as friendships. In no department of their life was I more successful in 'thinking black', or as it should more correctly be said 'feeling black', than in the sphere of witchcraft. I, too, used to react to misfortunes in the idiom of witchcraft, and it was often an effort to check this lapse into unreason.

We saw earlier how witchcraft is a participant in all misfortunes. Misfortune and witchcraft are much the same to a Zande, for it is only in situations of misfortune or of anticipation of it that the notion of witchcraft is evoked. In a sense we may say that witchcraft is misfortune, the procedure of oracle consultations and presentation of fowls' wings being the socially prescribed channel of response to misfortune, and notions of witchcraft-activity giving the requisite ideological background to make the response logical and coherent.

A witch attacks a man when motivated by hatred, envy, jealousy, and greed. Usually if he has no enmity towards a man he will not attack him. Therefore a Zande in misfortune at once considers who is likely to hate him. He is well aware that others take pleasure in his troubles and pain and are displeased at his good fortune. He knows that if he becomes rich the poor will hate him, that if he rises in social position his inferiors will be jealous of his authority, that if he is handsome the less favoured will envy his looks, that if he is talented as a hunter, a singer, a fighter, or a rhetorician, he will earn the malice of those less gifted, and that if he enjoys the regard of his prince and of his neighbours he will be detested for his prestige and popularity.

In the daily tasks of life there is ample scope for friction. In the household there is frequent occasion for ill-feeling between husband and wife and between wife and co-wife arising from division of labour and sexual jealousies. Among his neighbours a man is sure to have both secret and open enemies. There may have been quarrels about cultivations and hunting areas. There may have been suspicions about designs on a wife. There may have been rivalry at dances. One may have uttered unguarded words which have been repeated to another. A man may have thought that a song referred to himself. He may have been insulted or struck at court. He may be a rival for a prince's favour. All unkind words and malicious actions and innuendoes are stored in the memory for retaliation. A prince has only to show favour to one of his courtiers, a husband to one of his wives, and the others will detest him. I found again and again that I had only to be generous to, even very friendly with, one of my neighbours and he would at once be apprehensive of witchcraft, and any ill-luck which befell him would be attributed to the jealousy my friendship had aroused in the breasts of his neighbours.

Usually, however, a man who believes that others are jealous of him will do nothing. He continues to be polite to them and tries to remain on friendly terms. But when he suffers a misfortune he will at once believe that it is one of these men who has bewitched him, and will place their names before the poison oracle to ascertain who among them is responsible. Oracle consultations therefore express histories of personal relationships, for, as a rule, a man only places before an oracle names of those who might have injured him on account of some definite events which he believes to have occasioned their enmity. It is often possible by adroit questioning to trace back the placing of a name before the oracle to its source in some past incident.

VI

Since accusations of witchcraft arise from personal enmities it will at once be seen why certain people are left out of consideration when a sick man casts around him in his mind to select those who might be injuring him in order to place their names before the oracle. People do not accuse nobles and seldom accuse influential commoners of witchcraft, not merely because it would be inadvisable to insult them but also because their social contact with these people is limited to situations in which their behaviour is determined by notions of status. A man quarrels with and is jealous of his social equals. A noble is socially so separated from commoners that were a commoner to quarrel with him it would be treason. Commoners bear ill-will against commoners and princes hate princes. Likewise a wealthy commoner will be patron to a poorer commoner and there will seldom be malice between them because the incentive to malice and the opportunity for creating it do not easily arise. A rich commoner will envy another rich commoner and a poor man will be jealous of another poor man. Offence is more easily taken at the words or actions of an equal than of a superior or inferior. In the same way, women come into contact with other women and not with men, save their husbands and kinsmen, so it is about other women that their friends consult the oracles, for since there is no social intercourse between men and unrelated women it is difficult for enmities to grow up between them. Likewise, as we have seen, children do not bewitch adults. This means that a child does not usually have relations with adults, other than with parents and kinsmen, that could breed hatred towards them in his heart. When an adult bewitches a child it is generally out of hatred for his father. It is among householders of roughly equal status who come into close daily relations with one another that there is the greatest opportunity for squabbles, and it is these people who most frequently place one another's names before the oracles when they or members of their families are sick.

Nevertheless, notions of witchcraft are evoked primarily by misfortune and are not entirely dependent on enmities. Thus a man who suffers a misfortune knows that he has been bewitched, and only then does he seek in his mind to find out who wishes him ill and might have bewitched him. If he cannot recall any incidents that might have caused a man to hate him, and if he has no particular enemies, he must still consult the oracles to discover a witch. Hence, even a prince will sometimes accuse commoners of witchcraft, for his misfortunes must be accounted for and checked, even though those whom he accuses of witchcraft are not his enemies.

It has been noted that witches only injure people in the vicinity, and that the closer they are to their victims the more serious are their attacks. We may suggest that the reason for this belief is that people living at a distance from one another have insufficient social contacts to produce mutual hatred, whereas there is ample opportunity for friction among those whose homesteads and cultivations are in close proximity. People are most likely to quarrel with those with whom they come into closest contact when the contact is not softened by sentiments of kinship or is not buffered by distinctions of age, sex, and class.

In a study of Zande witchcraft we must bear in mind, firstly, that the notion is a function of situations of misfortune, and, secondly, that it is a function of personal relations.

VII

The notion of witchcraft is not only a function of misfortune and of personal relations but also comprises moral judgement. Indeed, Zande morality is so closely related to their notions of witchcraft that it may be said to embrace them. The Zande phrase 'It is witchcraft' may often be translated simply as 'It is bad'. For, as we have seen, witchcraft does not act haphazardly or without intent but is a planned assault by one man on another whom he hates. Azande say that hatred, jealousy, envy, backbiting, slander, and so forth go ahead and witchcraft follows after. A man must first hate his enemy and will then bewitch him, and unless the witch be contrite of heart when he blows out water his action will be without effect. Now since Zande interest is not in witches as such—that is to say, the static condition of being a possessor of witchcraft—but only in witch-activity, there are two consequences. Firstly, witchcraft tends to become synonymous with the sentiments which are supposed to cause it, so that Azande think of hatred and envy and greed in terms of witchcraft and likewise think of witchcraft in terms of the sentiments it discloses. Secondly, a person who has bewitched a man is not viewed by him ever afterwards as a witch but only at the time of the misfortune he has caused and in relation to these special conditions. There is no fixed attitude towards witches as there is, for instance, towards nobles. A noble is always a noble and is treated as such in every situation, but there is no like sharpness or constancy about the social personality of a witch, for he is only regarded as a witch in certain situations. Zande notions of witchcraft express a dynamic relationship of persons to other persons in inauspicious situations. Their meaning is so dependent on passing situations that a man is scarcely regarded as a witch when the situation that evoked an accusation against him has disappeared.

Azande will not allow one to say that anybody who hates another is a witch, or that witchcraft and hatred are synonymous. All men are liable to develop sentiments against their neighbours, but unless they are actually born with witchcraft in their bellies they cannot do their enemies an injury by merely disliking them.

It is true that an old man may say that a youth may become ill from *ima abakumba*, the consequence of an elder being angry with him, but Azande do not believe that the anger of an old man can by itself do much harm, and if an old man speaks in this vein they say that he is telling them by innuendo that he will bewitch them if they vex him. For unless an old man is a witch or sorcerer no harm can befall an unrelated person against whom he speaks in anger. His ill-will might cause some slight inconvenience, and the oracles may become confused between hatred and possession of witchcraft unless they are warned to consider only the question of actual witchcraft.

Mere feeling against a man and uttering of words against him cannot by itself seriously harm him unless there is some definite social tie between them. The curses of an unrelated man can do you no harm, but nothing is more dreadful than the curses (*motiwa*) of father and mother and uncles and aunts. Even without ritually uttering a curse a father may bring misfortune on his son simply by anger and complaint. It is also said that if a prince is continuously angered and sorrowful at the departure of a subject it will not go well with him (*motiwa gbia*). One informant told me also that if a woman goes on a journey against her husband's wishes and he sulks and pines after her it may be ill with her on her journey.

If you have any doubts whether a man who dislikes you is merely hating you or is actually bewitching you, you can ask the poison oracle, or one of the lesser oracles, to quiet them. You caution the oracle not to pay attention to spitefulness, but to concentrate upon the single issue of witchcraft. You tell it you do not wish to know whether the man hates you, but whether he is bewitching you. For instance, you say to the rubbing-board oracle, 'You observe slander and put it aside, you observe hatred and put it aside, you observe jealousy and put it aside. Real witchcraft, consider that alone. If it is going to kill me, rubbing-board oracle stick (answer "Yes").'

Moreover, according to Zande ideas, it does not follow that a witch must injure people merely because he is a witch. A man may be born a witch but his witchcraft-substance may remain 'cool'. As Azande conceive witchcraft this means that, although the man is a witch, he is a decent fellow who is not embittered against his neighbours or jealous of their happiness. Such a man is a good citizen, and to a Zande good citizenship consists in carrying out your obligations cheerfully and living all times charitably with your neighbours. A good man is good tempered and generous, a good son, husband, and father, loyal to his prince, just in his dealings with his fellow-men, true to his bargains, a law-abiding man and a peace-maker, one who abhors adultery, one who speaks well of his neighbours, and one who is generally good natured and courteous. It is not expected of him to love his enemies or to show forbearance to those who injure his family and kinsmen or commit adultery with his wives. But if a man has suffered no wrong he ought not to show enmity to others. Similarly, jealousy is evil unless it is culturally approved as is rivalry between princes, between witch-doctors, and between singers.

Behaviour which conflicts with Zande ideas of what is right and proper, though not in itself witchcraft, nevertheless is the drive behind it, and persons who offend against rules of conduct are the most frequently exposed as witches. When we consider the situations that evoke notions of witchcraft and the method adopted by men to identify witches, it will at once be seen that the volitional and moral character of witchcraft is contained in them. Moral condemnation is predetermined, because when a man suffers a misfortune he meditates upon his grievance and ponders in his mind who among his neighbours has shown him unmerited hostility or who bears unjustly a grudge against him. These people have wronged him and wish him evil, and he therefore considers that they have bewitched him, for a man would not bewitch him if he did not hate him.

Now Zande moral notions are not very different from our own in their division of conduct into good and bad, but since they are not expressed in theistic terms their kinship with the codes of behaviour expounded in famous religions is not at once apparent. The ghosts of the dead cannot be appealed to as arbiters of morals and sanctions of conduct, because the ghosts are members of kinship groups and only exercise authority within these groups among the same people over whom they exercised authority when they were alive. The Supreme Being is a very vague influence and is not cited by Azande as the guardian of moral law which must be obeyed simply because he is its author. It is in the idiom of witchcraft that Azande express moral rules which mostly lie outside criminal and civil law. 'Jealousy is not good because of witchcraft, a jealous man may kill someone,' they say, and they speak likewise of other antisocial sentiments.

VIII

Azande say, 'Death has always a cause, and no man dies without a reason,' meaning that death results always from some enmity. It is witchcraft which kills a man, but it is uncharitableness that drives a witch to murder. Likewise greed may be the starting-point for murder, and men fear to refuse requests for gifts lest a sponger bewitches them and they say that 'a man who is always asking for gifts is a witch'.

Those who always speak in a roundabout manner and are not straightforward in their conversation are suspected of witchcraft. Azande are very sensitive and usually on the lookout for unpleasant allusions to themselves in apparently harmless conversation. This is a frequent occasion of quarrels, and there is no means of determining whether the speaker has meant the allusions or whether his hearer has supplied them. For example, a man sits with some of his neighbours and says, 'No man remains for ever in the world.' One of the old men sitting nearby gives a disapproving grunt at this remark, hearing which the speaker explains that he was talking of an old man who has just died; but others may think that he meant that he wished the death of one of those with whom he was sitting.

A man who threatens others with misfortune is certain to be suspected of witchcraft should the misfortunes befall them. A man threatens another in anger and says to him, 'You will not walk this year,' and then some short while afterwards the man may fall sick or have an accident and he will remember the words which were spoken to him in passion and will at once consult the oracles, placing before them the name of the speaker as the first on his list of suspects.

A spiteful disposition arouses suspicions of witchcraft. Glum and ill-tempered people, those who suffer from some physical deformity, and those who have been mutilated are suspected on account of their spitefulness. Men whose habits are dirty, such as those who defecate in the gardens of others and urinate in public, or who eat without washing their hands, and eat bad food like tortoise, toad, and house-rat, are the kind of people who might well bewitch others. The same is thought of unmannerly persons who enter into a man's hut without first asking his permission; who cannot disguise their greed in the presence of food or beer; who make offensive remarks to their wives and neighbours and fling insults and curses after them; and so on.

Not everyone who displays these unpleasant traits is necessarily regarded as a witch, but it is these sentiments and modes of behaviour which make people suspicious of witchcraft, so that Azande know that those who display them have the desire to bewitch, even if they do not possess the power to do so. Since it is these traits which antagonize neighbours against those who show them it is their names which are most frequently placed before the oracles when the neighbours fall sick, and they are therefore likely to be accused frequently of witchcraft and to acquire a reputation as witches. Witches tend to be those whose behaviour is least in accordance with social demands. For though Azande do not consistently think of neighbours who have once or twice bewitched them as witches, some people are so frequently exposed by oracles that they gain a sustained reputation for witchcraft and are regarded as witches outside specific situations of misfortune. Those whom we would call good citizens—and, of course, the richer and more powerful members of society are such—are seldom accused of witchcraft, while those who make themselves a nuisance to their neighbours and those who are weak are most likely to be accused of witchcraft.

Indeed, it is desirable to state that weakness, as well as hatred and jealousy, invites accusations of witchcraft, for there can be no doubt in the mind of anyone who has lived for long among Azande that they are averse from consulting oracles about influential persons and prefer to inquire about men without influence at court and about women—that is to say, about persons who cannot easily retaliate later for the insult contained in an accusation of witchcraft. This is more evident in the oracular disclosures of witch-doctors than in the revelations of oracles. A Zande would not agree to my statement. Certainly influential men are sometimes accused of witchcraft, and often poor men are not, or very seldom, accused. I describe only a general impression of a tendency which qualifies what I have said about accusations of witchcraft being a function of equal status, for it is only a wide division of status that excludes enmities likely to lead to accusations of witchcraft.

Where Zande moral notions differ profoundly from our own is in the range of events they consider to have a moral significance. For to a Zande almost every happening which is harmful to him is due to the evil disposition of someone else. What is bad for him is morally bad, that is to say, it derives from an evil man. Any misfortune evokes the notion of injury and desire for retaliation. For all loss is deemed by Azande to be due to witches. To them death, whatever its occasion, is murder and cries out for vengeance, for the event or situation of death is to them the important thing and not the instrument by which it was occasioned, be it disease, or a wild beast, or the spear of an enemy.

In our society only certain misfortunes are believed to be due to the wickedness of other people, and it is only in these limited situations of misfortune that we can retaliate through prescribed channels upon the authors of them. Disease or failure in economic pursuits are not thought by us to be injuries inflicted on us by other people. If a man is sick or his enterprises fail he cannot retaliate upon anyone, as he can if his watch has been stolen or he has been assaulted. But in Zandeland all misfortunes are due to witchcraft, and all allow the person who has suffered loss to retaliate along prescribed channels in every situation because the loss is attributed to a person. In situations such as theft or adultery or murder by violence there is already in play a person who invites retaliation. If he is known he is sued in the courts, if unknown he is pursued by punitive magic. When this person is absent notions of witchcraft provide an alternative objective. Every misfortune supposes witchcraft, and every enmity suggests its author.

Looked at from this aspect it is easier to understand how Azande fail to observe and define the fact that not only may anybody be a witch, which they readily admit, but that most commoners are witches. Azande at once challenge your statement if you say that most people are witches. Notwithstanding, in my experience all except the noble class and commoners of influential position at court are at one time or another exposed by oracles as having bewitched their neighbours and therefore as witches. This must necessarily be the case, since all men suffer misfortunes and every man is someone's enemy. But it is generally only those who make themselves disliked by many of their neighbours who are often accused of witchcraft and earn a reputation as witches.

Keeping our eyes fixed on the dynamic meaning of witchcraft, and recognizing therefore its universality, we shall better understand how it comes about that witches are not ostracized and persecuted; for what is a function of passing states and is common to most men cannot be treated with severity. The position of a witch is in no way analogous to that of a criminal in our own society, and he is certainly not an outcast living in the shadow of disgrace and shunned by his neighbours. On the contrary, confirmed witches, known for miles around as such, live like ordinary citizens. Often they are respected fathers and husbands, welcome visitors to homesteads and guests at feasts, and sometimes influential members of the inner-council at a prince's court. Some of my acquaintances were notorious witches.

A witch may enjoy a certain amount of prestige on account of his powers, for everyone is careful not to offend him, since no one deliberately courts disaster. This is why a householder who kills an animal sends presents of meat to the old men who occupy neighbouring homesteads. For if an old witch receives no meat he will prevent the hunter from killing any more beasts, whereas if he receives his portion he will hope that more beasts are killed and will refrain from interference. Likewise a man will be careful not to anger his wives gratuitously, for if one of them is a witch he may bring misfortune on his head by a fit of bad temper. A man distributes meat fairly among his wives lest one of them, offended at receiving a smaller portion than the others, should prevent him from killing more game.

Belief in witchcraft is a valuable corrective to uncharitable impulses, because a show of spleen or meanness or hostility may bring serious consequences in its train. Since Azande do not know who are and who are not witches, they assume that all their neighbours may be witches, and are therefore careful not to offend any of them without good cause. The notion works in two ways. A jealous man, for instance, will be suspected of witchcraft by those of whom he is jealous and will seek to avoid suspicion by curbing his jealousy. In the second place, those of whom he is jealous may be witches and may seek to injure him in return for his enmity, so that he will curb his jealousy from fear of being bewitched.

Azande say that you can never be certain that anyone is free from witchcraft. Hence they say, 'In consulting oracles about witchcraft no one is left out,' meaning that it is best to ask the oracles about everyone and to make no exceptions, and hence their aphorism 'One cannot see into a man as into an open-wove basket,' meaning that it is impossible to see witchcraft inside a man. It is therefore better to earn no man's enmity, since hatred is the motive in every act of witchcraft.

CHAPTER IV

Are Witches Conscious Agents?

I

ONE of the most remarkable features of European witchcraft was the readiness with which witches sometimes, not under duress, confessed their guilt and gave lengthy accounts of their crimes and their organization. It seems that, to some degree at any rate, people living in a community in which the facts of witchcraft are never doubted may convince themselves that they possess the power with which others credit them. However this may be, it is of interest to ask whether Azande ever confess that they are witches.

To Azande the question of guilt does not present itself as it would to us. As I have already explained, their interest in witchcraft is aroused only in specific cases of misfortune and persists only while the misfortune lasts. The only witch they pay attention to is the witch who is actually causing them misfortune. When their mishap is ended they cease to regard the man as a witch, for, as we have seen, anyone may be a witch, but a Zande is only concerned with a witch whose witchcraft is significant to himself. Also, witchcraft is something they react to and against in misfortune, this being the main meaning it has for them. It is a response to certain situations and not an intricate intellectual concept. Hence a Zande accused of witchcraft is astonished. He has not conceived of witchcraft from this angle. To him it has always been a reaction against others in his own misfortunes, so that it is difficult for him to apprehend the notion when he himself is its objective in the misfortunes of other people.

This problem is exceedingly difficult. Some African peoples appear to bridge over the difficulty which arises between a proven act of witchcraft and the witch's avowed ignorance of the act by asserting that a witch may act without volition. But Zande notions do not readily permit this thesis. Ask any Zande the straightforward question whether a man knows that he is a witch and bewitches in full consciousness of his action, and he will reply that it is impossible that a witch should be ignorant of his condition and of his assaults upon others. Neither in reply to such a question, nor on the many occasions upon which I have witnessed oracular consultations about witchcraft and seen fowls' wings being taken to those exposed by the poison oracle, have I ever heard it suggested that a man might be ignorant of being a witch or might have used his powers unconsciously. For Azande think that witches lead a secret life and share their confidences with other witches laughing about their misdeeds and boasting of their exploits against those whom they hate.

Yet Azande are inconsistent in this matter. Although they assert the moral guilt of others, nevertheless, when accused of witchcraft themselves they plead innocence, if not of the act—for they cannot well do that in public—at least of intention. To an outsider it appears that there is a contradiction between denial of volition in one's own case and insistence upon volition in the cases of others. But the situation in which a Zande is placed determines which of a number of beliefs comes into play, and the fact that this belief contradicts his usual ideas does not trouble him. He assumes that witches are responsible for their actions just as we assume that the criminal is responsible for his crimes. When he is himself accused of witchcraft this is a peculiar and special case.

We must remember that a Zande has only his own individual experience to judge by, for one does not discuss matters of this kind with one's friends. Public opinion accepts that a witch is a conscious agent, but on a particular occasion when the poison oracle denounces a certain man for having performed an act of witchcraft he is aware of his lack of intention. So far as he knows he has never visited the home of the sick man whom he is said to have injured, and he is forced to conclude that either there must have been an error or that he has acted unconsciously. But he believes his own case to be exceptional and that others are responsible for their actions. People have always been of the opinion that witches plan their assaults, and the fact that he himself has not acted with intent is no reason to suppose that others do not act consciously. Indeed, a man in these circumstances must feel that if it is true that he is a witch he is certainly not an ordinary witch, for witches recognize each other and co-operate in their undertakings, whereas no one has a secret understanding with him nor seeks his aid.

I have frequently observed that the attitude of my Zande friends, as shown in their behaviour rather than in their statements, was different when someone was accused of injuring them by witchcraft from their attitude when they themselves were accused of injuring others. Again, their response to a direct question whether a witch knows his own condition and injures others of his own free will (that is when I evoked a statement of accepted opinion) was different to the information they sometimes volunteered when the question was not explicitly raised. The particular situation in which they found themselves pointed their statements and coloured their opinions.

In the course of discussions upon other subjects I have sometimes found that informants will admit that it is possible that some witches may sometimes, in certain circumstances, be ignorant of their condition, and that their ignorance is generally admitted in the cases of witch-children and of adult witches who have been accused of witchcraft on one or two occasions only. Also, when a man's witchcraft is 'cool', as Azande say, or as we should say when it is inoperative, he may well be ignorant of his condition.

I think, in fact, that it would not be reading too much into the ideas Azande sometimes express on this subject to describe them as follows: A man cannot help being a witch; it is not his fault that he is born with witchcraft in his belly. He may be quite ignorant that he is a witch and quite innocent of acts of witchcraft. In this state of innocence he might do someone an injury unwittingly, but when he has on several occasions been exposed by the poison oracle he is then conscious of his powers and begins to use them, with malice.

When a man or one of his family or kin is sick he is very annoyed. To understand his feelings about the moral responsibility of the man whose name the oracle discloses as responsible for the sickness, it must be recollected that he places before it the names of those people whom he dislikes most, so that the witch is likely to be someone with whom he has been for some time on bad terms. Old animosity is reinforced by new resentment. It is therefore useless to suggest to him that the witch is unaware of his witchcraft, for he is disinclined to consider such a possibility when he has long known of the man's hatred and desire to do him an injury. In such a situation as this, moral responsibility of witches is assumed without qualifications. It is contained in the processes of selection and accusation and has no need to be stated.

But the same persons who have so strongly asserted the malice and volition of others when they are the injured party will speak in a different manner when they are recipients of fowls' wings. I have often had an opportunity to observe the same persons in both situations. Having considered what are the usual opinions held by Azande about responsibility of witches, and how their reaction to injury brings out the notion of responsibility in its most uncompromising form, we may now observe how the witch responds to an accusation.

If he is short-tempered he may make a scene when a fowl's wing is placed before him. He may tell the messenger to take it away and may curse the people who sent it, and say that they are simply trying to humiliate him out of malice. Such scenes are rare, but I have either witnessed or had good knowledge of several, and men have been known to injure a messenger. A man who behaves in this manner is acting contrary to custom and is insulting the chief's deputy who ordered the wing to be laid before him. He will be laughed at as a provincial who is ignorant of the manners of polite society, and may gain the reputation of a hardened witch who admits his witchcraft by the anger he displays when it is found out. What he ought to do is to blow out water and say: 'If I possess witchcraft in my belly I am unaware of it; may it cool. It is thus that I blow out water.'

It is difficult to judge from a man's public behaviour his real feelings when presented with a fowl's wing, for even if he is certain of his innocence he will perform this simple ceremony, since it is the proper thing for a gentleman to do; for it is not only laid down by custom that he must blow out water, but the phrases in which he is expected to express his regret are more or less stereotyped, and even the earnest and apologetic tone of voice in which he utters them is determined by tradition.

When I have had the opportunity I have spoken to the accused man as shortly as possible after the presentation of a fowl's wing to him in order to discover his views. Often enough the accused was one of my servants, informants, or personal friends, so that I was able to do so in private and without shyness. I found that they either declared that the accusation was silly, even malicious, or they accepted it with resignation. Those who resented the accusation would say that their accusers had not consulted the oracles at all, but had just killed fowls and stuck their wings on a stick, or that if they consulted the poison oracle it must have made a mistake owing to witchcraft having influenced its verdict or a taboo having been broken. These suggestions would not be made in public. A man may add in private that he has never been accused of witchcraft before, and that it is therefore unlikely that he would start bewitching people now. A man who is able to point to several of his close kinsmen who have been subject to post-mortem examination and have been found to lack witchcraft-substance in their bellies will instance these cases to show that it is wellnigh impossible for him to be a witch. However, such a man will blow on the wing in order to end the matter and avoid unpleasantness. He would say to me afterwards: 'If I am a witch I know nothing about it. Why should I wish to injure anyone? But since they gave me the fowl's wing I blew on it to show that I bear no one ill-will.'

Judging from these private conversations with Azande after they have received fowls' wings I would say that it is mainly difference of temperament which decides the emotional reaction to an accusation of witchcraft. In public everybody reacts in a like manner for, however offended a man may be, he ought to act with standardized meekness.

I once heard a man give his son sound advice on this matter. From time to time the youth had been presented with fowls' wings by a neighbour and had vigorously protested against what he considered insults and nothing more. His father told him that the accusations were, of course, absurd, as several of his kinsmen had been examined post mortem and no witchcraft-substance had been found in their abdomens. Nevertheless, it did no harm to blow water. He said that it was not only polite to do so when requested but also showed an absence of ill-feeling which ought to characterize all good citizens. It is better for an innocent man to comply with good grace.

But though many men declare in private that they are not witches and that there must have been a mistake, my experience of Azande when presented with hens' wings has convinced me that some think, for a short time at any rate, that perhaps after all they are witches. Tradition about witchcraft, so definite about what cannot normally be tested—e.g. the concrete nature of witchcraft-substance—is vague and indeterminate about what might be proved or disproved, namely, the operation of witchcraft. The manner in which witches carry out their exploits is a mystery to Azande, and since in waking life they have no evidence upon which to base a theory of action, they fall back upon the transcendental notion of soul. Dreams are largely perceptions of witchcraft and in dreams a man may see and talk to witches, yet to a Zande dream life is a world of shadowy doubts. It is possible to understand, therefore, that a man accused of bewitching another may hesitate to deny the accusation and even convince himself for a short while of its evident untruth. He knows that often witches are asleep when the soul of their witchcraft-substance flits on its errand of destruction. Perhaps when he was asleep and unaware something of the kind happened and his witchcraft led its independent life. In these circumstances a man might well be a witch and yet not know that he is one. Yet I have never known a Zande admit his witchcraft.

But a man will be very lucky if he escapes occasional accusations, and after the poison oracle has declared on several occasions that a man has bewitched others he may doubt his immunity. 'The poison oracle does not err' is every Zande's *credo*. Its authority is backed by the political power of the princes and by tradition. Moreover, the fact that a man has publicly to enact a confession of guilt by blowing on a fowl's wing must render him at least doubtful about the existence of witchcraft in his belly.

II

I sometimes asked a man, if I knew him very well, 'Are you a witch?' I expected a prompt unqualified denial couched in offended tone, but received often a humble reply, 'Ai, master, if there is witchcraft in my belly I know nothing of it. I am no witch because people have not seen witchcraft in the bellies of our kin.' However, it was less the replies I received than the tone and manner in which they were given that gave me an impression of doubt. Had I asked them whether they were thieves the tone and manner of their reply would have been decided and angry.

In one of my texts an old man prays to Mbori, the Supreme Being, at dawn before making his early morning ablutions, saying that he has stolen no man's possession, that he has not committed adultery with any man's wife, that he bears no man ill-will, but desires to live in charity with his neighbours; and he adds, 'Even if I possess witchcraft in my belly may I not harm the gardens of any man. May the mouth of my witchcraft cool; let it rather vent its spleen on those animals in the bush that daily dance on the graves of my kinsmen.'

It is usual, and considered polite and friendly, for a man who visits a sick friend to pause near his friend's hut and ask his wife to bring water in a gourd. He takes a draught of this water and, after swilling his mouth with it, blows it in spray to the ground and says, 'O Mbori, this man who is sick, if it is I who am killing him with my witchcraft let him recover.' It must be remembered, however, that this speech is a mere formality, and whilst it suggests a cultural recognition of the possibility of a man injuring another unawares, it would be wrong to assume that the man who spoke the words had any doubts about his own immunity from witchcraft at the time. According to Zande notions, a witch would almost certainly not visit a man whom he had bewitched.

When consulting the rubbing-board oracle about a sick kinsman or wife a man may ask it about his neighbours to discover who is bewitching the sick person. Sometimes before placing the names of these people before the oracle one will hear him ask, 'Is it I who am to blame?' Here again the question shows a recognition of the possibility of unawareness of witchcraft, but there is no reason to suppose that the man who asks it considers for a moment that he might be responsible. His question is a pure formality. It looks well to show himself open-minded in his inquiry, and he may do so without fear of the rubbing-board oracle accusing him, since either he or a friend is the operator. A man would not ask this question of the poison oracle.

It is said that when a man goes to war his wives take a draught of water and blow it out on the foot of the ghost-shrine in the centre of his homestead, and say: 'May nothing happen to him. May my witchcraft cool towards him. O fellow-wives, may nothing happen to our husband. Be cool towards him.'

It will be remembered also that before making an autopsy on a dead kinsman his relatives will first ask the poison oracle for an assurance that his belly does not contain witchcraft-substance.

III

One would imagine that if witchcraft is hereditary, then a man must surely have a good idea whether he is a witch or not from the records of his father, his paternal uncles, and his grandfather. He must know whether they have ever paid compensation for murder, received fowls' wings, and undergone unsuccessful post-mortem examination. But, whilst a man will certainly bring up cases in which the corpses of his kinsmen were examined for witchcraft and found to contain none in order to boast his own immunity, the fact that a man's forebears were witches is not stressed. It is generally not even known, for it has no significance either to their sons or to other people since no one is interested in the question whether a man is a witch or not. To a Zande this appears an entirely theoretical question and one about which he has not informed himself. What he wants to know is whether a certain man is injuring him in a particular situation at a particular time. Hence the doctrine of hereditary witchcraft probably has little influence towards indicating to a man his possession of witchcraft.

This lack of precision in identification of witchcraft is rendered even more obvious by British rule, which does not permit direct vengeance upon a witch, nor accept the legality of his paying compensation for an imaginary crime. In the old days when witchcraft became a criminal charge—that is to say, when murder had been committed—there was no doubt who were witches. If a man was executed or paid compensation for murder he was a witch, and he must have felt assured of his own guilt and his kinsmen must have accepted the stigma that attached itself, at any rate for a time, to their name on account of this enaction of justice. But today a witch is never accused of a crime. At the worst he can be told that his witchcraft is injuring someone, but he will not be told that he has killed him, and there is no reason to suppose that a man who has been exposed by the poison oracle as having caused a man sickness was also the man who actually killed him, although he died from the same sickness. Hence a witch and his kinsmen will remain in complete ignorance that he has committed murder. The relatives of a dead man will eventually kill someone with vengeance-magic, but the general public and the relatives of the slain witch will remain ignorant of the cause of his death. His kinsmen will suppose that he has also died from witchcraft, and they in their turn will try and avenge themselves on a witch. No man or woman today has to face an accusation of murder by witchcraft, that is to say, an accusation by a prince's oracle, so that this factor in the creation of self-knowledge of witchcraft is now absent.

At the present time there are no longer means of bringing a witch to the fore by an act of public vengeance. All is vagueness and confusion. Each small group of kinsmen act in private slaying witches by their magic unknown to the rest of the world. Only the prince knows what is happening, and he is silent. The same death is considered by neighbours as death and little more, by kinsmen as an act of witchcraft, by the kinsmen of other dead men as an act of their magic. In matters other than death it is possible for one set of people to say that their oracle has exposed a man for bewitching one of their kinsmen, while the friends and relatives of the accused may easily deny the imputation and say that he blew out water as a mere matter of form because there is no certainty that the oracle has spoken the truth or even has ever been consulted at all, for it is not a prince's oracle. Hence it is, perhaps, not extraordinary that I should never have heard a confession of witchcraft.

CHAPTER V

Witch-Doctors

I

IT may have occurred to many readers that there is an analogy between the Zande concept of witchcraft and our own concept of luck. When, in spite of human knowledge, forethought, and technical efficiency, a man suffers a mishap, we say that it is his bad luck, whereas Azande say that he has been bewitched. The situations which give rise to these two notions are similar. If the misfortune has already taken place and is concluded Azande content themselves with the thought that their failure has been due to witchcraft, just as we content ourselves with the reflection that our failure is due to our hard luck. In such situations there is not a great difference between our reactions and theirs. But when a misfortune is in process of falling upon a man, as in sickness, or is anticipated, our responses are different to theirs. We make every effort to rid ourselves of, or elude, a misfortune by our knowledge of the objective conditions which cause it. The Zande acts in a like manner, but since in his beliefs the chief cause of any misfortune is witchcraft, he concentrates his attention upon this factor of supreme importance. They and we use rational means for controlling the conditions that produce misfortune, but we conceive of these conditions differently from them.

Since Azande believe that witches may at any time bring sickness and death upon them they are anxious to establish and maintain contact with these evil powers and by counteracting them control their own destiny. Although they may at any moment be struck down by witchcraft they do not despair. Far from being gloomy, all observers have described Azande as a cheerful people who are always laughing and joking. For Azande need not live in continual dread of witchcraft, since they can enter into relations with it and thereby control it by means of oracles and magic. By oracles they can foresee future dispositions of witchcraft and change them before they develop.

By magic they can guard themselves against witchcraft and destroy it.

The Zande witch-doctor is both diviner and magician. As diviner he exposes witches; as magician he thwarts them. But chiefly he is a diviner. In this capacity he is often known as *ira avure*, possessor of *avure*, the word *avure* being contained also in the expression *do avure*, 'to dance *avure*', which describes the dance of witch-doctors and in a more general sense the whole seance at which they perform. When he acts as a leech he is known as a *binza*, but this word and *ira avure* are interchangeable in reference to his divinatory functions, though *binza* is alone used in reference to his leechcraft. In both roles his task is the same—to counteract witchcraft. As a diviner he discovers the location of witchcraft, and as a leech he repairs its ravages.

Azande regard witch-doctors as one of their many oracles though they do not normally speak of them as oracles. They consider their prophecies and revelations to have equal value with the disclosures of the rubbing-board oracles but to be less reliable than the poison oracle and the termites oracle. I have already described how a sick man, or kinsmen acting on his behalf, consults various oracles, ending with the poison oracle, to determine who among his enemies is bewitching him. But instead of commencing therapeutic operations with the rubbing-board oracle they may summon one or several witch-doctors to divine on behalf of a sick man, or about economic failure. Though great attention is paid to the declarations of witch-doctors their revelations have no legal value, and it is even considered inadvisable to approach a witch by the customary procedure on the strength of a witch-doctor's statement unsupported by a corroborative verdict of the poison oracle.

II

The Zande corporation of witch-doctors is a specialized profession with vested interests in knowledge of medicines, so that many of their activities are not easily observed. Therefore I preface my description of witch-doctors with a short statement of the way in which I collected my information.

In studying the Zande corporation of witch-doctors it was necessary to divide the field of inquiry into two sections and to employ different methods in the investigation of each. One section comprised their activities in relation to the rest of Zande society, the part they play in communal life, their place in national tradition, their contacts with the princes, and the current beliefs and stories associated with them in the public mind. It was easy to record this part of their life, for there was no difficulty about witnessing public performances which are open to all comers. It was likewise easy to obtain a commentary on what is abstruse in the ritual from regular informants and casual bystanders alike. In this section it was, in fact, possible to employ the usual methods of fieldwork investigation—direct and repeated observation of behaviour, cross-questioning of natives, both in the situation of ritual when their attention is directed to the performance about which information is sought and in more leisurely conversations in tent, or hut, collection of texts, and even mild participation in native activities by the ethnographer himself.

On the other hand, the corporation has an esoteric life from which the uninitiated are excluded, and this forms the second section of our study. Not only are knowledge of medicines and tricks of the trade hidden from outsiders, but much of the inner social life of the corporation and many of its beliefs are unknown to them. The usual methods of inquiry were here largely ineffective and the ordinary system of controls inoperative. I could have observed directly only by becoming myself a witch-doctor, and while this would have been possible among the Azande, I doubt whether it would have proved advantageous. Previous experience of participation in activities of this kind had led me to the conclusion that an anthropologist gains little by obtruding himself into ceremonies as an actor, for a European is never seriously regarded as a member of an esoteric group and has little opportunity of checking to what extent a performance is changed for his benefit, by design, or by the psychological responses of the participants to the rites being affected by his presence. It is, moreover, difficult to use the ordinary methods of critical investigation when one is actually engaged in ceremonial and is supposed to be an eager member of an institution. The many practical difficulties of a European being actively engaged in the trade of an African witch-doctor were also weighty enough to act as a deterrent to this mode of inquiry, especially as members of the noble class (Avongara) do not become witch-doctors.

The course of inquiry which immediately suggested itself was to try to win the goodwill of one or two practitioners and to persuade them to divulge their secrets in strict confidence. This I attempted and made some headway in my inquiries before it became evident that I was not likely to proceed very far. My informants were prepared to give information which they knew could be obtained without great difficulty from other sources, but were reticent about their principal secrets to the point of refusal to discuss them. It would, I believe, have been possible by using every artifice to have eventually wormed out all their secrets, but this would have meant bringing undue pressure on people to divulge what they wished to hide, so I dropped inquiry into this part of Zande life altogether for several months. Subsequently I adopted the only alternative course, of using a substitute, to learn all about the technique of witch-doctors. My personal servant, Kamanga, was initiated into the corporation and became a practising witch-doctor. He gave me full accounts of procedure from the commencement of his career step by step as it developed.

This might not be thought a very good method of inquiry, and I had doubts about its fertility when I began to employ it, but it proved, in event, to be fruitful. While Kamanga was slowly being initiated by one practitioner, it was possible for me to utilize his information to draw out of their shells rival practitioners by playing on their jealousy and vanity. Kamanga could be trusted to tell me everything he had learnt in the course of his tuition, but I felt sure that, while he would be told much more than I would obtain from my own inquiries, part of his training would be cut out by his teacher since we acted straight-forwardly in telling him that his pupil would pass on all information to me. It was difficult for him to lie directly to Kamanga, since he was aware that his statements would be tested with rival witch-doctors in the locality and with practitioners from other districts, but he could, on the other hand, keep information from him with fair success, and this is what he did do. In the long run, however, an ethnographer is bound to triumph. Armed with preliminary knowledge nothing can prevent him from driving deeper and deeper the wedge if he is interested and persistent.

This is the kind of inquiry which needs leisurely pursuit.

Results can only be obtained by a patient approach and a long wait upon favourable conditions. I never intruded upon private conversations between Kamanga and Badobo, his teacher, however dilatory their conduct. The astuteness of the teacher would have surprised me more had it not been that I was well acquainted with the extreme credulity of his pupil, whose deep faith in magicians never ceased to astonish me, though I had daily evidence of it. Subtle procrastination might well have persuaded me to jettison my inquiry into the technique of witch-doctors in favour of other anthropological cargo had it not been for the arrival of a noted witch-doctor on a professional tour from a distant district. This man, named Bögwözu, was arrogant towards the local practitioners, whom he treated with alternating contempt and condescension. Badobo bore his conceit less easily than the other witch-doctors since he was used to the deference now paid to his rival.

Here was an opportunity to be seized at once, since it might not recur. I flattered Bögwözu's self-esteem, suggested that he should take over the tuition of Kamanga, and offered to pay him munificently so long as he taught his pupil all he knew I explained to him that I was tired of Badobo's wiliness anc extortion, and that I expected my generosity to be reciprocatec by the equipment of Kamanga with something more than exoteric knowledge of a witch-doctor's technique. To Badobo I excused myself on the grounds that this new practitioner was distinguished in his profession and had qualified among the neighbouring Baka people, who are renowned for their magic, as well as among Azande, so that he could teach Kamanga the medicines of two cultures. At the same time Badobo was to continue his instruction and receive remuneration for his services.

When informants fall out anthropologists come into their own. The rivalry between these two practitioners grew into bitter and ill-concealed hostility. Bögwözu gave me information about medicines and magical rites to prove that his rival was ignorant of the one or incapable in the performance of the other. Badobo became alert and showed himself no less eager to demonstrate his knowledge of magic both to Kamanga and to myself. They vied with each other to gain ascendancy among the local practitioners. Kamanga and I reaped a full harvest in this quarrel, not only from the protagonists themselves but also from other witch-doctors in the neighbourhood, and even from interested laymen.

But, in spite of their rivalry and my persistence, the two practitioners mentioned above did not divulge to Kamanga the method by which they extracted objects from the bodies of their patients, a surgical operation performed by witch-doctors all over Africa, for they well understood that he was a sponge out of which I squeezed all the moisture of information which they put into it. I mention this fact because, although I caught them out and compelled them through force of awkward circumstances to divulge their exact mode of trickery, it shows that in spite of the methods of investigation which I employed, my informants did not communicate their entire knowledge to me, even indirectly, and suggests that there were other departments of their knowledge which they did not disclose. This may have been the case. It was inevitable that I should learn sooner or later how objects are removed from the bodies of sick persons by Zande witch-doctors, since I knew beforehand what happens among other African peoples, but it is possible that in other matters where there was not the same basis for inquiry the witch-doctors, if they wished to hide anything, concealed it with greater success. I have only to add that Kamanga's sustained interest and industry enabled me to take down the gist of his experiences in a large number of native texts, given week after week for many months, and that my constant association with him enabled us to discuss these texts informally and at leisure. A single informant known intimately is often a more reliable source of information than the pooled statements of many informants less well known.

III

A European in Zandeland is likely to come across witch-doctors for the first time at a seance, at which they dance and divine, because seances are held in public and heralded and accompanied by drums. These public performances are local events of some importance, and those who live in the neighbourhood regard them as interesting spectacles well worth a short walk. It may be supposed, indeed, that attendance at them has an important formative influence on the growth of witchcraft-beliefs in the minds of children, for children make a point of attending them and taking part in them as spectators and chorus. This is the first occasion on which they demonstrate their belief, and it is more dramatically and more publicly affirmed at these seances than in any other situations.

Seances are held on a variety of occasions, but generally at the request of a householder who is suffering, or fears, a misfortune. Perhaps he or his wife is ill or he fears his children will sicken. Perhaps his hunting is consistently unsuccessful or he wants to know where in the bush he is likely to find animals. Perhaps blight has begun to mar his ground-nuts or he is merely uncertain where to sow his cleusine. Perhaps his wife has not given him a child or he feels that someone is about to speak ill of him to his father-in-law.

One meets witch-doctors as they proceed by ones or twos towards a troubled homestead, each wearing his hat decorated with feathers and carrying his large hide bag containing skins, horns, magic whistles, belts, leglets and armlets made from various wild fruits, and seeds. In olden days before European administration only two or three witch-doctors would attend a meeting in any one district, but today most government settlements can muster half a dozen, while occasionally at popular seances, as when a new magician is being initiated into the corporation, as many as a dozen will assist.

When they meet at their destination they exchange greetings and discuss in low tones among themselves the affairs of the seance while preparing the ground for dancing. In these conversations and preparations the lead is taken by an experienced magician who has generally been a witch-doctor for a longer period than the others, and who may have initiated many of the other performers into the craft. His authority is not great.

Members of the ruling class never, to my knowledge, become practitioners. A noble would at once lose prestige by associating with commoners at their joint meals of medicine and public dances. I have even heard contemptuous remarks about a commoner headman who occasionally took part in these proceedings, as it was considered beneath the dignity of a man holding a political position from his prince to demean himself in this manner. It was thought more fitting that he should restrict himself to political life and remain a spectator of these activities, participation in which must lessen the social distance which divided him from those who owed him allegiance as the representative of his prince. Consequently the political pattern of Zande social life has left no imprint upon the institution of their witch-doctors, for had princes entered into the corporation they must necessarily have done so as leaders.

It is very seldom that women become witch-doctors. A few are qualified to act as leeches, and occasionally a woman gains a considerable reputation among her patients, usually persons of her own sex, and is appointed practitioner to a prince's harem. Men also visit women leeches to be treated for ailments. It is very rare, however, for a woman to take part in dances of witch-doctors. They do not take part in the communal meals of witch-doctors, nor are they initiated into the craft through ritual burial. Women witch-doctors and leeches are always past their youth and are often widows.

IV

Preparations for a dance consist in marking out an area of operations and, when that has been done, of robing. Starting from the drums, a large circle is drawn on the ground, and this is generally made more conspicuous by white ashes being sprinkled along it. No layman is supposed to enter into this circle reserved for the witch-doctors' dance, and were he to do so he would risk having a black-beetle or piece of bone shot into his body by an outraged magician. Each practitioner, having unslung from his shoulder his leather bag, produces from it a number of horns of waterbuck, bushbuck, dik-dik, bongo, and other animals, and thrusts these in the earth along the circular ash-line. On one of these straightened horns often rests a pot of water into which witch-doctors gaze in order to see witchcraft. Interspersed among the horns are gnarled pieces of magical wood, and from both these and the horns magical whistles sometimes dangle. The place where his horns are stuck in the earth and the space in front of them are regarded by a witch-doctor as his own particular field of operations upon which he will resent encroachment by any other witch-doctor.

The horns, straightened out by being heated in the fire and bent, while hot, on the ground, are filled with a paste, made from ashes and juices of various herbs and shrubs mixed with oil, and they are replenished from time to time when the supply is running short or becoming dry. These medicines have great importance, for knowledge of the medicines means knowledge of the art of a witch-doctor. It is not magic words nor ritual sequences which are stressed in initiation into the corporation of witch-doctors, but trees and herbs. A Zande witch-doctor is essentially a man who knows what plants and trees compose the medicines which, if eaten, will give him power to see witchcraft with his own eyes, to know where it resides, and to drive it away from its intended victims. The Zande witch-doctor exercises supernatural powers solely because he knows the right medicines and has eaten them in the right manner. His prophecies are derived from the magic inside him. His inspiration does not spring from the Supreme Being nor from the ghosts of the dead.

The professional robes with which witch-doctors adorn themselves while the dancing ground is being marked out consist of straw hats topped with large bunches of feathers of geese and parrots and other marsh and bush birds. Strings of magic whistles made from peculiar trees are strung across their chests and tied round their arms. Skins of wild cats, civet cats, genets, servals, and other carnivora and small rodents, as well as of monkeys (especially the colobus), are tucked under their waist-strings so that they form a fringe which entirely covers the bark-cloth worn by all male Azande. Over the skins they tie a string of fruits of the doleib palm (*Borassus flabellifer*). A wooden tongue has been inserted into each of these fruits making of them dull-sounding bells which rattle together from the waist on the least movement. They tie round their legs and ankles, and sometimes round their arms also, bundles of orange-coloured seeds. In their hands they hold rattles, iron bells attached to wooden handles, and they shake these up and down in the performance. As he dances each witch-doctor is in himself a complete orchestra, which rattles and rings and bangs to the rhythm of the drums.

v

Besides the witch-doctors there are many other people present at a seance, and we may refer to them according to their functions as spectators, drummers, and chorus of boys. Men and boys sit under a tree or granary near the drums. Women sit in another part of the homestead a long way removed from the men, for men and women never sit together in public. Seances are generally well attended by the neighbourhood, some people coming with questions to be put to the witch-doctors, others coming to hear local scandal and to look at the dancing. To a woman especially it is a relief from the monotony of the family life to which she is tied by her duties, and from the drab routine of the household to which the jealousy of her husband confines her. As a rule the owner of the homestead will throw it open to all comers, since a large audience flatters the performers and their host alike.

Those who wish to put questions to the witch-doctors bring small presents with them in order to place them before the man of whose oracular powers they desire to make use. These presents include small knives, rings, piastres and half-piastres, but consist most commonly of small heaps of eleusine and bundles of maize-heads and bowls of sweet potatoes.

The host has to provide gong and drums, and since it is only here and there that one finds a household possessing these instruments he will almost certainly have to spend a part of the morning borrowing them from neighbours and carrying them to his own residence. He has also to supervise the various household arrangements consequent upon a visit of witch-doctors. If there are only one or two magicians a generous householder will entertain them to a meal and will probably ask a few of the more influential spectators as well. He must prepare a few small presents for the witch-doctors as a reward for their services when the afternoon's work is over. He spends most of the afternoon sitting with his guests.

Drummers are not specially summoned, but are recruited among youths and boys on the spot. They are chosen, if selected at all, for their ability in the art, but generally there is no choice of drummers, and he who can first get possession of an instrument plays it. There ·is often much competition among boys and youths to act the part of drummer, so that squabbles sometimes result. Only if a drummer tires or proves inefficient will someone else take his place, unless, as often happens, he is prepared to let a friend take turns at the drums with himself. In exchange for their services witch-doctors will sometimes give the drummers one or two inspired revelations without demanding a fee.

Before commencing to dance and sing witch-doctors often order out of the crowd of spectators all the small boys and range them on the ground near the drums to back up their songs. Everyone in the crowd to some extent backs up the songs of the performers, but these boys may be considered as constituting a special chorus as they are placed for this purpose where they can easily be seen by the witch-doctors and admonished if they are not singing lustily enough. If a magician is annoyed with them he will shoot a bone or black-beetle into one of the boys and then extract it to show what he can do if he is really exasperated by their slackness.

VI

A seance consists of a witch-doctor or witch-doctors dancing and singing in accompaniment to drums and gong and answering questions put to them by spectators. It takes some time before the performers are warmed up. They commence slowly with sedate hops and then gather momentum, leaping and whirling with remarkable agility and force. Weighted down with excessive clothing and exposed to the full glare of the sun perspiration pours off them. After a short dance one of them rushes up to the drums and shakes his hand-bells at them to stop. When they cease he lectures the drummers and tells them that they must beat the drums better than that. They commence again. Drums and gong resound, hand-bells go *wia wia*, wooden bells strung round waists clatter, and anklets click in a confusion of sound but with a rhythmic pattern since the dancers move hands, legs, and trunks to the beat of gong and drums. One of the witch-doctors goes over to the drummers and orders them to cease beating. He faces the crowd and harangues them, especially the chorus of boys: 'Why are you not backing up my songs properly, everyone must sing the chorus; if I see anyone slacking I will injure him with my magic; I will seize him as a witch. Now, does everyone hear what I am saying?' Always there are such preliminaries before the witch-doctors commence to reveal hidden things.

They begin to sing and dance again. One magician performs at a time in front of the drums, leaping and turning with his full vigour, while the others keep their positions in a row behind him, dancing with less violence and supporting his songs. Sometimes two or three of them will advance together up to the drums and give a joint performance. When a member of the audience wishes to put a question he or she puts it to a particular witch-doctor who responds by dancing alone up to the drums and there giving a spirited solo performance. When he is so out of breath that he can dance no longer he shakes his hand-bells at the drummers for them to cease beating, and he doubles up his body to regain breath, or stumbles about the place as though intoxicated. This is the moment for giving an oracular reply to the question put to him. Usually he commences to do this in a far-off voice and with faltering speech. It appears as though the words come to him from without and that he has difficulty in hearing and transmitting them. As he proceeds with his utterances the witch-doctor begins to throw off his air of semi-consciousness and to give forth his revelations with assurance, and eventually with truculence. When he has finished what he has to say he dances again to obtain further knowledge of the matter about which he is being questioned, since full information may not have come to him during his first dance, or he may dance to another question if he considers that he has satisfactorily dealt with the first one.

Sometimes at these meetings the performers dance themselves into a state of fury and gash their tongues and chests with knives. I have witnessed scenes which remind one of the priests of Baal who 'cried aloud, and cut themselves after their manner with knives and lancets, till the blood gushed out upon them'. I have seen men in a state of wild excitement, drunk with the intoxicating orchestral music of drums and gong, bells and rattles, throw back their heads and gash their chests with knives, till blood poured in streams down their bodies. Others cut their tongues and blood mixed with saliva foamed at the corners of their lips and trickled down their chins where it was carried away in a flow of sweat. When they have cut their tongues they dance with them hanging out of their mouths to show their art. They put on ferocious airs, enlarge the whites of their eyes, and open their mouths into grimaces as though contortions, due to great physical tension and exhaustion, were not gruesome enough.

What is the meaning of all this fury and grotesque expression? This we shall only discover by dissecting it and making a careful analysis of its parts.

VII

Seances are held when a householder has suffered some misfortune. It may be asked why in these circumstances he does not consult one of the oracles in private rather than go to the trouble of summoning several practitioners to a more expensive public performance, especially, as we shall see later, since other oracles are generally considered to be more reliable as sources of revelation than witch-doctors, and since he will in any case have to ask them for a confirmation of a witch-doctor's utterances before he can act upon them. The reason may be that public seances increase the social prestige of a householder who initiates them, and that revelations of witch-doctors have a peculiar social value in that, although considered more liable to error than several other oracles, they have the special advantage which an open investigation gives in delicate personal matters. Moreover, the witch-doctor functions at these seances not only as an oracular agent but also as a fighter against witchcraft, so that he can not only tell a person in which direction he must look for the witch who is injuring him and what steps he may take to counteract the influence of witchcraft, but also by his dances he wages immediate war on witches and may succeed in driving them from his patient, so that, by showing them he is aware of their identity they are scared for ever from his homestead. But I believe that the first of these reasons, the desire to enhance one's reputation by giving a public entertainment, is the most important. To those present a seance is a very good show which is amusing to watch, now and again exciting, and always provides material for comment and gossip for a long time afterwards. To the master of the homestead it is a means of finding out who is troubling his welfare; of warning the witch, who is probably present in person at the seance, that he is on his tracks; and of gaining public support and recognition in his difficulties, and esteem and publicity by throwing open his house to the countryside and by employing performers.

An account of a seance which I wrote myself on returning home in the evening after witnessing it will amplify the

preceding text and tell what happened from a European's point
of view.

One of the witch-doctors steps forward after a short dance
and demands silence. He calls out the name of one of those
present—'Zingbondo, Zingbondo, that death of your father-in-
law, listen, that death of your father-in-law, Mugadi, Mugadi
is dead, it is true Mugadi is dead, you hear?' He speaks as
though in a trance, his speech laborious and disconnected.
'Mugadi is dead, his daughter (your wife) is in your homestead,
her mother has come to live with you. Listen, they must not
go and weep near the grave of Mugadi. If they continue to do
this then one among you will die, do you hear?' Zingbondo
replies meekly, 'Yes, master, I hear, it is indeed as you have
spoken, you have spoken the truth.' (Zingbondo is very pleased
at this announcement as he resents his wife having an excuse,
which cannot be denied, for frequent absence from his household.)

Another witch-doctor steps forward smiling with
confidence—he is an old hand—and turns to the local headman, named Banvuru, and addresses him thus, 'Chief, your
companions are slandering you, they are speaking evil of you
and wish to injure you; be careful to consult the rubbing-board
oracle about them frequently.' The headman does not reply,
but someone who wishes to curry favour with him and to show
that it is not he who is playing traitor calls out, 'Tell us the
names of these men.' (This is more difficult, for the witch-doctor
wishes to avoid making enemies by personal accusations.) He
retires, saying that he will dance to the question. He signals
to the drummers to commence beating the drums, to which he
dances and leaps about wildly; his bells go *wia wia wia*, the
doleib fruits knock together around his waist; sweat pours from
his body, he and his companions utter wild yells. He pants for
breath and, exhausted, stumbles towards the drums which he
silences by a downward stroke of his bells. In sudden silence
he stands for a long while in front of the headman. He does
not speak. In a moment he falls helplessly to the ground as
though in a faint, and for several minutes he writhes there, face
to the earth, with the movements of one who suffers great pain.
Then he makes a dramatic recovery, bounds to his feet, and
utters a revelation. 'Those men', he says, 'who are injuring you

with witchcraft, who are slandering you, they are so-and-so'
(he mentions the name of the headman who preceded the
present holder of the office), 'and so-and-so' (he gives the name
of a man from whom the headman has lately taken away his
daughter to give in marriage to someone else). The witch-
doctor hesitates. He utters 'and . . .', then pauses, looking fixedly
at the ground beneath his feet as though searching for something there, while everyone awaits another disclosure. One of
his companions comes forward to his assistance and says in an
assured voice '. . . and so-and-so, he also is injuring you, there
are three of them.' He mentions the two persons whose names
had previously been disclosed and the one which he has just
added to his list. Another witch-doctor interrupts him. 'No,'
he says, 'there are four of them, so-and-so is also bewitching
you' (he mentions the name of one of his personal enemies
whom he wishes to place out of favour with the headman for
his own purposes. The other practitioners understand his
motives, but witch-doctors never contradict one another at a
public seance; they present a united front to the uninitiated.)

The headman on his part listens to what he has been told,
but he does not speak a word. Later he will place these four
names before the poison oracle and learn the truth. He thinks—
a Zande told me—that after all the witch-doctors ought to be
correct in what they say, for they are witches themselves and
ought to know their own mothers' sons.

Oracles having been delivered for the benefit of the chief
person present the dance is resumed and continued for hour
after hour. An old man calls out the name of a witch-doctor
and gives him some maize-heads. He wants to know whether
his eleusine crop will succeed this year. The witch-doctor runs
to look into his medicine-pot. He gazes for a little while into
the medicated water and then springs forward into a dance.
He dances because it is in the dance that medicines of the witch-
doctors work and cause them to see hidden things. It stirs up
and makes active the medicines within them, so that when they
are asked a question they will always dance it rather than
ponder it to find the answer. He concludes his dance, silences
the drums, and walks over to where his interlocutor sits. 'You
ask me about your eleusine, whether it will succeed this year;
where have you planted it?' 'Sir,' he replies, 'I have planted

it beyond the little stream Bagomoro.' The witch-doctor solilo-
quizes. 'You have planted it beyond the little stream Bagomoro,
hm! hm! How many wives have you got?' 'Three.' 'I see witchcraft ahead, witchcraft ahead, witchcraft ahead: be cautious,
for your wives are going to bewitch your eleusine crop. The
chief wife, it is not she, eh! No it is not the chief wife. Do you
hear what I say? It is not the chief wife. I can see it in my belly,
for I have great medicine. It is not the chief wife, not the chief
wife, not the chief wife. Do you hear it? Not the chief wife.' The
witch-doctor is now entering into a trance-like condition and
has difficulty in speaking, save in single words and clipped sentences. 'The chief wife, it is not she. Malice. Malice. Malice.
The other two wives are jealous of her. Malice. Do you hear,
malice? You must guard yourself against them. They must blow
water on to your eleusine. Do you hear? Let them blow water
to cool their witchcraft. Do you hear? Jealousy is a bad thing.
Jealousy is a bad thing, it is hunger. Your eleusine crop will
fail. You will be troubled by hunger; you hear what I say,
hunger?'

I have reconstructed a seance from an account which I wrote
when I had just witnessed it, but I have not attempted to give
all the questions asked and answered during the afternoon.
They are too numerous to record and, moreover, it is not possible to note every statement made by witch-doctors at a meeting where often two of them are functioning at the same time,
for it is not easy to keep pace with more than one inquiry.
Also, even when there is only one witch-doctor present it is difficult to understand what he is talking about unless one is aware
of the exact nature of the question asked because his replies are
not concise and straightforward, but long-winded, rambling,
broken discourses. It is common for witch-doctors to give
revelations to members of their audience without being
requested to do so. They often volunteer gratuitous information
about pending misfortunes.

A performance at court is somewhat different from a performance in a commoner's homestead. Generally the prince sits
by himself, with perhaps a few small sons and pages on the
ground beside him, while deputies, leaders of companies, and
other men of good social position, who happen to be at court,
sit opposite him at a good distance away. Women are not

present. There is no special chorus of boys, and though the spectators, with the exception of the prince himself, may sometimes back up the songs in low voices, generally the witch-doctor sings solo. I have never seen more than one witch-doctor performing at a court. A prince has one or two practitioners among his subjects whom he always summons when he requires the professional services of witch-doctors. The seance is a command performance and the demeanour of everyone present is characterized by the quietness and good form exacted at court. The witch-doctor dances about the prince's business alone and when he has discovered a witch or traitor he walks up to the prince and whispers the name in his ear. There is none of the boasting and display which I have described at performances at commoner homesteads, and a witch-doctor never uses the bullying tones he so often adopts when speaking to commoners. As far as I have observed courtiers do not ask questions of the witch-doctor about their private affairs though they may shout encouragement to him, and, to show their loyalty to their prince, are often loud in their demands that he shall disclose the names of any persons whom he may discover to be threatening the prince's welfare. It is a great honour to be summoned to divine at court and witch-doctors who have performed there are esteemed in the whole province as persons whose revelations may be trusted.

However, the descriptions given in this chapter are of seances at homesteads of commoners and the analysis which follows refers to the behaviour of witch-doctors and their audiences away from court.

VIII

I wish to direct attention to the mode and content of a witch-doctor's revelations. Special notice should be taken of the manner in which a witch-doctor makes his declarations, since I shall have to refer back to it later when considering the whole field of belief in connexion with their activities. They have two main modes of utterance, and both differ from the speech forms of everyday life. The first is one of truculence. They are overbearing with their audiences, taking liberties with them which would at once be resented in ordinary life. They assert themselves in an overweening manner, browbeating drummers, chorus of boys, and spectators alike, telling them to stop talking, ordering them to sit down, admonishing them sharply to pay attention, and so on. All this is taken in good part by those present and no one takes offence at what would, on other occasions, be considered unpardonable rudeness. The same blatant confidence envelops their oracular utterances, which they accompany with all sorts of dramatic gestures and extravagant poses, abandoning ordinary speech for the braggart tones of a diviner imbued with powerful magic from which are derived words which cannot be doubted. They impress their revelations on their hearers with assurance and much repetition.

When they drop their overbearing attitude they lapse into tones even more abnormal. After a spirited dance they disclose secrets or prophesy in the voice of a medium who sees and hears something from without. They deliver these psychic messages in disconnected sentences, often a string of separate words not strung together grammatically, in a dreamy, far-away voice. They speak with difficulty, like men talking in a trance, or like men talking in their sleep. This, as we shall see later, is only partly a pose, for it is also in part a product of physical exhaustion and of faith in their medicines.

How does this mode of delivery affect the content of their utterances? Their revelations and prophecies are based on a knowledge of local scandal. It must be repeated that in Zande belief the possession of witchcraft gives a man power to harm his fellows but is not the motive of crime. We have seen how the drive behind all acts of witchcraft is to be looked for in emotions and sentiments common to all men—malice, jealousy, greed, envy, backbiting, slander, and so on. Now the scandal of native society is largely common property, and witch-doctors, being recruited from the neighbourhood, are well informed about local enmities and squabbles. A witch-doctor who is on a visit from a distant province will take advice on these matters from local witch-doctors before and during a seance. Therefore, when a man asks them to account for some sickness or misfortune which has befallen him they will produce as the cause of the trouble the name of someone who bears their questioner ill-will, or whom their questioner imagines to bear him ill-will. A witch-doctor divines successfully because he says what his listener wishes him to say, and because he uses tact.

It is fairly easy for the witch-doctor, because there are a number of stock enmities in Zande culture; between neighbours, because they have a greater number of contacts and hence more opportunities for quarrelling than those whose homesteads are separated by considerable distances; between wives, because it is a commonplace among Azande that the polygamous family spells friction among its members; and between courtiers, whose political ambitions are bound to clash. A witch-doctor asks his client for the names of his neighbours, wives, or fellow-courtiers as the case may be. He then dances with the names of these people in mind and discloses one of them, if possible by implication rather than directly, as a witch. It is erroneous to suppose that a witch-doctor guesses at random the name of a witch. This would be absurd from the Zande viewpoint, since a grudge of some kind is an essential motive of an act of witchcraft. On the contrary, he takes the names of a number of people who wish his client ill or who have reason for wishing him ill, and decides by means of his magic who of these have the power to injure him and are exercising it; that is, those who have witchcraft-substance in their bellies. Witch-doctors do not merely exercise cunning to find out those who are on bad terms with their clients and produce these names as witches to please those who pay them and cannot see through their subtlety. Everyone is fully aware of the manner in which they discover witches, and their procedure is a necessary outcome of ideas about witchcraft current in their culture.

It is important to note how a witch-doctor produces his revelations. First of all he cross-examines his client. He may want to know the names of his neighbours or wives or of those who took part in some activity with him. Now, it should be noticed that these names are put forward by the client and not by the witch-doctor himself and therefore involve selection on his client's part.

The witch-doctor also gets his listeners into a suitable frame of mind for receiving his revelations by lavish use of professional dogmatism. Having obtained from his client a number of names, he says he will dance to them. After his first two or three dances he repeats, rather than answers, the question put to him, assuring his client that he will discover everything before long. He struts about telling his audience that they will hear the truth today because he has powerful magic which cannot fail him, and he will remind them of earlier prophecies which have been fulfilled. After another bout of dancing he gives a partial answer couched in a negative form. If it is a question about sickness of a child he will tell the father that two of his wives are not responsible and that he will dance to the others. If it is a question about a bad crop of some food plant he will assure the owner of the gardens that those neighbours of his who live in a certain direction from his homestead are not responsible, but that he will now dance to the other directions. Thus I have witnessed witch-doctors dance for half a day about a question of unsuccessful hunting. After dancing for a long time they informed the owner of the hunting area (myself) that they had discovered that it was neither the women nor the young men who were spoiling the sport, and that they would surely ferret out the real culprit before sunset. They danced again, and at the end of the dance they gave the information that those responsible were certainly married men. Later in the day they said that the same witchcraft which had ruined hunting the year before still hung over the hunting area, so that those married men who had entered the district since could at once be exonerated. After further dancing they stopped the drums and announced, without giving their names, that they had discovered three men responsible for the bad hunting. They danced again and told their audience that they had discovered a fourth culprit and that they had ascertained that there were no others besides these four men. Towards evening they divulged that the reason for these four men using witchcraft to injure hunting was that the year before they had not been asked to take part in the activity. It was this which had first occasioned their envy. Although the question about who was injuring the hunting area was put to the witch-doctors in the morning, it was not till after the sun had gone down that they whispered the names of those responsible to their client, this being the usual procedure at court.

Often witch-doctors avoid even whispering names and convey their revelations by innuendo, by *sanza*, as the Azande call it. This conveyance of meaning by hints was extremely difficult for me to follow since I always stood to some extent outside the inner life of the community. It was a form of speech which my knowledge of ordinary linguistic usage enabled me to understand only in part. Even native listeners sometimes miss the full meaning of a witch-doctor's words though it is understood by the man who is asking about his troubles. Words which convey no meaning to the ethnologist and doubtful meaning to other bystanders receive ready interpretation by the questioner, who alone has a full understanding of the situation. A man asks the practitioner who is causing blight on his groundnuts, and is informed that it is no one outside his household, nor the chief wife in the household, who is responsible, but one of the other wives, who bears the chief wife malice. The witch-doctor may not give an opinion about which of the other wives it is, but the householder himself will have his own ideas about the matter, as he has full knowledge of the feelings of members of his homestead towards one another, of the whole history of their mutual contacts, and of any recent events which have disturbed the calm of his household life. When he knows that it is not an outsider who is doing him injury, but one of his wives, he guesses which of them it is, and can check his surmise by consulting the poison oracle, while strangers without the same knowledge of conditions are left in the dark. This is a very simple illustration, but it will serve. Often a witch-doctor's innuendo and its interpretation in the mind of his client are much more involved.

Hence we see how at both ends of an inquiry the layman goes far to meet the witch-doctor. At the beginning he selects to some extent the names of those persons about whom the witch-doctor is to dance, and at the end he supplies in part an interpretation of the witch-doctor's utterances from his own peculiar social circumstances and mental content. I think also that as a witch-doctor brings out his revelations bit by bit, at first, almost as suggestions, even inquiries, he watches carefully his interlocutor to observe whether his answer is in accordance with the questioner's own suspicions. He becomes more definite when he is assured on this point.

A witch-doctor very seldom accuses a member of the aristocracy of witchcraft, just as a commoner does not consult oracles about them. He may give an important prince information about attempts to use sorcery against him by members of his family or clan, but he does not suggest that they are witches.

Princes, however jealous of each other they may be, always maintain class solidarity in opposition to their subjects and do not allow commoners to bring contempt upon any of their relatives. I do not think a witch-doctor would ever have disclosed the name of a noble as a witch in the past, but today I have on rare occasions observed nobles accused of witchcraft, though they have not been closely related to ruling princes.

Discretion is also advisable in revealing names of commoners as witches since Azande do not always take an accusation quietly. I have seen a man rise from his place in the audience and threaten to knife a witch-doctor who was rash enough to accuse him of witchcraft, and so forcibly did he make his protest that the witch-doctor danced again and admitted an error. He said privately that he did not really make a mistake but merely withdrew his statement to save a scene. The man was a witch and proved his guilt by his behaviour.

Witch-doctors often divulge names of witches to ordinary clients in privacy after the seance has ended and the spectators have returned to their homesteads. In public they try to avoid direct statements and, above all, to keep clear of names. It is only when denouncing women and weak people that they are less scrupulous about mentioning names in public. It must be remembered that, apart from the possibility of an immediate scene, a witch-doctor is on other occasions an ordinary citizen and has to live in close daily contact with his neighbours, and therefore has no desire to alienate them by a public insult. Also, we must not forget that witch-doctors believe in witches quite as firmly as a layman. It is true that while dancing at a seance they are safe, since they are well primed with medicines and are on the alert against attack, but when they are unprotected and off their guard they may easily succumb to a witch who desires to avenge public exposure. On the other hand, if they whisper the names of witches to their clients it need never be known whom they have denounced, for their clients do not immediately disclose them, but first place them one by one before the poison oracle for corroboration, so that it is as a verdict of the poison oracle and not of a witch-doctor that the name is finally made public. Even when a man's name is mentioned in public by a witch-doctor it is seldom directly stated that he is a witch. The witch-doctor says only that this man wishes someone ill or is speaking ill of him. Everyone knows that he is accusing the man of witchcraft, but he does not say so.

It is not difficult to see that a witch-doctor's revelations are largely based on local scandal, and that to some extent he thinks out his answers to questions while dancing and strutting about. Azande are aware of this fact. Nevertheless, I feel strongly that we must allow the Zande witch-doctor a measure of intuition and not attribute his utterances solely to his reason. The witch-doctor and his client consciously select between them a number of persons likely to have caused sickness or loss. The witch-doctor then commences to dance with the names of these persons in his memory until he is able to decide who of them are injuring his client, and I believe that in this secondary process of selection he is very little influenced by logic. If you ask a Zande, layman or practitioner, he will tell you that the witch-doctor begins to dance with the names of three or four likely persons in his mind, and that he dances to these people and goes on dancing until the medicines which he has previously eaten produce in him a realization of witchcraft in one of them. It is indeed almost impossible to be more explicit, but I am convinced that they select one of the names through what is largely unconscious mental activity. In the first place, they dance themselves into a condition bordering on dissociation. They are intoxicated with music created by themselves and others and are physically prostrated. As far as I can gather from what witch-doctors have told me, they keep the names in their memory and repeat them now and again, but otherwise allow their minds to become a complete blank. Suddenly one of the persons to whom he is dancing obtrudes himself upon the witch-doctor's consciousness, sometimes as a visual image, but generally by an association of the idea and name of the witch with a physiological disturbance, chiefly in a sudden quickening of the heart-beats.

IX

A witch-doctor does not only divine with his lips, but with his whole body. He dances the questions which are put to him. A witch-doctor's dance contrasts strikingly with the usual ceremonial dance of Azande. The one is spirited, violent, ecstatic, the other slow, calm, restrained. The one is an individual performance organized only by traditional movements and rhythm, the other a collective performance. It is true that several practitioners may perform together, and when they do so they generally conform to a rough common movement, i.e. they keep in line and make similar steps to rhythm of gong and drums. But in this case they often form themselves into a professional chorus which backs up the songs of an individual performer and gives him a supporting background. Usually only one, or two at the most, will be actually 'dancing questions' put to them at the same time. Very often there is only one witch-doctor present at a seance.

These dances provide an additional reason why no aristocrat could become a witch-doctor, since what is a proper ritual expression in others would be for him an undignified display. On those rare occasions when a woman witch-doctor takes part in a seance she keeps in the background and performs a sedate dance of her own. She does not attempt to imitate the violent dancing of the men, as this would be regarded as unseemly conduct.

It is important to notice that witch-doctors not only dance but make their own music with hand-bells and rattles, so that the effect in conjunction with gong and drums is intoxicating, not only to the performers themselves, but also to their audience; and that this intoxication is an appropriate condition for divination. Music, rhythmic movements, facial grimaces, grotesque dress, all lend their aid in creating a proper atmosphere for the manifestation of esoteric powers. The audience follow the display eagerly and move their heads to the music and even repeat the songs in a low voice when they are pleasing themselves rather than adding to the volume of chorus. It would be a great mistake to suppose that there is an atmosphere of awe during the ceremony. On the contrary, everyone is jovial and amused, talking to each other and making jokes. Nevertheless, there is no doubt that the success of the witch-doctor's profession is largely due to the fact that he does not rely entirely upon the settled faith of his audience, but makes belief easier by compelling their surrender to sensory stimuli.

We have to remember, moreover, that the audience is not observing simply a rhythmic performance, but also a ritual enactment of magic. It is something more than a dance, it is a fight, partly direct and partly symbolic, against the powers of evil. The full meaning of a seance as a parade against witch-craft can only be grasped when this dancing is understood. An observer who recorded only questions put to the witch-doctors and the replies which they gave would leave out the whole mechanism by which the answers are obtained, and even the answers themselves. A witch-doctor 'dances the questions'.

Before the commencement of a seance the performers eat some of their medicines which give them power to see the un-seen and to enable them to resist great fatigue. I have been told by witch-doctors that it would not be possible to stand so much exertion had they not previously eaten medicines. Medicines prime them with power to resist witchcraft. It goes into their stomachs and dancing shakes it up and sends it all over their bodies, where it becomes an active agent, enabling them to pro-phesy. In this active state it tells them who are witches and even enables them to see spiritual emanations of witchcraft floating about as little lights. Against these evil powers they wage a tremendous fight. They rush backwards and forwards, stopping suddenly and listening intently for some sound or searching eagerly for some sight. Suddenly one of them sees witchcraft in a neighbouring garden, though it is invisible to the uniti-ated, and rushes towards it with gestures of resolution and dis-gust. He quickly runs back to get some medicine from his horn and dashes away again to smear it on a plant or tree where he has seen the witchcraft settle. They frequently make dashes into the bush in this way and eagerly search for witchcraft along a path in the grass, or from the top of a termite-hill.

Every movement in the dance is as full of meaning as speech. All this jumping and leaping embodies a world of innuendo. A witch-doctor dances in front of one spectator or gazes intently at another, and when people see this they think that he has spotted a witch, and the object of their attention feels un-comfortable. Spectators can never be quite certain about the meaning of a witch-doctor's behaviour, but they can interpret in a general way from his actions what he is feeling and seeing. Every movement, every gesture, every grimace, expresses the fight they are waging against witchcraft, and it is necessary for the meaning of a dance to be explained by witch-doctors as well as by laymen to appreciate its full symbolism.

CHAPTER VI

Training of a Novice in the Art of a Witch-Doctor

I

As far as I have been able to observe, it is usual for a youth to express his desire to become a witch-doctor to a senior member of the corporation in his district and ask him to act as his sponsor. Therefore, in speaking of the manner in which novices are taught, I shall have in mind this usual transference of magic from a witch-doctor to his youthful apprentice. I have, however, sometimes seen boys of under sixteen years of age, and even quite small children of four or five, being given medicines to eat. In these cases it is generally a father or maternal uncle who wishes his son or nephew to enter the profession and commences to train him from his earliest years in its technique, and to make his spirit strong with medicines. Thus I have seen small children dancing the witch-doctors' dance and eating their medicines, in which actions they copy the movements which they have seen their elders make at seances and communal magic meals. Their elders encourage them in a jovial way and the children regard the whole affair as a piece of fun. Such children become gradually accustomed to performing in this manner, and when they are about fifteen years of age their father will occasionally take them with him when he visits a homestead to dance there, and will let them take part in the proceedings, though they will not wear any of the ordinary ceremonial decorations of a witch-doctor. Knowledge of medicines and ritual behaviour is handed over in this way from father to son, bit by bit, over a long period of years.

When a youth applies to a witch-doctor for tuition the transference is much shorter and is complicated by payments, and by the formation of personal attitudes, which have to be built up outside family and household. The young man is asked by his future teacher whether he is quite certain that he wishes to be initiated and is exhorted to consider the dangers which may beset his relations and himself if he attempts to acquire the magic half-heartedly. He will also be reminded that the magic is rare and expensive, and, that his teacher will require frequent and substantial gifts. If he persists in his desire to become a practitioner the older man will consent to teach him the art. His relatives are unlikely to object if their poison oracle foresees no unfortunate outcome for the youth or themselves.

A novice begins to eat medicines with other witch-doctors to strengthen his soul and give him powers of prophesy; he is initiated into the corporation by public burial; he is given witchcraft-phlegm to swallow; and he is taken to a stream-source and shown the various herbs and shrubs and trees from which the medicines are derived. However, there is no fixed sequence in these rites.

II

I have often observed three or four witch-doctors, and sometimes as many as seven or eight, gather in the homestead of an experienced colleague, who knows all the medicinal herbs and trees from which a magic stew is made, and there partake of a communal meal. This senior witch-doctor, who is also generally the owner of the homestead at which the ceremony takes place, has already dug up in the bush a number of roots, and scraped and washed them preparatory to cooking. He places them with water in a pot and he and his colleagues gather round the fire to watch them boil. They chat and joke among themselves about a variety of secular subjects, though the affairs of their profession are also sometimes discussed. They display no outward manifestations of awe and reverence. After the water has boiled for some time and become coloured from the juices of the plants, the witch-doctor who has gathered them and is cooking them, and whom I shall refer to as their owner, takes the pot off the fire and pours out the liquid into a second pot, which he places on the fire for further boiling. The roots from which the juices have been extracted are removed to a nearby hut, where they are stored for another occasion.

At this point the witch-doctors commence to rivet their attention upon the business in hand, drop their secular conversation, and develop a noticeable degree of concentration on the medicinal juices now boiling on the fire. This is the first sign in their behaviour that they are dealing with magical forces. Spells from this point accompany various phases of the cooking and continue seriatim till the end of the ceremony. When the owner is pouring out his medicinal juices into a second pot for their further boiling he generally addresses them in a few words, asking for the welfare of witch-doctors as a whole and for the success of their professional interests. He then divides up a ball of paste, made from oil-bearing seeds ground down with a magic root, into several small round balls, one for each witch-doctor present. The owner places these along the periphery of the pot and first he and then each witch-doctor in order of seniority flicks his ball into the pot. The owner now takes a little wooden stirrer and slowly stirs the oil in the juices, addressing the medicines as he does so, partly on his own behalf and partly on behalf of the novice whom he is initiating:

May no evil fall upon me, but let me rest in peace. May I not die. May I acquire wealth through my professional skill. May no relative of mine die from the ill-luck of my medicines; may my wife not die; my relatives are animals, my relative is eleusine, may my eleusine be fruitful.

(About his pupil.) When you dance in the witch-doctors' dance may you not die. May your home be prosperous and may no witchcraft come to injure your friends. May none of your relatives die. Your relatives are animals, your father is an elephant, your father's elder brother is a red pig, your wives are cane-rats, your mother is a bushbuck, your maternal uncles are duikers, your grandfather is a rhinoceros.

(About himself.) If witchcraft comes here to my home let it return whence it came. If a man makes sorcery against me let him die. If a man bears ill-will towards my home let him keep away, and may disgruntled fellows who come to show their spite in my home receive a nasty surprise. Let my home be prosperous.

(About his pupil.) Let evil go over there, over there; let medicine make things prosperous for you. If anyone refuses you payment for your services may he not recover from his sickness. When you go to dance with witch-doctors and they gaze into your face may they not be angry with you, but let them be contented so that people may give you presents. When you go to a seance may many presents be given you. When you dance may you not make an error in locating witchcraft. When you blow your whistle against wild cats[1] may you

---

[1] Cf. pp. 237–8.

not die. When you blow your *zunga* whistle let the soul of a man come back to him so that he may not die.

The senior witch-doctor now hands the stirrer to his pupil, who utters a few words over the medicine as he stirs it:

You medicine which I am cooking, mind you always speak the truth to me. Do not let anyone injure me with his witchcraft, but let me recognize all witches. Do not trouble my relatives, because I have no relatives. My relatives live in the bush and are elephants and water-buck; my grandparents are buffaloes and all birds. When I dance with senior witch-doctors do not let them shoot me with their shafts. Let me be expert at the witch-doctor's craft so that people will give me many spears on account of my magic.

Another witch-doctor now takes the stick from his hand and commences to stir and address the medicines:

May no misfortune come upon me. May none of my relatives die; my relatives are all animals, warthog, antelope, elephant, and harte-beeste; my domestic fowls are partridges. If anyone comes to injure me with witchcraft, may he die. If anyone comes with envy and malice to my home may that envy and malice return to their owner. May I live long with the medicine of witch-doctors to dance five years, ten years, twenty years, for years and years and years. May I grow old in dancing the dance of divination. May the other witch-doctors not hate me nor think evil of me to injure me with their medicines. Let all men come to hear my prophecies. When I dance with medicine inside me may they come with spears and knives, with rings and piastres, with eleusine and maize and ground-nuts that I may eat them, and beer that I may drink it. May I dance in the east in the kingdom of Mange and in the west in the kingdom of Tembura. May men hear my renown in the kingdom of Renzi to the south and in the far north among the foreigners at Wau. (He lets the stirrer fall on the side of the pot which lies in the direction which he mentions as he speaks of east, west, south, and north.)

Each witch-doctor who wishes to stir and address the medi-cines on the fire in this manner does so and the owner adds salt to the mixture. After a while the oil boils to the edge of the pot, and when he perceives this he removes the pot from the fire and decants the oil into a gourd and afterwards replaces the pot, which still contains a thick, oily paste. This is again addressed and stirred by those witch-doctors who care to do so. When there are only two or three fully qualified witch-doctors and no novices present, each stirs and addresses the medicines and eats of them without necessarily making a preliminary payment to their owner, but when there are a large number of witch-doctors, including several novices, present, it is customary for the owner not to allow them free spells, but to demand a fee from each person who partakes of the communal meal. He tells them that he will not take the pot off the fire until everyone has made a payment. Whereupon each witch-doctor produces half a piastre, or a small knife, or a ring, and places it on the ground in front of the fire or even in the pot itself. These payments must be placed in the sight of the medicines, which normally must be bought or they will not be potent. Purchase is a part of the ritual conditioning of the magic which gives it potency. I have even seen a witch-doctor who was treating a patient for nothing place a piastre of his own on the ground, and when I asked him what he was doing he explained that it would be a bad thing if the medicine did not observe a fee, for it might lose its potency. If anyone fails to produce a gift the owner may threaten to leave the medicine on the fire and let it burn, or, it is said, he may sometimes remove it from the fire, but not let any of his colleagues eat it till they have made sufficient payments. The medicines are his. He gathered them in the bush and prepared them and cooked them in his own utensils. He is their owner and they must be purchased from him. It must be remembered that since magic which is not purchased in this manner is of doubtful potency it is to the advantage of the eater to pay a small fee, as well as to the advantage of the owner to receive it, for not only does payment of a fee form an integral part of the magic ritual, but also in Zandeland it is thought essential that when magical powers are transmitted from one person to another their seller should be satisfied with the deal, since otherwise they will lose their powers in the transference. The goodwill of the owner is also a relevant condition in the sale of magic, and his goodwill can be assured by a small payment.

When presents have been made to him the owner removes the pot from the fire and decants the oil which has exuded from the paste during its second boiling, and then places the pot on one side for the residuum to cool. If there is a novice present on whose special behalf they are cooking medicines, the pot is placed in front of him and he puts his face in the steam, taking care to keep his eyes open meanwhile so that it enters into them. Other witch-doctors do the same, and some of them utter a few words to the magic as they hold their faces in the mouth of the pot. When the paste has cooled its owner serves it, usually helping the novice before the others. The method of serving is a regular feature of magic meals among Azande. The server scrapes some medicine with a stick from the bottom of the pot and directs it to the mouth of one man, but when this man is about to eat it he quickly removes it and places it in the mouth of another. He feeds each practitioner in turn in this manner, and when each has been served they all crowd round the pot itself and eat the residue of the medicated paste with their hands as they would eat any other food.

When it is finished, the owner takes the oil which he has earlier decanted and adds to part of it some ashes of burnt *ngbimi zawa* (a parasite of *Lophira alata*) and stirs it into a black fluid. He hands round the rest of the oil to the witch-doctors to drink. He then takes a knife and makes incisions on their chests and above their shoulder-blades and on their wrists and faces, and rubs some of the black fluid into the cuts. As he rubs it into a man's wrist he says:

Let this man treat his patients successfully and do not let objects of witchcraft elude him.

As he rubs it into a man's breast he says:

If this man sees a witch let his heart shake in cognizance of witchcraft.

As he rubs it into his back above the shoulder-blades he says:

Don't let anyone shoot this man with magic shafts from behind, and if anyone does shoot him from behind, may the assailant perish. May anyone who sheds his blood die at once. If a witch comes to injure him in the night, even though he approaches from behind, may this man see him, let not the witch conceal his face.

They also drink some of this black fluid, and if there is a quantity of it they pour some of it into their horns, where they keep a permanent store of medicine.

After a senior witch-doctor has treated his colleagues in this

way he impresses on them the desirability of making him frequent payments, and admonishes them not to play the fool with
their magic or it will not remain steadfast in their bodies, but
will lose its power.

III

A novice begins to take part in these communal meals, generally
held on the morning of a seance, early in his apprenticeship,
since the primary object of his career is to become imbued with
medicine which will enable him to identify witchcraft. It is
well to emphasize again that this is a simple magical process.
The man eats medicines and becomes physically strong so that
he is able to resist fatigue at a seance, and spiritually strong
so that he is able to resist the onslaught of witches. The medicines in themselves produce results without the consumer of
them being fully initiated and while he is still ignorant of their
composition. When a little child eats them, for instance, they
are supposed to move him to prance in the manner of a witch-
doctor, and an adult who has such medicines in his body will
sometimes shake and jump and belch violently as he is sitting
in his homestead. I have sometimes seen witch-doctors twitch
spasmodically and belch in this way, but I have little doubt
that they do it to show off before laymen, though there may
be a genuine psycho-physical disturbance induced by suggestion and by the action of the medicines. Exactly the same medicines are also used to treat the sick.

   Nevertheless, a man who has eaten medicines only a few
times is not qualified to take a prominent part in the activities
of a seance, or to prophesy at it. Occasionally witch-doctors
practise dancing in the homestead of one of them in order to
train a novice in the art.

   As soon as a youth has eaten medicine he begins to dance,
so that I often saw one or two novices dancing at a seance,
though they made no attempt to divine. They were not suffi-
ciently experienced, for they had only eaten a small quantity of
medicine, had not yet been initiated, and had not learnt the roots
from which the medicines are extracted. Every novice hopes
sooner or later to reach a position in the corporation when he will
be able to initiate pupils of his own, and he can only acquire
this status when he has learnt the proper herbs and trees.

There is no chance of recognizing these plants from observing their roots at a communal meal, and consequently there is no objection to laymen being present at these meals as well as specialists, and I have often seen lay friends of the magicians sitting beside them as they eat their paste, though I have never observed them partaking of the meal.

Witch-doctors are said to be very careful lest anyone should find out what plants they dig up for magical use. They remove their stalks and leaves and hide them in the bush some way from where they have dug them up lest anyone should follow in their tracks and learn their medicines. A plant is known by its stalk and leaves and not by its roots.

IV

Magic must be bought like any other property, and the really significant part of initiation is the slow transference of knowledge about plants from teacher to pupil in exchange for a long string of fees. A teacher may show them casually to his pupil at any time when they are both out in the bush together, as on a hunting trip, or he may specially take him out for the purpose. Unless the medicines are bought with adequate fees there is a danger that they will lose their potency for the recipient during the transference, since their owner is dissatisfied and bears the purchaser ill-will. Also, it is always possible for a teacher, if he does not think that he has received sufficient payment for his medicines, to make magic to cancel them so that they will no longer function in the body of their purchaser. This can be done either by a witch-doctor cooking medicines and uttering a spell over them to deprive a novice of the power of the magic which he has consumed, or by the performance of a special rite to the same effect. He takes a forest creeper, called *ngbanza*, and attaches one end of it to the top of a flexible withy stuck in the earth, and fastens the other end in the ground so that it is like the string of a bow. He then brings magic of thunder and drops some of it on the lower end of the creeper in order that thunder may roar and strike the creeper and cut it in two, the top part flying up on high and the lower part remaining in the earth. As the top part flies on high so does the medicine fly out of the man who has consumed it.

In the case of Kamanga, the payment of fees was not quite

normal, since I made presents of spears to his teacher, though he supplemented these gifts from his own property. A man is supposed to give his teacher twenty *baso*. *Baso* is the Zande word for spears, but it is often used, as in this connexion, for any kind of wealth. Actually a pupil, being generally a young man, has very little property of his own, so that he will pay by instalments over a number of years, and he and his teacher will keep a record in their heads of what he has paid. He may raise one or two spears, but for the most part his *baso* consist of rings, knives, piastres, pots of beer, baskets of food, meat, and other objects of small value. Some of these gifts come into his hands by ritual exchange or gift on ceremonial occasions, others he begs from his relatives, and yet others he may earn by performing Government labour, such as porterage. Most of them are presented to his teacher at his initiation.

If a novice is keen and clever he is soon able to start practising on his own account, though he is expected to give his first fees to his teacher, and to make him occasional presents afterwards.

A man does not learn from his teacher all the medicines which it is possible to learn, for no man knows all of them. Different persons know different medicines, and when a man meets someone who knows a plant of which he is ignorant he may try to buy the knowledge. If the man who knows the plant is a friend and the plant is not an important one he may show it to him for nothing, but otherwise he will expect a small payment. As the years go on, and a witch-doctor comes into wider contact with other members of his profession, he gradually adds to his store of medicines. This fact enables us to understand how keen to discover each other's medicines were the two rival witch-doctors Badobo and Bögwözu, and why each of them asked Kamanga to show him the plants which the other had taught him. The plants mentioned in the succeeding paragraphs are the better-known and more essential medicines, and most of them are taught to a novice shortly before or after his initiation ceremony.

Badobo and Kamanga used to show me plants which are employed by witch-doctors when I was hunting with them in the bush, but I did not collect them for identification. I have only once been out with Badobo when he was showing Kamanga some of these plants, on which occasion he told him in a few words the purposes and names of a few plants. I shall therefore rely almost entirely on Kamanga's account of his expedition to the source of a stream to learn medicines of witch-doctors.

v

Zandeland is covered with a network of streams which flow along either side of the Nile–Congo Divide. These streams rise in springs which have eaten out of the earth dark chasms, shaded by tall trees and obscured with dense brushwood. Sometimes this erosion has burrowed short tunnels into the earth, which lead off from the main cavern, buttressed with roots of gigantic trees and roofed with thick foliage of shrub and creeper. Azande fear these caverns, which house snakes and are the homes of ghosts and of the Supreme Being.

Before Kamanga set out he told me that the party would consist of Badobo, Alenvo, and himself. He and Badobo would creep along the ground on all fours and the ghosts would come and show them the plants for which they were looking. He said they might have to enter into several of these dark tunnels in their search for plants, but that the ghosts would eventually reveal them. They would then both catch hold of them and drag them out of the soil and retire backwards with them. Badobo would show them to Kamanga, so that he in his turn would one day be able to show them to his pupils. Meanwhile Alenvo would stand outside the cavern, ringing his hand-bells, and they would make their way towards the sound in the darkness. If it were not for these bells they would be lost.

Kamanga was in some doubt about the exact nature of the ghosts which haunt these dark, damp regions. He knew that they were ordinary ghosts of dead persons, but he believed also that they were ghosts of dead witch-doctors.

I give Kamanga's description of what happened:

We walked a long way to the source of a stream along a tiny path which led to it. We went on for about as far as that tree over there and then they[2] stopped and said to me that they were about to go with me into the earth to the place where live the ghosts of medicine and the Supreme Being, so what about giving them a present? It was not likely that they would accompany me there empty-handed. I

[2] i.e. his teacher Badobo and the other witch-doctor, Alenvo.

stopped at this and thought for a while, and then I took a piastre
and gave it to them. Badobo then said that they would continue and
show me medicines. We continued for some time until we reached
the mouth of a cavern, ever such a big cavern, where they said: 'Let
us enter.'

Badobo told me to straddle his back as he proceeded on all fours,
so I sat astride his back, and clasped him with my hands. He told
me that he was about to take me ahead and that I was not to be
afraid. We entered into this cavern. Suddenly he placed his head to
the ground, resting it on the back of his hands. All this time I was
on his back. We went on farther, and Badobo again rested his face
on the back of his hands. The whole floor of the cavern vibrated, '*li
li li li li*'. We continued and approached another entrance to the
cavern, where he performed his final crouchings to the ground. He
said to me: 'When I make a sudden spring and seize a plant, you
seize hold of it as well.' I assented.

He crouched down thus, then suddenly leapt up, suddenly started
off, and seized a plant in the middle of the cavern, and I seized it
too. He said to me: 'This is the plant which I was going to show you.'
He told me that if it was anybody else, he would most certainly ask
him for a payment, especially as the ghosts had not done us any harm
on the floor of the cavern and we had heard no wailing while he was
showing me this medicine, so that it appeared that my initiation
prospered; for if my initiation had not prospered, then the ghosts
would have been angry and we should have heard them wailing:
'*Bazogare oooo.*'[3] Doubtless I would also have seen a snake in the
cavern. But since I had accompanied him, and he had taken me with
him, into the place of the Supreme Being, I had not heard wailing.
I had not heard the speech of ghosts. A great serpent had not attacked
us. Then he said to me: 'This plant which I am showing to you is
a very powerful medicine of witch-doctors.' He then told me to bend
down my head and look towards the earth into a deep pool which
was there.

I asked him: 'What is the name of this medicine which you have
pulled up?' and he answered: 'It is called *bagu* because it does not sleep
still, but its leaves murmur all the night "*guuuuuu*".' He told me that
there is another powerful medicine called *nderoko* at the edge of
streams, and that I would see its tentacled roots spread out at the
entrance of this cavern, and he told Alenvo to cut one of them with
his knife. Alenvo cut it and broke it off and cried: 'Spears! spears!
spears! spears!' For whenever we dug up a plant together at this
stream they always said when they pulled it up: 'Spears! spears!

---

[3] The wailing song of women mourners.

spears!'⁴ They spoke in this way about all the medicines of the witch-doctors. `

(Badobo shows Kamanga other medicines.)

We then went and stood in the middle of the stream where Badobo said to me: 'I want you to show me, while we are both here together, what plants among all these plants Bögwözu taught you as those in use among Baka witch-doctors.'

I told him the names of these plants which Bögwözu had taught me and, when I reached this point, Badobo said to me: 'Yes. He taught you much. All our medicines are the same. Those medicines which he taught you are also my medicines, but there are still three medicines which he did not teach you.' Badobo then began to teach me further medicines, namely: the *ziga*⁵ of witch-doctors which is *zerengbondo*. He said to me that he was showing me the *ziga* of witch-doctors so that when I began to cook medicines often, and became an important witch-doctor, I would know its leaf among other plants. He told me not to scrape its wood towards the east, but only towards the west. When I cooked it and uttered a spell over it I should say: 'May no one kill me as a result of my professional activities. May my wives not leave my homestead. May my wife not die as a result of the practice of my craft.' He told me that I should utter a spell in this manner, and that when I had cooked the medicines I should take their residue (i.e. the woods which had been boiled to extract their juices) and bury it in the threshold of my hut and in the place where my household fire burns. He said that I should then eat the medicinal paste and anoint my wives and children with its oil. He said that whenever I went to dance the dance of divination might no evil happen to me and might my wife not die on account of my professional activities, because it is for this reason that they cook the *ziga* lest the ill-luck of the medicines should fall upon their wives, so that no wife of a witch-doctor would live long. He then finished his talk about medicines with what he had said about the *ziga*.

I have not recorded the events of Kamanga's initiation in the order in which they occurred, for he was ritually buried before he swallowed witchcraft-phlegm and he swallowed witchcraft-phlegm before he paid his visit to stream-sources, but the order in which I have given them is more suitable to

⁴ In reference to payments made to a teacher by his pupil.

⁵ Many Zande medicines have a *ziga* or antidote. In this case the antidote is eaten in order to prevent misfortune falling on the family of the novice, since, as explained in an earlier footnote, it is considered that the acquisition of a powerful magic may cause the death of one of his family or kin. It is hoped that the object of their ill-luck, if anyone, will be a distant relative.

the texture of my account, and their exact chronology is not a matter of importance. Each rite is a self-contained investment of magic powers which, in their totality, compose the full equipment of a witch-doctor.

VI

Kamanga's tuition advanced by gradual stages. He learnt one medicine today and another perhaps a month or two later, and as Badobo generally managed to extract a small fee from him in exchange for each piece of knowledge he taught him as slowly as possible. A youth may spend years before his teacher has exhausted his stock of information about herbs and trees, part of which he hands over long after public initiation, though in Kamanga's case I exercised pressure to get his tuition completed within a couple of years, since otherwise I would not have been able to follow its course. Besides teaching his pupil medicines, a witch-doctor is expected to give him a few skins and rattles to start his professional outfit.

I believe that the teachings of Badobo and Bögwözu in respect to medicines were perfectly genuine, and usually it was possible to check from other sources the information they supplied to Kamanga. Moreover, Kamanga himself was anxious to check their statements by reference to other witch-doctors, since he did not feel certain that they were teaching him all the medicines they knew. He had opportunities for comparing notes with independent practitioners, a large number of whom he met after he had begun to eat magical meals and to take part in seances.

Nevertheless, our inquiry stuck firmly at one point. Neither Badobo nor Bögwözu would teach him how to remove objects of witchcraft from his patients. They told him of medicines which would enable him to perform operations, and they left him with the impression that, having partaken of these medicines, he had only to make an incision on a patient's body, place a poultice over it, and massage it for objects of witchcraft to appear.

Doubtless the witch-doctors would have completed Kamanga's training after I had left the country, for it is obvious that something must have been done or he would have suffered a series of ignominious failures in his attempts to produce objects from the bodies of his patients, an exposure surely without precedent. By this time, however, I was tired of Badobo's chicanery and Bögwözu's bluff. I had already ceased to give Badobo presents, but there was still an outstanding account to settle with Bögwözu since I had promised him the princely gift of ten spears if he trained Kamanga fully. He now wanted to return to his home, which was a day and a half's journey away, and asked for his present and dismissal. When I urged that Kamanga was not properly trained he informed me that his pupil knew everything there was to be known.

As a boy of my household was slightly sick at the time, I suggested that Kamanga should operate on him that evening, and I told Bögwözu that if his pupil were able to perform the operation successfully I would gladly give him his ten spears and let him return home on the following morning. Bögwözu prepared a poultice of *kpoyo* bark, and while Kamanga was making an incision on the sick boy's abdomen, he inserted a small piece of charcoal into it. I was sitting between Bögwözu and Kamanga. When the teacher handed over the poultice to his pupil I took it from him to pass it to Kamanga, but in doing so I felt for the object which it contained and removed it between my finger and thumb while pretending to make a casual examination of the kind of stuff a poultice consisted of and commenting on the material. I am not certain whether Bögwözu saw what I had done, but I think that he suspected my motive in handling the poultice, for he certainly looked suspicious. It was a disagreeable surprise for Kamanga when, after massaging his patient's abdomen through the poultice, in the usual manner of witch-doctors, and after then removing the poultice, he could not find any object of witchcraft in it. While Kamanga was still searching and hoping to identify every little piece of hard vegetable matter in the poultice with an object of witchcraft, I observed out of the corner of my eye Bögwözu moving the palm of his hand over the ground, seeking for another piece of charcoal to make up for the deficiency. I considered that the time had now come to stop proceedings and I asked Kamanga and his teacher to come to my hut a few yards away, where I told them that I had removed the charcoal from the poultice, and asked Bögwözu to explain how it had got there. For a few moments he pretended incredulity and asked to see the object, since he said that such a thing was impossible, but he was clever enough to see that further pretence would be useless, and, as we were in private, he made no further difficulty about admitting the imposture. He received two spears for his trouble and returned home next day without the other eight, which he forfeited for not fulfilling his part of the bargain.

The effect of these disclosures on Kamanga was devastating. When he had recovered from his astonishment he was in serious doubt whether he ought to continue his initiation. He could not at first believe his eyes and ears, but in a day or two he had completely recovered his poise and developed a marked degree of self-assurance which, if I was not mistaken, he had not shown before this incident. In future he, like his colleagues, excused to me their sleight-of-hand on the grounds that it is not the pretended extraction of bones, pieces of charcoal, spiders, black-beetles, and other supposed objects of witchcraft from the bodies of their patients which cures them of their diseases, but the *mbiro* medicine which they administer internally and externally at the same time. If their surgery is fake, their physic is sound.

VII

After this episode Bögwözu left us and we fell back on Badobo again. As there was no longer any point in concealing his sharp practices, he readily taught them to Kamanga. I give his teaching in the latter's own words:

Badobo told me that before I commence to treat a patient I must cut a piece of *togoro ranga* and shape it with a knife until it is like an object of witchcraft. I must conceal this between my fingers, or, alternatively, put it under my nail. He said I must sit still and do nothing, and let a layman prepare the poultice. When he hands it to me I must take it from him quickly and squeeze it between my fingers so as cunningly to insert into it the little object from under my fingernail. I must see that it is well set in the poultice, and place it on the affected part of my patient.

First I ought to rub some *mbiro* medicine across the mouth of my patient and afterwards to take a mouthful of water, gargle it, and blow it out. I ought then to massage the patient, to remove the poultice, and, holding it in my hand, to search it until I discover an object of witchcraft in it. When I find an object I must show it to the onlookers so that they may see it and say: 'Heu! Well I never! So that's the thing from which he was dying.'

A man performs this act of surgery with one object about three times. When he has removed it from the poultice he places it on the stump of a nearby tree and warns everyone not to touch it because it is a thing connected with witchcraft. Then he takes it again and hides it once more under his nail, and for a second time performs a surgical operation with it. A man who is good at cheating makes use of the same object about three times.

Thus they said to me about it, 'Witch-doctors treat a sick man and deceive him, saying that they have taken an object of witchcraft from his body whereas they have not taken it at all; but, on the other hand, they have put medicine into the sick man's mouth and cut his skin at the part of the body where he is in pain and have rubbed their medicine across the cut.' When the man has recovered people say that indeed witch-doctors are skilful healers, whereas it is the medicine which really cures people, and it is on account of medicine that people recover when they are treated by witch-doctors. The people think that healing is brought about by the extraction of objects, and only witch-doctors know that it is the medicine which heals people. The people themselves do not learn the truth because only witch-doctors know it, and they keep it a secret. They do not spread their knowledge abroad, but tell it only to those who have first eaten their medicines, because their treatment is very deceitful.

I felt rather sorry for Kamanga at this time. He had always shown sublime faith in witch-doctors; no arguments of mine had made any lasting impression on him since he countered them by answering that there was nothing new in the suggestion of fraud, but that it covered only part of the phenomena and not all of them. Moreover, he was never really convinced that any witch-doctors cheat till he became a witch-doctor himself. Yet I do not think that even this experience convinced him thoroughly that all witch-doctors are frauds. He now knew that those with whom he came into contact cheated their patients, but he still thought that witch-doctors exist who have strong enough magic genuinely to discover and extract objects of witchcraft.

But it must be realized that there are wide differences of mental approach between different laymen; and, indeed, differences of attitude of the same man in different situations. By way of illustration I cite a text spoken by another informant, Kisanga:

When a man becomes sick they send for a witch-doctor. Before the witch-doctor comes to the sick man he scrapes down an animal's bone and hammers it till it is quite small and then drops it into the medicines in his horn. He later arrives at the homestead of the sick man and takes a mouthful of water and swills his mouth round with it and opens his mouth so that people can look into it. He also spreads out his hands to them so that everyone can see them, and speaks thus to them: 'Observe me well, I am not a cheat, since I have no desire to take anything from anyone fraudulently.'

He gets up and takes his medicine in its horn and puts it down beside him, shoves a little stick into it, and licks the stick, at the same time taking a little bone into his mouth. He applies his mouth to the affected part of the sick man's body, sucks it for a long time, and then takes his mouth away and spits out the little bone into the palm of his hand and shows it to everyone, saying: 'This is the thing which is causing him sickness.' He goes on doing this in the same manner until all the bones which he has taken into his mouth are used up.

But those witch-doctors who are themselves witches know who is injuring the sick man. Before he goes to see the sick man such a witch-doctor first of all visits the witch and pleads with him, saying: 'Will you do me the favour of leaving that man alone so that he may get well from his sickness, and everyone may speak well of me and say that truly I am a trustworthy witch-doctor.'

The witch says to him: 'All right, I will be generous on your account. If it were any other witch-doctor I would certainly refuse the request. But when you go to the sick man remember that you must bring back all the presents you receive so that we can share them.' The witch-doctor replies: 'I will bring all the presents here to you and we will share them. I only want to increase my reputation among the people, and that is why I have come to ask you to do me a favour so that when I have treated the sick man he may get completely well.'

The witch consents to the witch-doctor's proposal and the witch-doctor goes off with his faked objects to the sick man, deceives him, and goes home. The sick man at once recovers, because the witch has already released his hold of him. The witch-doctor hears that the sick man has recovered and sends a messenger for his present, since he cured him. The relatives of the sick man will certainly not refuse to give him a present, because they think that it is he who has saved their relative. They give him his present as he desires: even if it is two spears they give them to him. Witch-doctors always cheat with witches in order to get presents from people. But a witch-doctor who is not himself a witch knows nothing, and people will always call him a cheat.

This account was given by a man of unusual brilliance, but

at the same time it represents popular opinion. Two points emerge clearly from it. The first is that people not only know that witch-doctors can produce objects from the bodies of their patients by fraud, but also that they are aware of the kind of fraud they employ. The second point is that this knowledge does not conflict with great faith in witch-doctors, because it is believed that a considerable number of them do actually produce remarkable cures through their traffic with witches. The skill of a witch-doctor depends on the quality of the medicines he has eaten and on his possession of *mangu*. If he is not himself a 'witch' nor has eaten powerful enough medicines he will be a witch-doctor only in name. Hence, if you criticize their witch-doctors, Azande will agree with you.

It is important to note that scepticism about witch-doctors is not socially repressed. Absence of formal and coercive doctrines permit Azande to state that many, even most, witch-doctors are frauds. No opposition being offered to such statements they leave the main belief in the prophetic and therapeutic powers of witch-doctors unimpaired. Indeed, scepticism is included in the pattern of belief in witch-doctors. Faith and scepticism are alike traditional. Scepticism explains failures of witch-doctors, and being directed towards particular witch-doctors even tends to support faith in others.

Azande have to state their doubts of the mystical powers of witch-doctors in mystical terms. A witch-doctor is a cheat because his medicines are poor. He is a liar because he possesses no 'witchcraft'. Their idiom is so much of a mystical order that criticism of one belief can only be made in terms of another that equally lacks foundation in fact. Thus Kisanga told us in the text cited above how witch-doctors cheat. He not only explained precisely and accurately how they cheat but even explained how it comes about that a sick man believes himself to have been cured by a cheating leech. He knows that he was sick, was treated, and is well, and assumes that the treatment cured him. Whereas he was cured, not by the therapeutic treatment of the witch-doctor, but by a bargain struck between the witch-doctor and the witch.

VIII

We have seen that Azande are aware of deception practised

by their witch-doctors in the role of leeches and of their inefficiency in the role of diviners. As in many other of their customs, we find a mingling of common sense and mystical thought, and we may ask why common sense does not triumph over superstition.

A partial explanation must, no doubt, be sought in the training in trickery Kamanga has described. Some such training is essential, for two reasons. In the first place, the Zande has a broad streak of scepticism in his attitude towards his leeches, who have therefore to be careful that their sleight-of-hand is not observed. In the second place, if the treatment is to be effective it must be performed in a traditional manner, which is thought to obviate any possibility of trickery and which alone, in consequence, can stimulate a patient's faith in his doctor. We have seen that the Zande does not believe in the therapeutic powers of witch-doctors through a special ability to believe in things supernatural, but that he always refers your scepticism to the test of experience. If the treatment is carried out in a certain manner, as when *bingba* grass is used as a poultice, he will be frankly suspicious. But if the witch-doctor sits down on a stool and calls upon a third person to cut *kpoyo* bast and make a poultice of it, rinses his mouth with water, and holds his hands for inspection, suspicions will be allayed. The Zande answers further scepticism in a rational and experimental way by giving you a corpus of cases which have come within his social horizon in which cures have been effected.

If you accompany a witch-doctor on one of his visits you will be convinced, if not of the validity of his cures, at least of his skill. As far as you can observe, everything which he does appears to be above-board, and you will notice nothing which might help you to detect a fraud. When you have lived for some time in Zandeland you will also have ample evidence of the therapeutic value of the kind of treatment which witch-doctors employ. Every native can give you from his own experience convincing accounts of how he and his relatives and friends have been cured by the extraction of bones or worms from their bodies. If one witch-doctor fails to cure a Zande he goes to another in the same way as we go to another doctor if we are dissatisfied with the treatment of the first one whom we have consulted. Similarly, Azande whom I have treated for a number of illnesses have often thrown over my treatment and visited their own practitioners, in whose medicines they have had greater faith. I have on several occasions dosed my friends for stomach-ache without diminishing their pain, and have afterwards seen them visit their own witch-doctors and return home greatly relieved, if not altogether freed, from pain. So we have to bear in mind that, in spite of the trickery of witch-doctors, their methods are, within a limited compass, successful.

There are, however, other ways in which faith is supported. Rhythm, mode of utterance, content of prophecies, all assist in creating faith in witch-doctors; yet even they do not entirely explain belief. Weight of tradition can alone do that. Witch-doctors have always been part of Zande culture. They figure in the oldest traditions of their nation. Their seances occasion one of the few types of social gatherings outside family life, and from an early age children have taken part in them as spectators, chorus, and drummers. Azande do not consider what their world would be like without witch-doctors any more than we consider what it would be like without physicians. Since there is witchcraft there are naturally witch-doctors. There is no incentive to agnosticism. All their beliefs hang together, and were a Zande to give up faith in witch-doctorhood he would have to surrender equally his belief in witchcraft and oracles. A seance of witch-doctors is a public affirmation of the existence of witchcraft. It is one of the ways in which belief in witchcraft is inculcated and expressed. Also, witch-doctors are part of the oracle-system. Together with the rubbing-board oracle they provide questions for the poison oracle which corroborates their revelations. In this web of belief every strand depends upon every other strand, and a Zande cannot get out of its meshes because this is the only world he knows. The web is not an external structure in which he is enclosed. It is the texture of his thought and he cannot think that his thought is wrong. Nevertheless, his beliefs are not absolutely set but are variable and fluctuating to allow for different situations and to permit empirical observation and even doubts.

IX

The last section of a witch-doctor's initiation which I have to describe is his ritual burial. I have witnessed this ceremony on two occasions, once when Kamanga was initiated, and once on a previous occasion.

The first time I witnessed an initiation the witch-doctors, after dancing for some hours, dug a hole in the centre of the homestead where the ceremony was being held. The owner of the homestead advanced to the hole with his wives and the initiate's father. There each took a draught of beer and blew it out to the ground to bless the novice's professional path. The witch-doctors then danced. Later they poured medicine from a small leaf filter on to the novice's fingers and toes. They squeezed some of the same liquid up his nostrils and he leant forward to let it run out of them. Finally, they squeezed medicine into his eyes. Afterwards he lay on his belly with the upper half of his body bent into the hole and covered over with a mat on which earth was heaped, and with the lower half of his body sticking out above the ground. He remained in this position for about half an hour, while witch-doctors jumped and danced over his body. One of them occasionally put his head under the mat to speak to the buried novice and then withdrew it. At the end of this time he was raised in an exhausted condition and supported to a seat of leaves near the dancing-ground. Kamanga's initiation was conducted in a similar manner.

This ceremony bears the imprint of a typical initiation ceremony. The neophyte is in a tabooed state for two or three days before the rites take place. He wears a cord made from the bast of the *dakpa* tree round his waist and he abstains from sexual intercourse and from various foods. He then goes through a ritual enactment of death and burial and resurrection, though a Zande would not describe it in this way.

When a witch-doctor has been initiated he takes a new name which he only uses professionally when engaged in divining and leechcraft. Thus Badobo, like his rival, was called Bögwözu; Kamanga, like our settlement headman, took the name Böwe; Ngbaranda, another of our local witch-doctors, took the name Semene; and so on.

CHAPTER VII

The Place of Witch-Doctors in Zande Society

I

A CLEVER witch-doctor is an important person in Zande society. He can locate and combat witchcraft which to the Zande is an ever-present menace. He can cure the sick and warn all over whom hang impending dangers. He is one of the means by which hoe-culture and hunting may yield their fruits to human labour, since through his magic they are freed from witchcraft which blasts all endeavour. Magic gives him power to see into the hearts of men and to reveal their evil intentions. Also a practitioner may be himself a witch. In this case he possesses *mangu* and *ngua*, witchcraft and magic. He can harm or protect, kill or cure. He is therefore a man who commands respect, and we have seen how respect is demanded during seances, when he compels people to give him their attention and acquires for the time being authoritative status. I think that no Zande is absolutely certain that he is not a witch and, if this is so, no one can be sure that his name will not be revealed during the seance, a condition that undoubtedly enhances a witch-doctor's prestige. Having on many occasions observed the behaviour of people at seances, I am sure that they are to some extent thrilled by the display. Witchcraft is hovering near them, for it is seen by the witch-doctors who attack it with their medicines; magic is operative all round them, and magical shafts are flying from point to point; the dancers are in a state of frenzied exaltation, which produces a sympathetic reaction in the behaviour of their audience; a battle of two spiritual powers is enacted before their eyes, magic versus witchcraft. In such situations the witch-doctor enjoys his greatest influence. When he is no longer functioning as a magician his social position cannot be said to be above that of an ordinary citizen.

His prestige does not depend so much on the practice of his craft as on his personal reputation in it. Today there are many practitioners, but few attain eminence. Fame is not, moreover, based solely on restricted professional knowledge of the witch-doctor's art, in its aspects of divination and leechcraft, but also on the fact that a noted witch-doctor is generally also a noted magician in other respects. Many of those who practise as witch-doctors also possess powerful magic of other kinds, such as *bagbuduma*, vengeance-magic, and *iwa*, the rubbing-board oracle. People may possess all kinds of magic without at the same time being witch-doctors, but the witch-doctor is essentially the magician of Zande society, the repository of all sorts of medicines.

II

Many people say that the great majority of witch-doctors are liars whose sole concern is to acquire wealth. I found that it was quite a normal belief among Azande that many of the practitioners are charlatans who make up any reply which they think will please their questioner, and whose sole inspiration is love of gain. It is indeed probable that Zande faith in their witch-doctors has declined since European conquest of their country, on account of the large increase in membership of the corporation. In the old days only two or three men in a province used to function as witch-doctors, whereas today they number scores. I have noticed again and again in other departments of Zande magic that faith tends to lessen as ownership spreads. Today a witch-doctor has little scruple about teaching as many pupils as he can obtain and charging them ridiculously small fees in comparison with old-time standards. Moreover, the same risk does not now attach to the profession as used to be the case, when an error of judgement might entail serious consequences. In the general cultural disequilibrium due to the social changes consequent on conquests and administration, belief in magic and witchcraft has ceased to function adequately, and a witch-doctorhood tends to become more a pastime than a serious profession. Nevertheless, there are many evidences which show decisively that scepticism is not a new phenomenon.

I particularly do not wish to give the impression that there is anyone who disbelieves in witch-doctorhood. Most of my acquaintances believed that there are a few entirely reliable practitioners, but that the majority are quacks. Hence in the case of any particular with-doctor they are never quite certain whether reliance can be placed on his statements or not. They know that some witch-doctors lie and that others tell the truth, but they cannot at once tell from his behaviour into which category any witch-doctor falls. They reserve judgement, and temper faith with scepticism.

It is always possible to check the statements of a witch-doctor by putting them before the poison oracle, which, not being under human control, may contradict them, so that it is not surprising that Azande have developed doubts. I have heard even witch-doctors themselves admit that not all members of their corporation are reliable and honest, but only those who have received proper medicines from persons qualified to initiate them.

Zande doctrine holds that one witch can see another witch and observe what he is doing in the world of witchcraft, whilst laymen can only unearth witch activity through their oracles. Hence, a witch-doctor who is also a witch may be relied upon to give correct information about his companions. Surely, say Azande, they ought to know all about their own mother's sons. Witch-doctors naturally do not admit this interpretation of their powers, which they attribute solely to their magic. They admit that members of their corporation have *mangu* in their bellies, but it is *mangu* generated by magic and of quite a different nature to *mangu* of witches, which is a biological inheritance. The layman is not entirely convinced by this subtle distinction and prefers to state plainly that it is ordinary *mangu* in their own bellies which enables successful practitioners to see it in the bellies of others.

I have many times heard people openly say that successful witch-doctors are witches. A man would not deliberately offend a practitioner by casting this opinion in his teeth, but I have heard Azande, especially princes, chaffing witch-doctors about their witchcraft. It is one of the traditional ideas associated with the corporation. Everyone knows it.

Another way in which we can measure popular belief in witch-doctors is by ranging them alongside other oracular agencies. Nobody would suggest that revelations of witch-doctors are as reliable as those of the poison oracle. The highest compliment which you can pay a witch-doctor is to tell him that he is prophesying 'just like *benge*', i.e. with complete accuracy. Nor can witch-doctors be considered on the same level as the termites oracle. Rather Azande compare them with the rubbing-board oracle which is manipulated by man and is known to make many mistakes. Thus we again find scepticism about witch-doctors expressed in this gradation of oracles. The Zande shows his supicions of the human element in oracles by placing greater reliance on the poison oracle and the termites oracle, which work through natural agencies, than on the rubbing-board oracle or witch-doctors, the one manipulated by human direction, the other in itself a human agency.

It must be remembered that rivalry among witch-doctors also plays a part; thus, the professional jealousy between Badobo and the intruder Bögwözu runs through the whole account of Kamanga's training and initiation. In any such training, a large number of the medicines taught to a novice have as their function the equipment of defensive and aggressive powers against professional rivals. There is little jealousy between junior witch-doctors; but when a man has gained a professional reputation it is certain to clash with the interests of others who have been longer established in the district. These doctors try to build up for themselves practices among laymen, and as they derive both wealth and reputation from them they are envious of the encroachment of others. The jealousy of witch-doctors is, indeed, proverbial among Azande. A witch-doctor tries to defeat his rivals, not only by equipping himself with special medicines and magically "shooting" small objects into his colleagues when dancing with them, but also by slander and denigration. Thus, the jealousies which lead witch-doctors to cast aspersions on one another must also lessen their prestige among laymen.

III

In any case, the reputation of witch-doctors, as of all other Zande magicians, is completely overshadowed by the political power of the royal Vongara house and nobles abstain from witch-doctors' activities which are entirely a commoner practice and mainly a commoner interest. Witch-doctors have no political power, and commoners with political power and ambitions do not become witch-doctors. It can easily be understood that in these circumstances the witch-doctor's social position is never an exalted one.

At the same time, princes respect witch-doctors and give them patronage. Princes, like everyone else, have their interests to protect from witchcraft. They have, indeed, a wider range of interests, since political interests are added to those of householder, husband, and producer. It is one of the special cares of a witch-doctor summoned to court to inform his master of any unrest in his kingdom or principality. A prince, owing to his large harem, is also more susceptible than a commoner to attacks by women witches, since he has a greater range of contacts with women and has consequently greater opportunity for arousing feminine ill-will.

Nobles patronize witch-doctors because their magic is good magic. It causes no one an injury and protects many from harm. It is not an ally of jealousy or spite, but their enemy. All Azande are agreed that the witch-doctor is harmless, and everyone praises his medicines. Witch-doctors may, it is true, fight among themselves, but that is their affair. They do not injure others so that people are not hostile to them. Their squabbles and magic combats among themselves are a source of great amusement to Azande.

But, though knowledge of medicines brings Zande witch-doctors no political power and no great social influence, nevertheless, witch-doctorhood shows a degree of social specialization. This has its economic side, for a first-class witch-doctor is constantly being summoned to court or to the homes of affluent commoners or to those of friends or relatives, and in consequence he is not able to give the same attention to economic pursuits as laymen can give to them. He makes up for his loss by his earnings as leech and diviner, which are either paid to him in food and tools or in metal wealth which can be exchanged for the one or converted into the other.

This social differentiation has its ritual side also, for the witch-doctor performs for a large number of people at a seance what each would otherwise have to do himself by means of oracles and various forms of protective magic. On these occasions the community trusts to him to look after their interests by keeping an eye on witches, exposing their intentions, and frustrating them.

Division of social labour has its psychological side, for it is clear that in some respects a witch-doctor's mentality differs from that of laymen. He has a wider range of general knowledge in the first place. Thus his profession introduces him to a large number of plants and trees, of which laymen do not know the full uses. He has, moreover, a wider range of behaviour-forms than laymen have. It will have been clear from the account I have given of a seance that he acts and feels in a way in which laymen never act and feel. To the behaviour-forms which are imposed upon him equally with every other member of Zande society are added new ones, which are novel both in their content and in the manner of their acquisition. His social contacts are also more varied. He travels more and farther than most members of his locality, and he enters society not only as an ordinary visitor, but also sometimes as a leech and at other times as a diviner. When he goes to dance at the court of a prince or at the home of a rich commoner his professional position gives him privilege which makes his relations with his patrons less crude than those existing between them and laymen of lower social position. Their relations become more varied and hence more complicated and delicate. Finally, the witch-doctor is cut off from the rest of the community in which he lives by his secret knowledge of the way in which objects are produced from the bodies of the sick, and it is possible that the scepticism which I have described is to be attributed largely to a spread-over of disbelief from professionals to laymen, for, however well witch-doctors may keep their secrets, they live their lives in daily intimacy with their uninitiated fellows, who cannot fail to be influenced by their contact.

Since we know that witch-doctors are aware of one piece of reality which is unknown to the rest of their society we may wonder whether they have not a wider appreciation of the nature of other things in the world around them. I did not reach this conclusion. Nevertheless, I was impressed with their ability, and believe that when one knows Azande well one can often detect the expert magician, especially the successful witch-doctor. My evidence is not full enough to demonstrate with assurance, but I consider it probable, that as a rule men who show a strong desire to become witch-doctors have a higher degree of intellectual curiosity and greater social ambition than the ordinary Zande possesses. Their personality is certainly developed by new modes of social behaviour which demand tact, courage, foresight, knowledge of human feelings, and a very considerable degree of mental agility if their professional activities are to be successfully carried out. I have no doubt, judging from the few witch-doctors whom I have known personally, that they show greater ability than most laymen, and this can be observed not only in their ritual functions, in which they display great cleverness, but also in their all-round competence in social intercourse, in their quick grasp of new situations, in their knowledge of custom, in their econ omic knowledge, and in their power to impress and manage men.

Yet the Zande witch-doctor, in spite of his extra knowledge, is as deep a believer in magic as his slightly less-informed fellows. He knows that he cheats laymen but does not know how he is cheated by his own ignorance. Just as laymen express their scepticism in a mystical idiom so witch-doctors express their knowledge in mystical terms. They know that their extraction of objects from the bodies of their patients is a fake, but they believe that they cure them by the medicines they administer. They know that the objects they are supposed to shoot into people are hidden in their hands, yet they think that they somehow, nevertheless, injure their rivals by assailing them with psychical ammunition. Here, as everywhere, we are confronted with the same tangle of knowledge and error. It is especially evident in the manner of divination employed by witch-doctors: they seem to reason so acutely, to weigh probabilities of enmity so evenly. Yet they believe as firmly in witch-craft as their clients and believe as steadfastly that the medicines they have eaten enable them to identify witches. They display an intellectual acuteness which might have expressed itself in scepticism and disillusionment were they not enclosed in the same network of thought, the same web of witchcraft, oracles, and magic, as are laymen. Within the limited situations of their professional practice they are able to think differently from laymen, but their thought is limited by the same cultural conditions outside these special situations.

It is difficult to know what mainly influences a youth in choosing to become a witch-doctor. Azande who are inclined to be cynical about such matters often declare that it is love of gain, but it is difficult to treat this opinion seriously because even noted witch-doctors, apart from selling their knowledge to novices, gain very little wealth by their divination and leech-craft, and it must be many years before a man recuperates from the expenses of his initiation. It was my impression that the most important incentives are desire to obtain medicines and desire to display oneself.

Many Azande show a great desire for medicines and take every opportunity to acquire new ones because they give security against witches and sorcerers and because they give a sense of power and ownership. Witch-doctors like to feel that they possess medicines denied to the rest of the community.

Those who are not attracted to court and political life have little means of displaying themselves in public before an attentive audience other than that offered by the profession of witch-doctor. A seance gives a witch-doctor opportunity to draw attention to himself in a role that allows him to assert his superiority and to dramatize his behaviour. Most Azande would be far too shy to dance and sing as witch-doctors do at seances, and some witch-doctors are quiet and shy on other occasions when people dance and sing. The opportunity to display themselves in a situation when display is socially applauded is a great incentive to some youths to take up the career of a witch-doctor.

Many men have simply taken over the art from their fathers and occasionally from their maternal uncles. But a father only teaches one of his sons the medicines, and I have noticed that he selects the son who, in his opinion, is the most suitable to practise as a witch-doctor and who shows that he is keen to become one.

I have never known a youth fail to qualify as a witch-doctor because he was too stupid to learn and practise the art. It is perhaps significant that a witch-doctor does not at once accept a youth as pupil but inquires from him with stress whether he is quite certain that he wishes to learn the art. Consequently only those who are keen and serious persist in their request to be initiated.

CHAPTER VIII

The Poison Oracle in Daily Life

I

ORACLES are a more satisfactory means of ascertaining the future, and hidden things of the present, than are witch-doctors. Witch-doctors are useful as sleuths for seeking out the many affairs of a group of homesteads, and their chief value is that they generally clear the atmosphere of witchcraft. On this account they are often asked to dance before a big hunt because this is a joint undertaking, many persons are involved, and the interests of a district are at stake. A public attack by witch-doctors, who act as ritual skirmishers to report on and to counter the mystical forces in opposition, is appropriate. When the seance is over people feel that witches have been scared from their undertaking.

But as diviners witch-doctors are not regarded as furnishing more than preliminary evidence, and in all matters of moment a man takes a witch-doctor's statement and places it before one of the greater oracles for corroboration. This is, moreover, necessary if a man wishes to take any public action. He cannot try to exact vengeance for homicide on the evidence of a witch-doctor alone. A witch-doctor would never be consulted on such a matter. A man would be very ill-advised even to present a fowl's wing to a witch accused solely by witch-doctors. The accused might mock the bearer of the wing and would not lose esteem for doing so. Hence Azande say that witch-doctors, like the rubbing-board oracle, are useful because they can answer quickly many questions and sort out suspects in a preliminary manner before men approach the poison oracle, but that they are not dependable.

II

The method of revealing what is hidden by administering poison to fowls has a wide extension in Africa; but just as the Azande are the most north-easterly people who have the notion of witchcraft as a material substance in the belly, so also is their culture the north-easterly limit of the distribution of this type of oracle. They are the only people in the Anglo-Egyptian Suddan who employ it.

The poison used is a red powder manufactured from a forest creeper and mixed with water to a paste. The liquid is squeezed out of the paste into the beaks of small domestic fowls which are compelled to swallow it. Generally violent spasms follow. The doses sometimes prove fatal, but as often the fowls recover. Sometimes they are even unaffected by the poison. From the behaviour of fowls under this ordeal, especially by their death or survival, Azande receive answers to the questions they place before the oracle.

The botanical nature of the poison has not been determined, but its chemical nature has been roughly analysed. Some of the oracle poison which I brought back to England was examined by Professor R. Robinson who informs me that:

The quantity of *benge* was insufficient to enable me to establish with certainly the nature of the active principle. All that can be said about it is that the toxic substance is alkaloidal in character and appears to be related chemically to strychnine. It is almost certainly not homogeneous, and this accounts for the difficulty of isolation in a pure condition. Thus, all I can say is that it is strychnine-like in many of its reactions, and that probably two or more bases are present.

III

The poison oracle, *benge*, is by far the most important of the Zande oracles. Zande rely completely on its decisions, which have the force of law when obtained on the orders of a prince. A visitor to Zandeland hears as much of the poison oracle as he hears of witchcraft, for whenever a question arises about the facts of a case or about a man's well-being they at once seek to know the opinion of the poison oracle on the matter. In many situations where we seek to base a verdict upon evidence or try to regulate our conduct by weighing of probabilities the Zande consults, without hesitation, the poison oracle and follows its directions with implicit trust.

No important venture is undertaken without authorization of the poison oracle. In important collective undertakings, in all crises of life, in all serious legal disputes, in all matters strongly affecting individual welfare, in short, on all occasions regarded by Azande as dangerous or socially important, the activity is preceded by consultation of the poison oracle.

I do not wish to catalogue all situations in which the oracle may be consulted since this would mean a list of social situations in every sphere of Zande life, and when each sphere is described the part played by oracles is more fitly recorded than in the present place. Notwithstanding, it is desirable to list some of the occasions on which the oracle must be consulted in order to give the reader a clear idea of its significance to Azande. When I say that the poison oracle, or some other oracle, must be consulted on the occasions listed below, I mean that if a Zande were not to consult it he would be acting contrary to custom and might suffer in social prestige. He might even incur legal penalties. The following situations are typical occasions of consultation:

To discover why a wife has not conceived.
During pregnancy of wife, about place of delivery, about her safety in childbirth, and about the safety of her child.
Before circumcision of son.
Before marriage of daughter.
Before sending son to act as page at court.
In sickness of any member of family. Will he die? Who is the witch responsible? etc.
To discover the agent responsible for any misfortune.
At death of kinsman in the old days. Who killed him? Who will execute the witch? etc.
Before exacting vengeance by magic. Who will keep the taboos? Who will make the magic? etc.
In cases of sorcery.
In cases of adultery.
Before gathering oracle poison.
Before making blood-brotherhood.
Before long journeys.
A man before marrying a wife.
Before presenting a prince with beer.
Before large-scale hunting.
A commoner in choosing a new homestead site.
Before accepting, or allowing a dependant to accept, European employment.
Before becoming a witch-doctor.

Before joining a closed association.

A man before he and his adult sons go to war.

In cases of disloyalty to a prince.

A prince before making war.

To determine disposition of warriors, place and time of attack, and all other matters pertaining to warfare.

A prince before appointing governors, deputies, or any other officials.

A prince before moving his court.

A prince to discover whether a communal ceremony will terminate drought.

A prince to determine the actions of the British District Commissioner.

A prince before accepting presents and tribute.

IV

It is not only about what we would consider the more important social activities that Azande consult their oracles, but also about their smaller everyday affairs. If time and opportunity permitted many Azande would wish to consult one or other of the oracles about every step in their lives. This is clearly impossible, but old men who know how to use the rubbing-board oracle usually carry one about with them so that if any doubt arises they can quiet it by immediate consultation.

A typical occasion on which a man consults his rubbing-board oracle is when he is on a visit to a friend's homestead. When his visit is concluded he asks the oracle whether he had better leave openly during the daytime or depart secretly at night so that any witch who may wish to dispatch his witchcraft after him, to cause him some misfortune on the journey, may be ignorant that he has left. If the oracle advises him to depart at night he tells his host and leaves before dawn. Other members of the homestead understand what has happened and are not angry that he has not bid them farewell. Or the rubbing-board oracle may tell a man that he can depart in the daytime but must be careful about witchcraft on the way. In this case he strolls away from his host's homestead as though he were taking a short walk and throws a spear-shaft aimlessly in front of him so that people who observe him on the path think that he is playing and will shortly return from his stroll, since people departing on a journey do not meander at the start. When he is well out of sight he quickens his steps and hastens on his way. Sometimes he does not even inform his host of his departure, but the host understands the reason for his silence.

I found that when a Zande acted towards me in a manner that we would call rude and untrustworthy his actions were often to be accounted for by obedience to his oracles. Usually I have found Azande courteous and reliable according to English standards, but sometimes their behaviour is unintelligible till their mystical notions are taken into account. Often Azande are tortuous in their dealings with one another, but they do not consider a man blameworthy for being secretive or acting contrary to his declared intentions. On the contrary, they praise his prudence for taking account of witchcraft at each step and for regulating his conduct after the direction of his oracles. Hence it is not necessary for one Zande to explain to another his waywardness, for everybody understands the motives of his conduct.

Not all Azande are equally prone to consult oracles. I have frequently observed that some men are more keenly aware of danger from witchcraft than others and rely far more than others upon magic and oracles to counteract its influence. Thus while some men like to consult oracles and to blow magic whistles or perform some other magic rite before embarking upon even small adventures, other men only consult oracles about important legal issues and at real crises, such as marriage, serious sickness, and death. When they are socially compelled to consult oracles they do so, but not otherwise. In legal procedure everyone must make use of the poison oracle.

To understand Zande legal procedure one must know exactly how the poison oracle is operated, because in the old days it was in itself the greater part of what we know as rules of evidence, judge, jury, and witnesses. In the past the two main types of cases were witchcraft and adultery. Witchcraft cases were settled entirely through the oracles since there was no possibility of discovering mystical action except through the mystical power of the poison oracle. All a prince had to do was to confirm the names of witches discovered by the kinsmen of dead persons by placing their names before his own oracle. The compensation which a witch had to pay for his crime was fixed by custom.

All death to Azande is murder and was the starting-point of the most important legal process in Zande culture. Azande therefore find it difficult to see how Europeans can refuse to take cognizance of what is so manifest and so shocking to them.

In a case of adultery there might be circumstantial evidence, but in fact simple cases of this kind were rare. The chance discovery of lovers during a few minutes' congress in the bush or during the absence of a husband from his homestead was small. The only certain evidence upon which a suspicious husband could act was that provided by the poison oracle, for even if a wife repented of her infidelity and told her husband the name of her lover he might deny the accusation. The husband might, it is true, urge before the prince some other grounds for suspicion, but he would base his charge of adultery mainly upon the evidence of the oracle, and no further proof than this was required. The accused man would defend himself less by urging absence of circumstantial evidence than by offering to give a *ngbu* or test. He was asked to choose a man of substance among the regular attendants at court and to give him the test, telling him to place the question of adultery before his oracle. This man acted on behalf of his prince and the declaration of his oracle settled the case. To Zande eyes this is the perfect procedure in adultery cases and they do not approve of European methods, for in their opinion the only sure evidence of guilt or innocence is not allowed.

Accusing husbands and men accused share this opinion, the husbands because they often cannot produce evidence acceptable to government courts of adulteries for which they possess conclusive proof in the declaration of the poison oracle; accused persons, because they are condemned on the declaration of a woman without appeal to the one really reliable authority, the poison oracle.

Special care is taken to protect a prince's oracle poison from witchcraft and pollution because a prince's oracles reveal matters of tribal importance, judge criminal and civil cases, and determine whether vengeance has been exacted for death. A prince has two or three official operators who supervise his poison oracle. These men must be thoroughly reliable since the fate of their master and the purity of law are in their hands. If they break a taboo the whole legal system may become corrupted and the innocent be judged guilty and the guilty be judged innocent. An official consulter of a prince's oracles must also be a man of impeccable honesty since he is given sole charge of many legal cases and tests of vengeance. He can ruin subjects of his master by fabricating oracular statements. Finally, the consulter of a prince's oracle must know how to maintain silence about his master's affairs. There is no offence more serious in the eyes of a Zande prince than 'revealing the speech of the king's poison oracle'.

We who do not believe in the poison oracle think that the courts we have established are just because they recognize only evidence which we regard as such, and we flatter ourselves that they are native courts of justice because we allow natives to preside over them. But Azande think that they do not admit the only evidence which is really relevant to the cases which come before them, and the princes who have to administer justice do so with mechanical application of imported European rules of procedure, and without conviction, since the rules are not according to custom.

v

I never found great difficulty in observing oracle consultations. I found that in such matters the best way of gaining confidence was to enact the same procedure as Azande and to take oracular verdicts as seriously as they take them. I always kept a supply of poison for the use of my household and neighbours and we regulated our affairs in accordance with the oracles' decisions. I may remark that I found this as satisfactory a way of running my home and affairs as any other I know of. Among Azande it is the only satisfactory way of life because it is the only way of life they understand, and it furnishes the only arguments by which they are wholly convinced and silenced. Friends and neighbours would from time to time ask me to let them bring fowls to consult my oracles about their troubles. I was always pleased at this sign of their trust. Also, I had opportunity on a number of occasions to observe other people's oracles at work. In the course of many months I made repeated observations of oracular consultations and had ample opportunity to acquaint myself with details of technique and interpretation. An investigation into the use of the poison oracle, like an investigation into beliefs about witchcraft, does not require special informants. I could rely upon direct observation and could elicit commentary from any adult Zande when a point was not wholly clear to me. I can say the same about the rubbing-board oracle and, to a lesser degree, of the termites oracle.

For information on the following points, however, I had to rely mainly, or entirely, on verbal information: the process of collecting oracle poison; the administration of poison to human beings; and the use of the poison oracle in judicial procedure at the king's court. Poison is not administered to human beings at the present time. The poison oracle has no longer a primary role in court procedure, though it is still to some extent employed. It had been my ambition to observe oracle poison being gathered and I made an expedition into the Belgian Congo with this end in view but was defeated by combined dysentery and malaria, and was carried home again in extreme weakness.

VI

The usual place for a consultation is on the edge of cultivations far removed from homesteads. Any place in the bush screened by high grasses and brushwood is suitable. Or they may choose the corner of a clearing at the edge of the bush where crops will later be sown, since this is not so damp as in the bush itself. The object in going so far is to ensure secrecy, to avoid pollution by people who have not observed the taboos, and to escape witchcraft which is less likely to corrupt the oracle in the bush than in a homestead.

One does not consult the poison oracle during the heat of the day since strong sunlight is bad both for the poison and for the chickens. If the oracle is consulted late in the morning the basket of chickens is placed in the shade of a nearby shrub or covered with grass. When the poison has been for some time in strong sunlight it becomes very potent and they say then that, 'If a man gives one dose to a small fowl he has given it quite enough.' The normal time for consultations is from about eight to nine o'clock in the morning, because by this time the dew has evaporated and it is possible to sit down in the bush without great discomfort. Very occasionally elders who frequently consult the oracles and conduct long seances hold them at night.

The consultation may then take place in the centre of the homestead after the womenfolk have retired to bed. Consultations may take place on any day except the day after a new moon.

Oracle poison is useless unless a man possesses fowls upon which to test it, for the oracle speaks through fowls. In every Zande household there is a fowl-house, and fowls are kept mainly with the object of subjecting them to oracular tests. As a rule they are only killed for food (and then only cocks or old hens) when an important visitor comes to the homestead, perhaps a prince's son or perhaps a father-in-law. Eggs are not eaten but are left to hens to hatch out. Clay receptacles may be fashioned or baskets placed in one of the huts to encourage hens to nest in them, but often they lay their eggs in the bush and if they are fortunate will one day strut back to the homestead accompanied by their broods. Generally a Zande, unless he is a wealthy man, will not possess more than half a dozen grown fowls at the most, and many people possess none at all or perhaps a single hen which someone has given to them.

Small chickens, only two or three days old, may be used for the poison oracle, but Azande prefer them older. However, one sees fowls of all sizes at oracle consultations, from tiny chickens to half-grown cockerels and pullets. When it is possible to tell the sex of fowls Azande use only cockerels, unless they have none and a consultation is necessary at once. The hens are spared for breeding purposes. Generally a man tells one of his younger sons to catch the fowls the night before a seance. Otherwise they catch them when the door of the fowl-house is opened shortly after sunrise, but it is better to catch them and put them in a basket at night when they are roosting. For if the fowls elude capture in the morning and run away into nearby gardens it is much trouble to catch them. Two or three boys have to run them down, all the womenfolk know what is going on, the neighbours hear the noise, and a witch among them may follow the owner of the fowls to prevent the oracle from giving him the information he desires. When chickens are used this difficulty does not arise because they sleep in one of the huts, where they are immune from attacks by wild cats, and they are easily caught on the morning of a seance.

Old men say that fully grown birds ought not to be used in

oracle consultations because they are too susceptible to the poison and have a habit of dying straight away before the poison has had time to consider the matter placed before it or even to hear a full statement of the problem. On the other hand, a chicken remains for a long time under the influence of the poison before it recovers or expires, so that the oracle has time to hear all the relevant details concerning the problem placed before it and to give a well-considered judgement.

VII

Any male may take part in the proceedings. However, the oracle is costly, and the questions put to it concern adult occupations. Therefore boys are only present when they operate the oracle. Normally these are boys who are observing taboos of mourning for the death of a relative. Adults also consider that it would be very unwise to allow any boys other than these to come near their poison because boys cannot be relied upon to observe the taboos on meats and vegetables.

An unmarried man will seldom be present at a seance. If he has any problems his father or uncle can act on his behalf. Moreover, only a married householder is wealthy enough to possess fowls and to acquire poison and has the experience to conduct a seance properly. Senior men also say that youths are generally engaged in some illicit love affair and would probably pollute the poison if they came near it.

It is particularly the province of married men with households of their own to consult the poison oracle and no occupation gives them greater pleasure. It is not merely that they are able to solve their personal problems; but also they are dealing with matters of public importance, witchcraft, sorcery, and adultery, in which their names will be associated as witnesses of the oracle's decisions. A middle-aged Zande is happy when he has some poison and a few fowls and the company of one or two trusted friends of his own age, and he can sit down to a long seance to discover all about the infidelities of his wives, his health and the health of his children, his marriage plans, his hunting and agricultural prospects, the advisability of changing his homestead, and so forth.

Poor men who do not possess poison or fowls but who are compelled for one reason or another to consult the oracle will persuade a kinsman, blood-brother, relative-in-law, or prince's deputy to consult it on their behalf. This is one of the main duties of social relationships.

Control over the poison oracle by the older men gives them great power over their juniors and is one of the main sources of their prestige. It is possible for the older men to place the names of the youths before the poison oracle and on its declarations to bring accusations of adultery against them. Moreover, a man who is not able to afford poison is not a fully independent householder, since he is unable to initiate any important undertaking and is dependent on the goodwill of others to inform him about everything that concerns his health and welfare.

Women are debarred not only from operating the poison oracle but from having anything to do with it. They are not expected even to speak of it, and a man who mentions the oracle in the presence of women uses some circumlocutory expression. When a man is going to consult the poison oracle he says to his wife that he is going to look at his cultivations or makes a similar excuse. She understands well enough what he is going to do but says nothing. Occasionally very old women of good social position have been known to operate the poison oracle, or at least to consult it, but such persons are rare exceptions and are always august persons.

The poison oracle is a male prerogative and is one of the principal mechanisms of male control and an expression of sex antagonism. For men say that women are capable of any deceit to defy a husband and please a lover, but men at least have the advantage that their oracle poison will reveal secret embraces. If it were not for the oracle it would be of little use to pay bride-wealth, for the most jealous watch will not prevent a woman from committing adultery if she has a mind to do so. And what woman has not? The only thing which women fear is the poison oracle; for if they can escape the eyes of men they cannot escape the eyes of the oracle. Hence it is said that women hate the oracle, and that if a woman finds some of the poison in the bush she will destroy its power by urinating on it. I once asked a Zande why he so carefully collected the leaves used in operating the oracle and threw them some distance away into the bush, and he replied that it was to prevent women from finding them and polluting them, for if they pollute the leaves then the poison which has been removed to its hiding-place will lose its power.

When we consider to what extent social life is regulated by the poison oracle we shall at once appreciate how great an advantage men have over women in their ability to use it, and how being cut off from the main means of establishing contact with the mystical forces that so deeply affect human welfare degrades woman's position in Zande society.

Great experience is necessary to conduct a seance in the correct manner and to know how to interpret the findings of the oracle. One must know how many doses of poison to administer, whether the oracle is working properly, in what order to take the questions, whether to put them in a positive or negative form, how long a fowl is to be held between the toes or in the hand while a question is being put to the oracle, when it ought to be jerked to stir up the poison, and when it is time to throw it on the ground for final inspection. One must know how to observe not only whether the fowl lives or dies, but also the exact manner in which the poison affects it, for while it is under the influence of the oracle its every movement is significant to the experienced eye. Also one must know the phraseology of address in order to put questions clearly to the oracle without error or ambiguity, and this is no easy task when a single question may be asked in a harangue lasting as long as five or ten minutes. Not every man is proficient in the art, though most adults can prepare and question the oracle if necessary. Those who as boys have often prepared the poison for their fathers and uncles, and who are members of families which frequent the court and constantly consult the oracle, are the most competent. Some men are very expert at questioning the oracle, and those who wish to consult it like to be accompanied by such a man.

VIII

Any man who is invited by the owner of the oracle poison may attend the seance, but he will be expected to keep clear of the oracle if he has had relations with his wife or eaten any of the prohibited foods within the last few days. It is imperative that the man who actually prepares the poison shall have observed these taboos, and for this reason the owner of the poison, referred to in this account as the owner, generally asks a boy or man who is under taboos of mourning to operate the oracle, since there can be no doubt that he has kept the taboos, because they are the same for mourning as for oracles. Such a man is always employed when, as in a case of sudden sickness, it is necessary to consult the oracle without warning so that there is no time for a man to prepare himself by observation of taboos. I shall refer to the man or boy who actually prepares the poison and administers it to fowls as the operator. When I speak of the questioner I refer to the man who sits opposite to the oracle and addresses it and calls upon it for judgements. As he sits a few feet from the oracle he ought also to have observed all the taboos. It is possible for a man to be owner, operator, and questioner at the same time by conducting the consultation of the oracle by himself, but this rarely, if ever, occurs. Usually there is no difficulty in obtaining the services of an operator since a man knows which of his neighbours are observing the taboos associated with death and vengeance. One of his companions who has not eaten tabooed food or had sexual relations with women for a day or two before the consultation acts as questioner. If a man is unclean he can address the oracle from a distance. It is better to take these precautions because contact of an unclean person with the oracle is certain to destroy its potency, and even the close proximity of an unclean person may have this result.

The taboos which have invariably to be kept by persons who come into contact with oracle poison are on:

Sexual relations with women.
Eating elephant's flesh.
Eating fish.
Eating *mboyo* vegetable *(Hibiscus esculentus)*.
Eating *morombida* vegetable *(Corchorus tridens)*.
Smoking hemp.

Some men avoid eating animals of a light colour, and such would seem to be the rule imposed on those who come into contact with a prince's oracles. Elephant's flesh and fish are forbidden on account of the powerful smell emitted by a man who has eaten them. I think that it is their slimy nature that has brought *mboyo* and *morombida* under a ritual ban. They are glutinous, and when the edible parts are plucked they do not break off cleanly but are attached to the stem by glutinous fibres which have to be drawn out. When cooked they form a sticky mess which can be stretched like toffee. Before he comes into contact with oracle poison, or even into close proximity to it, a man ought to have refrained from sexual intercourse for five or six days and to have abstained from the forbidden meats and vegetables for three or four days. However, the length of time during which a man ought to observe these taboos prior to operating the oracle is not fixed, and different men give different estimates. Many are content to refrain from sexual intercourse for five or even four days. If a man who has had sexual relations is asked to operate the oracle he will say, 'I have eaten *mboyo*,' and everyone will understand that he is employing a euphemism for sexual intercourse. He may excuse himself in similar terms if he simply does not wish to be bothered with the work.

The owner does not pay the operator and questioner for their services. The questioner is almost invariably either the owner himself or one of his friends who also wishes to put questions to the oracle and has brought fowls with him for the purpose. It is usual to reward the operator, if he is an adult, by giving him a fowl during the seance so that he can place one of his own problems before the oracle. Since he is generally a man who wears a girdle of mourning and vengeance he will often ask the oracle when the vengeance-magic is going to strike its victim.

To guard against pollution a man generally hides his poison in the thatched roof of a hut, on the inner side, if possible, in a hut which women do not use, but this is not essential, for a woman does not know that there is poison hidden in the roof and is unlikely to come into contact with it. The owner of the poison must have kept the taboos if he wishes to take it down from the roof himself, and if he is unclean he will bring the man or boy who is to operate the oracle into the hut and indicate to him at a distance where the poison is hidden in the thatch. So good a hiding-place is the thatched roof of a hut for a small packet of poison that it is often difficult for its owner himself to find it. No one may smoke hemp in a hut which lodges oracle poison. However, there is always a danger of pollution and of witchcraft if the poison is kept in a homestead, and some men prefer to hide it in a hole in a tree in the bush, or even to build a small shelter and to lay it on the ground beneath.

This shelter is far removed from human dwellings, and were a man to come across it in the bush he would not disturb it lest it cover some kind of lethal medicine. It is very improbable that witchcraft will discover oracle poison hidden in the bush. I have never seen oracle poison under a shelter in the bush, but I was told that it is frequently housed in this manner.

Oracle poison when not in use is kept wrapped in leaves, and at the end of a seance used poison is placed in a separate leaf-wrapping to unused poison. The poison may be used two or three times and sometimes fresh poison is added to it to make it more potent. When its action shows that it has lost its strength they throw it away.

All good oracle poison is the same, whoever owns, operates, and consults it. But its goodness depends on the care and virtue of owner, operator, and consulter. As the greatest precautions are taken with a prince's poison, it is considered more reliable than the poison of commoners. All *benge* is the same material, but people speak of 'my *benge*' or of 'so-and-so's *benge*', and they say that the poison of one prince is absolutely reliable while that of another prince is not so reliable. They make these judgements partly on the evidence of subsequent events which prove oracles right or wrong in their statements, and partly on the verdicts of the king's oracle, which is the final authority. For in the past cases would occasionally go from a provincial governor's oracles to Gbudwe's oracle which might declare them to be in error.

IX

I will now describe the manner in which poison is administered to fowls. The operator goes ahead of the rest of the party in order to prepare for the test. He takes with him a small gourdful of water. He clears a space by treading down the grasses. Afterwards he scrapes a hole in the earth into which he places a large leaf as a basin for the oracle poison. From *bingba* grass he fashions a small brush to administer the poison, and from leaves he makes a filter to pour the liquid poison into the beaks of the fowls; and from other leaves he makes a cup to transfer water from the gourd to the poison when it needs to be moistened. Finally, he tears off some branches of nearby shrubs and extracts their bast to be used as cord for attaching to the legs of fowls which have survived the test so that they can be easily retrieved from the grass when the business of the day is finished. The operator does not moisten the poison till the rest of the party arrive. There may be only one man or there may be several who have questions to put to the oracle. Each brings his fowls with him in an open-wove basket. As it has been agreed beforehand where the oracle consultation is to take place they know where to foregather. As each person arrives he hands over his basket of fowls to the operator who places it on the ground near him. A man who is used to acting as questioner sits opposite to it, a few feet away if he has observed the taboos, but several yards away if he has not observed them. Other men who have not kept the taboos remain at a greater distance.

When everyone is seated they discuss in low tones whose fowl they will take first and how the question shall be framed. Meanwhile the operator pours some water from the gourd at his side into his leaf cup and from the cup on to the poison, which then effervesces. He mixes the poison and water with his finger-tips into a paste of the right consistency and, when instructed by the questioner, takes one of the fowls and draws down its wings over its legs and pins them between and under his toes. He takes his grass brush, twirls it round in the poison, and folds it in the leaf filter. He holds open the beak of the fowl and tips the end of the filter into it and squeezes the filter so that the liquid runs out of the paste into the throat of the fowl. He bobs the head of the fowl up and down to compel it to swallow the poison.

At this point the questioner, having previously been instructed by the owner of the fowl on the facts which he is to put before the oracle, commences to address the poison inside the fowl. He continues to address it for about a couple of minutes, when a second dose of poison is usually administered. If it is a very small chicken two doses will suffice, but a larger fowl will receive three doses, and I have known a fowl receive a fourth dose, but never more than four. The questioner does not cease his address to the oracle, but puts his questions again and again in different forms, though always with the same refrain, 'If such is the case, poison oracle kill the fowl,' or 'If such is the case, poison oracle spare the fowl.' From time to time he interrupts his flow of oratory to give a technical order to the operator. He may tell him to give the fowl another dose of poison or to jerk it between his toes by raising and lowering his foot (this stirs up the poison inside the fowl). When the last dose of poison has been administered and he has further addressed it, he tells the operator to raise the fowl. The operator takes it in his hand and, holding its legs between his fingers so that it faces him, gives it an occasional jerk backwards and forwards. The questioner redoubles his oratory as though the verdict depended upon his forensic efforts, and if the fowl is not already dead he then, after a further bout of oratory, tells the operator to put it on the ground. He continues to address the poison inside the fowl while they watch its movements on the ground.

The poison affects fowls in many ways. Occasionally it kills them immediately after the first dose, while they are still on the ground. This seldom happens, for normally a fowl is not seriously affected till it is removed from the ground and jerked backwards and forwards in the hand. Then, if it is going to die, it goes through spasmodic stretchings of the body and closing of the wings and vomits. After several such spasms it vomits and expires in a final seizure. Some fowls appear quite unaffected by the poison, and when, after being jerked backwards and forwards for a while, they are flung to the ground peck about unconcernedly. Those fowls which are unaffected by the poison generally excrete as soon as they are put to earth. Some fowls appear little affected by the poison till put to earth, when they suddenly collapse and die. It is very seldom that a fowl seriously affected by the poison finally recovers.

One generally knows what the verdict is going to be after the fowl has been held in the hand for a couple of minutes. If it appears certain to recover the operator ties bast to its leg and throws it to the ground. If it appears certain to die he does not trouble to tie bast to its leg, but lays it on the earth to die. Often when a fowl has died they draw its corpse in a semicircle round the poison to show it to the poison. They then cut off a wing to use as evidence and cover the body with grass. Those fowls which survive are taken home and let loose. A fowl is never used twice on the same day.

There is no stereotyped speech—no formula—in which the oracle must be addressed. Nevertheless, there are traditional refrains, pieces of imagery, compliments to the oracle, ways of formulating a question, and so forth which occur in every consultation.

The main duty of the questioner is to see that the oracle fully understands the question put to it and is acquainted with all facts relevant to the problem it is asked to solve. They address it with all the care for detail that one observes in court cases before a prince. This means beginning a long way back and noting over a considerable period of time every detail which might elucidate the case, linking up facts into a consistent picture of events, and the marshalling of arguments into a logical and closely knit web of sequences and interrelations of fact and inference. Also the questioner is careful to mention to the oracle again and again the name of the man who is consulting it, and he points him out to the oracle with his outstretched arm. He mentions also the name of his father, perhaps the name of his clan, and the name of the place where he resides, and he gives similar details of other people mentioned in the address.

An address consists usually of alternate directions. The first sentences outline the question in terms demanding an affirmative answer and end with the command, 'Poison oracle kill the fowl.' The next sentences outline the question in terms demanding a negative answer and end with the command, 'Poison oracle spare the fowl.' The consulter then takes up the question again in terms asking an affirmative answer; and so on. If a bystander considers that a relevant point has been left out he interrupts the questioner, who then makes this point.

The questioner has a switch in his hand, and while questioning the oracle beats the ground, as he sits cross-legged, in front of it. He continues to beat the ground till the end of his address. Often he will gesticulate as he makes his points, in the same manner as a man making a case in court. He sometimes plucks grass and shows it to the poison and, after explaining that there is something he does not wish it to consider, throws it behind him. Thus he tells the oracle that he does not wish it to consider the question of witchcraft but only of sorcery. Witchcraft is *wingi*, something irrelevant, and he casts it behind him. The imagery used is specially noteworthy. It is seldom that the oracle is addressed without analogies and circumlocutions.

Thus in asking whether a man has committed adultery one frames the question in some such manner as follows:

Poison oracle, poison oracle, you are in the throat of the fowl. That man his navel joined her navel; they pressed together; he knew her as woman and she knew him as man. She has drawn *badiabe* (a leaf used as a towel) and water to his side (for ablutions after intercourse); poison oracle hear it, kill the fowl.

While the fowl is undergoing its ordeal men are attentive to their behaviour. A man must tighten and spread out his bark-cloth loin-covering lest he expose his genitals, as when he is sitting in the presence of a prince or parent-in-law. Men speak in a low voice as they do in the presence of superiors. Indeed, all conversation is avoided unless it directly concerns the procedure of consultation. If anyone desires to leave before the proceedings are finished he takes a leaf and spits on it and places it where he has been sittng. I have seen a man who rose for a few moments only to catch a fowl which had escaped from its basket place a blade of grass on the stone upon which he had been sitting. Spears must be laid on the ground and not planted upright in the presence of the poison oracle. Azande are very serious during a seance, for they are asking questions of vital importance to their lives and happiness.

X

Basically, the system of question and answer in oracle consultations is simple. There are two tests, the *bambata sima*, or first test, and the *gingo*, or second test. If a fowl dies in the first test then another fowl must survive the second test, and if a fowl survives the first test another fowl must die in the second test for the judgement to be accepted as valid. Generally the question is so framed that the oracle will have to kill a fowl in the first test and spare another fowl in the corroborative test to give an affirmative reply, and to spare a fowl in the first test and kill another fowl in the corroborative test to give a negative reply; but this is not invariably the case, and questions are sometimes framed in an opposite manner. The killing of a fowl does not give in itself a positive or negative answer. That depends upon the form of the question. I will illustrate the usual procedure by an example:

A.

First Test. If X has committed adultery poison oracle kill the fowl. If X is innocent poison oracle spare the fowl. The fowl dies.

Second Test. The poison oracle has declared X guilty of adultery by slaying the fowl. If its declaration is true let it spare this second fowl. The fowl survives.

Result. A valid verdict. X is guilty.

B.

First Test. If X has committed adultery poison oracle kill the fowl. If X is innocent poison oracle spare the fowl. The fowl lives.

Second Test. The poison oracle has declared X innocent of adultery by sparing the fowl. If its declaration is true let it slay the second fowl. The fowl dies.

Result. A valid verdict. X is innocent.

C.

First Test. If X has committed adultery poison oracle kill the fowl. If X is innocent poison oracle spare the fowl. The fowl dies.

Second Test. The poison oracle has declared X guilty of adultery by slaying the fowl. If its declaration is true let it spare the second fowl. The fowl dies.

Result. The verdict is contradictory and therefore invalid.

D.

First Test. If X has committed adultery poison oracle kill the fowl. If X is innocent poison oracle spare the fowl. The fowl survives.

Second Test. The poison oracle has declared X innocent of adultery by sparing the fowl. If its declaration is true let it slay the second fowl. The fowl survives.

Result. The verdict is contradictory and therefore invalid.

In the two tests one fowl must die and the other must live if the verdict is to be accepted as valid. If both live or both die the verdict is invalid and the oracle must be consulted on the matter a second time on another occasion. If the supply of oracle poison is sufficient the two tests may be made during the same seance, especially when the matter is important and urgent. Very often, however, a test is not completed at a single seance, as will be observed in the tables that follow, for one of these reasons:

(1) The other part of the test may have been carried out previously or may be carried out at a future seance. Sometimes

a long interval elapses between two tests because the first one is considered sufficient justification for commencing an undertaking, but a second test has to be made before the undertaking is far advanced, e.g. a man is betrothed to a girl and begins to pay bride-spears to her father on the authority of a single test and leaves the corroborative test till months later. But the girl will not come to live with him permanently till both tests have been made. (2) One of the lesser oracles may have been consulted earlier so that a single verdict of the poison oracle is therefore regarded as an oracular confirmation. (3) Often Azande consider a single test sufficient, especially if the oracle gives its answer decisively by killing the fowl without hesitation. They are able to economize their oracle poison by this means. (4) Many confirmations of verdicts are contained in the oracle's answers to other questions, e.g. a man asks whether a witch will die if a certain kinsman observes taboos of vengeance-magic. The oracle says 'Yes'. He then asks whether the kinsman will die during the period he is under taboos. If the oracle says 'No' it confirms its previous verdict because the life of the kinsman is bound up with the accomplishment of vengeance. (5) Sometimes a single fowl is used to confirm different questions. If in answer to two different questions the oracle killed two fowls it may then be asked to spare a third fowl to confirm both its verdicts at the same time. (6) When a serious matter is not at stake Azande are sometimes content merely to know that the oracle is functioning correctly, and being assured of this, are prepared to accept its single statements and to dispense with repetitions of judgement. Thus five unconnected questions may be asked in a seance. The oracle spares fowls in answer to the first four questions and then kills a fowl in answer to the fifth question. This shows that the action of the particular bundle of poison is discriminating and therefore its first four verdicts may be assumed to be valid.

But two tests are essential in any question that concerns the relations between two persons, especially when they involve legal issues.

XI

The following consultations of the poison oracle are given to show the type of questions asked and the order of asking, and to enable the reader to judge for himself the proportion of fowls that die, the number of doses of poison they receive, and the order of deaths and survivals. I was present at both the seances recorded, and many of the questions concern persons connected with my household and their relatives.

SEANCE I

(1) Should X take on the taboos of mourning and vengeance for the death of Magadi till vengeance be accomplished? The fowl DIES, giving the answer 'Yes'.

(2) If X takes on the taboos of mourning for Magadi will he die in consequence (i.e. if, through carelessness in its use, the magical medicine he has sent out against Magadi's murderer should turn back upon X himself? This would also be a corroboration of the first question, since if X were to die then vengeance would not be accomplished during his period of mourning.) The fowl DIES, giving the answer 'Yes'. (These two verdicts contradicted one another and a short discussion followed. One man present said that since Magadi died of leprosy his death ought not to be avenged, and that for this reason the oracle had given contradictory verdicts. This opinion was rejected by others.)

(3) If Adiyambio, who is suffering from a deep-seated ulcer, remains in our government settlement, will he die? The fowl SURVIVES, giving the answer 'No'.

(4) If Bamina lives in the new homestead which he has just built for himself will he die? The fowl DIES, giving the answer 'Yes'.

(5) If Bamina remains in his old homestead will he die? The fowl DIES, giving the answer 'Yes'.

(6) If Bamina goes to live in the government settlement of Ndoruma will he die? The fowl SURVIVES, giving the answer 'No'.

(7) (Corroboration of the last question.) Did the oracle speak truly when it said that Bamina would not die if he went to live in the government settlement of Ndoruma? The fowl SURVIVES, giving the answer 'No'. (The answers to questions 6 and 7 therefore contradicted one another. Someone suggested that the oracle was tired like a chief who has been sitting for hours listening to cases in his court and is weary. Another man said that the oracle saw some misfortune ahead, which was not death yet was a serious misfortune, and had taken this way of warning Bamina. In any case, the verdicts taken together were considered a bad augury and there was a short discussion about who was threatening the welfare of Bamina. Mbira gave it as his opinion that the danger

was from sorcery and not from witchcraft since witchcraft does not pursue a man from one place to another in this manner but ceases to trouble him if he leaves his homestead and goes to live elsewhere.)

(8) They now ask the oracle about two men, one called Pilipili and the other a man of the Bangombi clan who had once married Bamina's daughter but whose bride-spears had been returned to him. Are either of these two men threatening Bamina with witchcraft or with bad magic? The fowl DIES, giving the answer 'Yes'.

The seance had to be closed at this point as there was not enough poison left to continue consultations.

SEANCE II

(1) Since by an earlier consultation it has been determined that the daughter of Mamenzi, the wife of Mekana, is in a bad 'condition', is the evil influence that hangs over her from the homestead of Mekana or from the homestead of her paternal grandfather (who had been given her bride-spears by her father as 'first-fruits')? If it is from Mekana's homestead, poison oracle spare the fowl. If it is from her grandfather's homestead, poison oracle kill the fowl. (It may be remarked that this is a very unusual way of putting a question to the oracle since it does not allow for a third alternative: that the witch is a member of some household other than the two mentioned. The procedure might even be regarded as incorrect. However, the husband was so certain that the evil influence which threatened his wife could only have arisen from jealousy in his own household, or from displeasure in the household of his parents-in-law, that the question appeared to him legitimate. Moreoever, it was always possible for the oracle to show that neither household was responsible by killing or sparing both fowls in the double test, or even by the way in which it affected the fowls during the tests.) The fowl DIES, saying that the evil influence is from the homestead of the girl's grandfather. (One dose of the poison was administered.)

(2) The rubbing-board oracle has said that a man named Sueyo made the magic which caused Kisanga such violent sickness. The question is now asked, 'Is the statement of the rubbing-board correct? If so, poison oracle kill the fowl!' The fowl SURVIVES, giving the answer 'No'. (Two doses administered.)

(3) X's mother lies seriously ill. Is her sickness due to Basa? If so, poison oracle kill the fowl. If Basa is not responsible, poison oracle spare the fowl. The fowl SURVIVES, giving the answer 'No'. (Two doses administered.)

(4) (Corroborative verdict to question No. (1).) If the evil influence that threatens his wife is due to Mekana's household, then poison oracle kill the fowl. If the evil influence emanates from the wives of his wife's grandfather, then poison oracle spare the fowl. The fowl SURVIVES, confirming that evil influence is from the homestead of the girl's grandfather. (Two doses administered.) (Mekana afterwards approached his father-in-law so that the womenfolk of his household might all collect and blow out water in sign of goodwill. He did not venture to single out any particular 'mother-in-law'.)

(5) Since the oracle (test No. (3)) said that the sickness of X's mother is not due to Basa, X now asks whether it is due to the wives of Y. If the wives of Y are responsible, poison oracle kill the fowl. The fowl DIES, giving the answer 'Yes'. (One dose administered.)

(6) (We now return to question No. (2).) It having been determined that Sueyo was not responsible for Kisanga's sickness, he asks whether the sorcerer lives on our side of the new part of the government settlement? If he lives there, poison oracle kill the fowl. The fowl SURVIVES, giving the answer 'No'. (Two doses administered.) (This verdict, combined with three previous verdicts on the matter, proved that the sorcerer did not live anywhere in our settlement.)

(7) (We return to the subject of Mekana's wife already dealt with in questions (1) and (4).) If there is anyone else besides the wives of his wife's grandfather who threatens her health, or if after the fowl's wing has been presented to them to blow water on to it they will still exercise an evil influence over her, then poison oracle kill the fowl. If, on the other hand, there is no one else to fear besides the wives of his wife's grandfather, and if they will blow out water on to the fowl's wing with sincerity and withdraw their evil influence, then poison oracle spare the fowl. The fowl SURVIVES, indicating that there will be nothing more to fear. (Two doses administered.)

(8) (We return to the question of X's mother already dealt with in tests Nos. (3) and (5).) It having been determined that the wives of Y are responsible for the sickness of his mother, X now asks whether they are alone responsible or whether Y himself has encouraged and assisted them in bewitching the old woman. If Y is guilty, then poison oracle kill the fowl. If Y is innocent, then poison oracle spare the fowl. The fowl DIES, saying that Y is responsible. (One dose administered.)

This second seance provides an example of a wholly successful consultation of the oracle. I would call attention to the manner in which an assortment of questions is arranged. There are three problems to be solved, and there are eight fowls by which to solve them. The questions concern the welfare of Mekana's wife, the health of a woman referred to as X's mother, and the identification of the sorcerer who has caused Kisanga such grievous sickness. When several persons have questions to put before the oracle one does not thrash out one problem and then turn to the next, but generally, as on this occasion, each person is allowed to ask a question in turn. In the second round each person tries to procure corroborative verdicts or asks subsidiary questions. If one man has more fowls than the others he is able to ask more questions, but he allows others to place their problems in between his queries. This is not simply a matter of courtesy but also rests on a notion that after a problem has been put to the oracle and it has given its answer it should be granted time to turn the matter over at leisure before it corroborates its first answer and gives a final verdict. The poison used at this seance was at once seen to be discriminating. It killed the first fowl and showed that it was not impotent because when *benge* is impotent all the fowls survive. It spared the second fowl, showing that it was not stupid, over-potent poison, for when it is such all the fowls die. It spared several other fowls, but at the finish killed the last fowl, showing that it maintained its potency. Azande look to these evidences in every test to establish that the poison is good.

XII

It remains to give an account of how human beings used to drink oracle poison in the old days. Some care is necessary in taking account of the Zande phrase *mo mbiri benge*, 'You drink oracle poison,' because this is a usual expression of a prince when he means no more than, 'You must submit your case to the poison oracle.' But in the past people sometimes, though very rarely, actually drank poison themselves. This might happen in two ways. A man accused of some serious offence might offer to drink poison after an oracular test with fowls had gone against him. Likewise, if a woman accused a man of having committed adultery with her he could demand that both he and the woman should drink poison.

Oracle poison was also occasionally administered to boy cap-

tives in important cases involving princes. The
made in the same idiom as an address to fowls. T
mixed with water in a gourd. The boy, seated
and wearing a girdle of *bingba* grass, drank the p
the questioner shook hand-bells and addressed th... ᵣ.
him. When he had finished his address he rubbed the gourd
on the boy's head and ordered him to rise. If the boy had
reached the fowl's wing and returned with it they would again
have addressed the poison within him and would then have told
him to replace the fowl's wing. They would afterwards have
uttered a third and final address and told the lad to fetch the
wing again. The test would then have ended.

If the poison were going to kill a boy it would not kill him
while he sat still on the ground, though he would suffer spasms
of pain that would make him stretch his arms backwards, gasp-
ing for breath. When a boy fell to the ground efforts were made,
with the king's consent, to revive him by administering a slimy
mixture made from the *mboyo* plant, the *kpoyo* tree, and salt.
This made him vomit the poison. Afterwards they carried him
to a brook-side and laid him in the shade and poured cold water
over his face.

CHAPTER IX

Problems arising from consultation
of the Poison Oracle

I

I HAVE described to many people in England the facts related in the last chapter and they have been, in the main, incredulous or contemptuous. In their questions to me they have sought to explain away Zande behaviour by rationalizing it, that is to say, by interpreting it in terms of our culture. They assume that Azande must understand the qualities of poisons as we understand them; or that they attribute a personality to the oracle, a mind that judges as men judge, but with higher prescience; or that the oracle is manipulated by the operator whose cunning conserves the faith of laymen. They ask what happens when the result of one test contradicts the other which it ought to confirm if the verdict be valid; what happens when the findings of oracles are belied by experience; and what happens when two oracles give contrary answers to the same question.

These same, and other, problems, naturally occurred to me in Zandeland, and I made inquiries into, and observations on, those points which struck me as being important, and in the present section I record my conclusions. Before setting them down I must warn the reader that we are trying to analyse behaviour rather than belief. Azande have little theory about their oracles and do not feel the need for doctrines.

I have translated the word *benge* as 'poison creeper', 'oracle poison', and 'poison oracle', in accordance with the context. But it is necessary to point out that Zande ideas about *benge* are very different from notions about poisons prevalent among the educated classes of Europe. To us it is a poison, but not to them.

It is true that *benge* is derived from a wild forest creeper and that its properties might be supposed to reside in the creeper, i.e. to be natural properties, but in Zande eyes it only becomes the *benge* of oracle consultations (and they have no interest in it outside this situation) when it has been prepared subject to taboos and is employed in the traditional manner. Properly speaking, it is only this manufactured *benge* which is *benge* at all in Zande opinion. Hence Azande say that if it is deprived of its potency for some reason or other it is 'just an ordinary thing, mere wood'.

Therefore, to ask Azande what would happen if they were to administer oracle poison to a fowl without delivering an address or, if they were to administer an extra portion of poison to a fowl which has recovered from the usual doses, or, if they were to place some of the poison in a man's food, is to ask silly questions. The Zande does not know what would happen, he is not interested in what would happen, and no one has ever been fool enough to waste good oracle poison in making such pointless experiments. Proper *benge* is endowed with potency by man's abstinence and his knowledge of tradition and will only function in the conditions of a seance.

When I asked a Zande what would happen if you went on administering dose after dose of poison to a fowl during a consultation in which the oracle ought to spare the fowl to give the right answer to the question placed before it, he replied that he did not know exactly what would happen, but that he supposed sooner or later it would burst. He would not countenance the suggestion that the extra poison would otherwise kill the fowl unless the question were suddenly reversed so that the oracle ought to kill the fowl to give a correct answer when, of course, it would at once die.

It is certain that Azande do not regard the reactions of fowls to *benge* and the action of *benge* on fowls as a natural process, that is to say, a process conditioned only by physical causes. The oracle is not to them a matter of chance, like the spinning of a coin, by which they are agreed to abide. Indeed, we may ask whether they have any notion that approximates to what we mean when we speak of physical causes.

Yet it might still be possible for Azande to have a crude common-sense notion of poisons. They might know that there are certain vegetable products that will kill men and beasts, without attributing supra-sensible properties to them. Certainly

Europeans often attribute knowledge of poisons to Azande and to other peoples of the Southern Sudan. No evidence for the homicidal use of poison has yet been produced, nor is likely to be. If there is one product possessed by Azande that is certainly poisonous it is *benge*, and daily its lethal properties are demonstrated on fowls, and sometimes have been demonstrated on men, yet they have no idea that it might be possible to kill people by adding it to their food. Though men are frequently suspected of using one kind or other of bad medicines to slay their neighbours, no one has ever conceived of a man using *benge* as a means of murder, and if you suggest it to him a Zande will tell you that *benge* would not be any good for the purpose.

Yet it is not always easy to reconcile Zande doctrines with their behaviour and with one another. They say that men will sometimes eat fowls after having cleansed them of poison, and this action would imply a knowledge of the natural properties of *benge* that they refuse to allow in other situations. The owner of a dead fowl may have its stomach and neck removed and the fowl prepared for food. My informants said that they try to remove all the poison from the carcass. Probably the practice is rare, since as a rule chickens are used which are too small for culinary purposes. Generally the fowls are thrown away or placed in a tree for birds to devour after their wings have been cut off. Moreover, a young man would not eat fowls killed by the oracle, so that the statement applies only to old men, and perhaps only to those who are not very particular about their food. When I protested against the statement that persons eat poisoned fowls I was asked, 'What harm can it do a man since no one addresses it?' Mekana once remarked to me that it would be rather a joke to address the oracle poison in the belly of an elder who had eaten a fowl which had died in an oracle test. One might say, he suggested, 'If so-and-so (naming the elder) slept with his wife last night, poison oracle kill him.' I think that Mekana was hardly serious in this suggestion. Nevertheless, the very fact of cleansing fowls of poison suggests that Azande are to some extent aware of its natural properties.

Some Azande hold that the poison will deteriorate with age, and all are aware that some poison is stronger than others and that it becomes more potent when exposed to the sun and less potent when diluted in water. They know that if a dog eats a fowl that has succumbed to the oracle it may die (it is possible that they conceive of the oracle still working inside the dog and answering the question put to it earlier, but I have no evidence that this is the case. It may also be possible that when men cleanse fowls killed by the oracle before eating them they are afraid lest the poison go on answering the question inside them and kill them. I have no doubt that a Zande might give so characteristically mystical a reason for his behaviour.)

II

Without laboratory experiments it is impossible to see any uniformities in the working of the oracle. Bare observation by itself is insufficient to explain why some fowls die and others survive. As a matter of fact, Azande act very much as we would act in like circumstances and they make the same kind of observations as we would make. They recognize that some poison is strong and other poison is weak and give more or fewer doses according to the kind they are using. One often hears it said during a seance, 'It is not strong enough,' 'You have given the fowl enough,' and like expressions. But Azande are dominated by an overwhelming faith which prevents them from making experiments, from generalizing contradictions between tests, between verdicts of different oracles, and between all the oracles and experience. To understand why it is that Azande do not draw from their observations the conclusions we would draw from the same evidence, we must realize that their attention is fixed on the mystical properties of the poison oracle and that its natural properties are of so little interest to them that they simply do not bother to consider them. To them the creeper is something other than the final product of manufacture used in ritual conditions, and the creeper scarcely enters into their notions about the oracle. If a Zande's mind were not fixed on the mystical qualities of *benge* and entirely absorbed by them he would perceive the significance of the knowledge he already possesses. As it is the contradiction between his beliefs and his observations only become a generalized and glaring contradiction when they are recorded side by side in the pages of an ethnographic treatise. But in real life these bits of knowledge do not form part of an indivisible concept, so that when a man thinks of *benge* he must think of all the details I have recorded here. They are functions of different situations and are uncoordinated. Hence the contradictions so apparent to us do not strike a Zande. If he is conscious of a contradiction it is a particular one which he can easily explain in terms of his own beliefs.

It is evident that the oracle system would be pointless if the possibility of *benge* being a natural poison, as an educated European would regard it, were not excluded. When I used at one time to question Zande faith in their poison oracle I was met sometimes by point-blank assertions, sometimes by one of the evasive secondary elaborations of belief that provide for any particular situation provoking scepticism, sometimes by polite pity, but always by an entanglement of linguistic obstacles, for one cannot well express in its language objections not formulated by a culture.

Azande observe the action of the poison oracle as we observe it, but their observations are always subordinated to their beliefs and are incorporated into their beliefs and made to explain them and justify them. Let the reader consider any argument that would utterly demolish all Zande claims for the power of the oracle. If it were translated into Zande modes of thought it would serve to support their entire structure of belief. For their mystical notions are eminently coherent, being interrelated by a network of logical ties, and are so ordered that they never too crudely contradict sensory experience but, instead, experience seems to justify them. The Zande is immersed in a sea of mystical notions, and if he speaks about his poison oracle he must speak in a mystical idiom.

If we cannot account for Zande faith in their poison oracle by assuming that they are aware that it is a poison and are willing to abide by the chance of its action on different fowls we might seek to comprehend it by supposing that they personify it. Given a mind, the Zande oracle is not much more difficult to understand than the Delphic Oracle. But they do not personify it. For, though it would seem to us that they must regard the oracles as personal beings, since they address them directly; in fact the question appears absurd when framed in the Zande tongue. A *boro*, a person, has two hands and two feet, a head, a belly, and so on, and the poison oracle has none of these things.

It is not alive, it does not breathe or move about. It is a thing. Azande have no theory about it; they do not know why it works, but only that it does work. Oracles have always existed and have always worked as they work now because such is their nature.

If you press a Zande to explain how the poison oracle can see far-off things he will say that its *mbisimo*, its soul, sees them. It might be urged that if the poison oracle has a soul it must be animate. Here we are up against the difficulty that always arises when a native word is translated by an English word. I have translated the Zande word *mbisimo* as 'soul' because the notion this word expresses in our own culture is nearer to the Zande notion of *mbisimo* of persons than any other English word. The concepts are not identical, and when in each language the word is used in a number of extended senses it is no longer possible to use the original expressions in translation without risk of confusion and gross distortion. In saying that the poison oracle has a *mbisimo* Zande mean little more than 'it does something' or, as we would say, 'it is dynamic'. You ask them how it works and they reply, 'It has a soul.' If you were to ask them how they know it has a 'soul', they would reply that they know because it works. They are explaining mystical action by naming it. The word *mbisimo* describes and explains all action of a mystical order.

[margin notes: mbisimo / *soul; / language / barrier]*

It becomes quite evident that Azande do not regard oracles as persons when we consider the rubbing-board oracle and the termites oracle. The rubbing-board is an instrument made by man out of wood and it only becomes an oracle when treated, and afterwards operated, in a certain manner, and if a taboo is broken it becomes once again merely shapen wood without power to see the future. Termites are certainly not corporeally or psychically persons. They are simply termites and nothing more, but if they are approached in the correct manner they are endowed with mystical powers.

It is difficult for us to understand how poison, rubbing-board, termites, and three sticks can be merely things and insects and yet hear what is said to them and foresee the future and reveal the present and past, but when used in ritual situations they cease to be mere things and mere insects and become mystical agents. And, since oracles are endowed with their powers by man himself, through man they may lose those powers. If a taboo is broken they become once again mere things, insects, and bits of wood.

III

It will at once occur to a European mind that a likely reason why one fowl dies and another lives is because more or larger doses of poison are administered to the one than to the other, and he is likely to jump to the conclusion that the verdict depends on the skill of the operator. Indeed, a European is prone to assume that the operator cheats, but I believe that he is wrong in this assumption. It is true that the number and size of doses given to fowls varies, and that even fowls of the same size do not always receive the same number of doses. But to suppose that Azande cheat is entirely to misunderstand their mentality. What would be the object in cheating? Today the declarations of the poison oracle are no longer recognized as evidence of murder or adultery, so that it can no longer be used as an instrument of justice and profit, and the usual questions placed before it concern the health and welfare of the questioner and his family. He wants to know always whether witchcraft is threatening his interests and, if so, who is the witch who has doomed him to some ill fate. Cheating, far from helping him, would destroy him, for instead of being able to approach the right witch and thus be released from his doom, he will approach the wrong person, or no person at all, and fall an inevitable victim to the fate that awaits him. It is entirely against his interests that trickery be used. It would probably result in his death. Even in questions of marriage where it might seem to the advantage of a Zande to obtain a favourable verdict in order that he might marry a certain girl, it would in fact be fatal to cheat, because were he to obtain an inaccurate verdict it would merely mean that his wife would die shortly after marriage.

It might, however, be urged that the consulter of the oracle is one person and the operator another, and that the feelings and purpose of the consulter are of less account than the cunning of the operator. This, as we shall see in the next chapter, may be a fair comment on the working of the rubbing-board oracle, but it is not apposite to the poison oracle for the following reasons: (1) The operator performs in public. His audience, all parties interested in the dispute or inquiry, sit a few feet away and can see what he does, and they largely direct his actions. (2) It was evident to me on the many occasions I witnessed consultations that the operator was just as little aware of what the result of a test was going to be as I or any of the other observers were. I judged from his actions, speech, and expression that he regarded himself as a mechanical server to, and in no way a director of, the oracle. (3) Sometimes the consulter of the oracle is the operator of it. A man who believes what Azande believe about witchcraft and oracles and then cheats would be a lunatic. (4) I have witnessed cases when it has been to the interests of the operator that the fowls shall live and they have died, and vice versa. (5) There is no special class of operators. They are not a corporation or closed association. Most adult males know how to operate the oracle, and anyone who wishes to operate it may do so. You cannot deceive one who practises your particular brand of deception. (6) The operators are generally boys of between 12 and 16, old enough to know and keep food taboos and young enough to be able to refrain from sexual intercourse. These innocents are the most unlikely people in Zandeland to know how to cheat, and are besides unconcerned, as a rule, with the adult problems that are presented to the oracle. (7) As often as not when there are two tests about a question the oracle contradicts itself. (8) Azande do not understand that *benge* is a natural poison and therefore do not know that trickery of this kind would even be possible. They will say of the rubbing-board oracle that a man has cheated with it, but one never hears it suggested that a man might have unfairly manipulated the poison oracle.

The difference in the number of doses given to fowls is due to certain technical rules in operating the oracle. There are a usual number of doses for fowls of different sizes, but the oracle gives its answers through the fowls, this being the only way in which it can speak; so that it is convenient that the fowl shall be seen to be affected by the poison, for then they know that it has heard the question, has considered it, and is replying to it. Therefore, if after two doses the fowl does not seem to be at all affected, even though this is the usual number of doses for a fowl of that size, they may give it a third dose. If the fowl

is still unaffected they know that the oracle is going to give a
clear verdict by sparing it and has answered without qualifications, for since it has killed other fowls on the same day it is
known to be good *benge* which can kill fowls if it wishes to do
so.

I have observed that Azande sometimes give fewer doses in
the second test, the *gingo*, than in the first test. They are not
trying to cheat but do not want to waste valuable poison. The
purpose of the second test is to ascertain that the oracle was
functioning correctly when it gave its first answer. It can
show this after one or two doses as clearly as after three or four
doses, and it is merely waste of good poison to give the extra
doses.

Azande realize that in civil disputes, concerning witchcraft
or adultery for example, it is possible for the man chosen to
consult the poison oracle about the point at issue to cheat in
another way. A man would not tamper with the poison because
he does not believe it possible to alter the verdict of an oracle
once the poison has been administered to a fowl, but he can
produce a hen's wing without ever consulting the poison oracle
at all, for he may merely kill a fowl and cut off its wing. Azande
say that this sometimes happens, but that the danger of its
occurrence is small because the elder who makes the test normally takes two or three witnesses with him. Moreover, it is possible for a man who is convinced that he has not been given
a fair test to appeal to the king, and if his poison oracle declares
the man to be innocent the king will send for the elder and
tell him that he is a cheat and a liar and may never again conduct official consultations.

IV

What explanation do Azande offer when the oracle contradicts
itself? Since Azande do not understand the natural properties
of the poison they cannot explain the contradiction scientifically; since they do not attribute personality to the oracle they
cannot account for its contradictions by volition; and since they
do not cheat they cannot manipulate the oracle to avoid contradictions. The oracle seems so ordered to provide a maximum
number of evident contradictions for, as we have seen, in important issues a single test is inacceptable and the oracle must slay

one fowl and spare another if it is to deliver a valid verdict. As we may well imagine, the oracle frequently kills both fowls or spares both fowls, and this would prove to us the futility of the whole proceeding. But it proves the opposite to Azande. They are not surprised at contradictions; they expect them. Paradox though it be, the errors as well as the valid judgements of the oracle prove to them its infallibility. The fact that the oracle is wrong when it is interfered with by some mystical power shows how accurate are its judgements when these powers are excluded.

The secondary elaborations of belief that explain the failure of the oracle attribute its failure to (1) the wrong variety of poison having been gathered, (2) breach of a taboo, (3) witchcraft, (4) anger of the owners of the forest where the creeper grows, (5) age of the poison, (6) anger of the ghosts, (7) sorcery, (8) use.

If at its first seance the oracle kills fowls without discrimination, slaying one after the other without sparing a single one, they say that it is 'foolish' poison. More often it happens at seances that the poison fails to affect the fowls and they say that it is 'weak poison' or 'dead poison'. If some four medium-sized fowls are in succession unaffected by the poison they stop the seance, and later the poison will be thrown away; since once it has lost its potency there are no means of restoring it, whereas if it is over-potent it may, after being kept for some time, become good, and by this Azande mean discriminating. Sometimes when the fowls appear totally unaffected by the poison they administer the usual doses to one of them while asking the oracle the straightforward question, 'If you are good oracle poison kill this fowl. If you are worthless oracle poison spare it.' If the poison is 'good poison' or 'strong poison' it can demonstrate its potency forthwith.

The poison may be over-potent because the gatherers collected it from the wrong kind of creeper, for there are two varieties of poison creeper, that called *nawada* and that called *andegi*. The *andegi* kills fowls without regard to the questions put to it. It is unnecessary to seek a cause, for people know at once by its action that it is *andegi* and they wrap it up in leaves and place it in hiding and wait some months for it to 'cool'. If at the end of this time it is still 'stupid' they either throw it away or seek to discover whether witchcraft or some other cause is now responsible for its failure to give correct judgements.

The explanation of why poison kills all the fowls by reference to *andegi* is only adduced when the poison is freshly gathered and being tested to determine its worth. If a packet of poison is passed as good *nawada* and at a later seance kills all the fowls some other explanation must be sought, and its behaviour is usually attributed to witchcraft.

If at its preliminary test or at any later test the poison is impotent and does not kill a single fowl Azande generally attribute its behaviour to breach of a taboo. Today when poison is often purchased from Azande of the Congo there is grave danger of it having been polluted by someone through whose hands it has passed, and once it has come into contact with an unclean person it is permanently ruined.

Witchcraft is often cited as a cause for wrong verdicts. It also may render the oracle impotent, though impotency is usually attributed to breach of taboo. Generally speaking, the presence of witchcraft is shown by the oracle killing two fowls in answer to the same question, or in sparing two fowls in answer to the same question when it has killed a fowl at the same seance. In such cases the poison is evidently potent and its failure to give correct judgements may be due to a passing influence of witchcraft. For the time being the seance may be stopped and resumed on another day when it is hoped that witchcraft will no longer be operative. Nevertheless, unless the oracle makes many consecutive errors Azande do not generally close the seance, because it often happens that witchcraft interferes with the working of the poison in relation to a single and particular question, and in no way influences it in relation to other questions. The witch is preventing the oracle from giving an accurate reply to a certain question that concerns him but is not seeking to interfere in questions that do not concern him nor to destroy the poison completely.

Sometimes the poison refuses to function properly on a certain day because the operator is in an unlucky state, 'his condition is bad', as Azande say, and this means that there is witchcraft about him and by coming into contact with the oracle poison he has transmitted the ill-luck to it, so that the 'condition' of the oracle is bad likewise. Sometimes they interrupt their questions to ask the oracle whether it is being troubled by witchcraft, and people say that it may then kill a fowl, after having shown itself unable to do so before, or spare a fowl, after having killed all the previous ones, in order to inform the questioner that there is witchcraft present. A man does not ask one packet of poison whether another packet is good.

If at its first testing after it has been gathered the oracle poison fails to operate, and the man who gathered it is certain that he kept the taboos required of him and that it did not come into contact with any polluting influence, its impotency may be attributed to the anger of the owners of the soil where it was dug up. Or it may be said that some foreigner must have polluted the poison, unknown to the gatherer, while the party were on their return journey. Such explanations are, however, seldom offered and would seldom be accepted. The man who puts them forward wishes to excuse himself from responsibility.

One sometimes hears it said that a packet of poison has lost its power because it has been kept too long. Men have, however, denied to me that this is possible, asserting that breach of taboo, or witchcraft, or some other cause must be responsible for loss of strength.

It is said that occasionally the ghosts are held responsible. Men say that if a man gathers oracle poison in the Congo and neglects to give part of it to his father as first-fruits the ghosts may corrupt it.

Finally, any poison will lose its power with use. A man generally prepares for a seance more poison than will be used in the tests. At the end of the seance he gathers up what is left and stores it apart from unused poison. Poison can be used at least twice and, if it is of good quality, sometimes three or four times. Sometimes they prepare a mixture of fresh and used poison. At length its strength is exhausted. Azande know this happens and they merely say 'It is exhausted' without advancing any mystical cause for its loss of potency.

Sometimes the poison acts in a peculiar manner inside the fowl and experience is necessary to interpret correctly its reactions. It sometimes happens that a fowl appears to have survived its ordeal but dies later when it is running about in the grass, or even after its owner has brought it back to his homestead. I have never observed a fowl revive after it has appeared to fall lifeless to the ground, but I was told that this occasionally occurs. Indeed, I have heard Mbira boast of having addressed an apparently lifeless hen for a long time with such vehemence and good sense that it finally survived. When such things happen young Azande do not always know how to interpret them, but old and experienced men are seldom at a loss to explain the fowl's behaviour. People do not care to act on a verdict of the oracle unless it is given without ambiguity.

If a fowl collapses very slowly and then suddenly recovers this means that there is some evil influence hanging over the operator. 'His condition is bad.' Fowls may die slowly in a long series of spasms as though the poison were uncertain whether to kill them or not, and this probably means that witchcraft is trying to influence the oracle.

The oracle must reply to the question in either an affirmative or a negative, but sometimes it sees more than it is asked and wants to let the people know what it has seen, e.g. they may ask it whether a man will be bewitched if he goes a journey, and the oracle knows that although he will not be bewitched his family will be bewitched during his absence or that he himself will be attacked by sorcery. Or they may ask whether a certain man will fall ill this month, and the oracle sees that although he will be in good health this month he will fall sick next month. It tries to tell people these facts and at the same time to answer the questions put to it.

v

It will have been noted that Azande act experimentally within the framework of their mystical notions. They act as we would have to act if we had no means of making chemical and physiological analyses and we wanted to obtain the same results as they want to obtain. As soon as the poison is brought back from its forest home it is tested to discover whether some fowls will live and others die under its influence. It would be unreasonable to use poison without first having ascertained that all fowls to which it is administered do not die or do not live. The oracle would then be a farce. Each seance must be in itself experimentally consistent. Thus if the first three fowls survive Azande will always be apprehensive. They at once suspect that the oracle is not working properly. But if then, afterwards, the fourth fowl dies, they are content. They will say to you, 'You see the poison is good, it has spared the first three fowls but it has killed this one.' Zande behaviour, though ritual, is consistent, and the reasons they give for their behaviour, though mystical, are intellectually coherent.

If their mystical notions allowed them to generalize their observations they would perceive, as we do, that their faith is without foundations. They themselves provide all the proof necessary. They say that they sometimes test new poison or old poison which they fear has been corrupted by asking it silly questions. At full moon they administer the poison to a fowl and address it thus:

Poison oracle, tell the chicken about those two spears over there. As I am about to go up to the sky, if I will spear the moon today with my spears, kill the fowl. If I will not spear the moon today, poison oracle spare the fowl.

If the oracle kills the fowl they know that it is corrupt.

And yet Azande do not see that their oracles tell them nothing! Their blindness is not due to stupidity: they reason excellently in the idiom of their beliefs, but they cannot reason outside, or against, their beliefs because they have no other idiom in which to express their thoughts.

The reader will naturally wonder what Azande say when subsequent events prove the prophecies of the poison oracle to be wrong. Here again Azande are not surprised at such an outcome, but it does not prove to them that the oracle is futile. It rather proves how well founded are their beliefs in witchcraft and sorcery and taboos. The contradiction between what the oracle said would happen and what actually has happened is just as glaring to Zande eyes as it is to ours, but they never for a moment question the virtue of the oracle in general but seek only to account for the inaccuracy of this particular poison.

Moreover, even if the oracle was not deflected from the straight path of prophecy by witchcraft or bad magic there are other reasons which would equally account for its failure. It may be that the particular venture about the success of which a man was consulting the oracle was not at the time of consultation threatened by witchcraft, but that a witch intervened at some time between the consultation and the commencement of the undertaking.

Azande see as well as we that the failure of their oracle to prophesy truly calls for explanation, but so entangled are they in mystical notions that they must make use of them to account for the failure. The contradiction between experience and one mystical notion is explained by reference to other mystical notions.

Normally there is little chance of the oracle being proved wrong, for it is usually asked questions to which its answers cannot well be challenged by subsequent experience, since the inquirer accepts the verdict and does not seek to check it by experiment. Thus were a man to ask the oracle, 'If I build my homestead in such-and-such a place will I die there?' or, 'If my son is sponsored by so-and-so in the circumcision ceremonies will he die?' and were the oracle to reply 'Yes' to either of these queries, he would not construct his homestead in the ill-omened place nor allow his son to be sponsored by the inauspicious man. Consequently he would never know what would have happened it he had not taken the advice of the oracle. Also, the verdict of the oracle is usually in accordance with the workings of nature, and were a man to receive the reply that it is safe for him to marry a certain girl because she will not die within the next few years, or that he is assured of his harvest of eleusine if he sows it in a certain spot in the bush, there would be little likelihood of the oracle being proved wrong, as the chances of the girl dying or of the hardy eleusine being totally destroyed would be small.

Furthermore, only certain types of question are regularly put to the oracle: questions relating to witchcraft, sickness, death, lengthy journeys, mourning and vengeance, changing of homestead sites, lengthy agricultural and hunting enterprises, and so forth. One does not ask the poison oracle about small matters or questions involving minute precision with regard to time. A man would not ask such a question as: 'Will I kill a bushbuck if I go hunting tomorrow?' and since men do not ask that sort of question they do not receive immediate detailed instructions which might go amiss and expose the falsity of the oracle.

Indeed, as a rule Azande do not ask questions to which answers are easily tested by experience and they ask only those questions which embrace contingencies. The answers either cannot be tested, or if proved by subsequent events to be erroneous permit an explanation of the error. In the last resort errors can always be explained by attributing them to mystical interference. But there is no need to suppose that the Zande is conscious of an evasion of clear issues. In restricting his questions to certain well-known types he is conforming to tradition. It does not occur to him to test the oracle experimentally unless he has grave suspicions about a particular packet of poison.

Moreover, the main purpose of the oracle lies in its ability to reveal the play of mystical forces. When Azande ask about health or marriage or hunting they are seeking information about the movement of psychic forces which might cause them misfortune. They do not attempt simply to discover the objective conditions at a certain point of time in the future, nor the objective results of a certain action, but the inclination of mystical powers, for these conditions and result depend upon them. Azande envisage a future, an individual's future that is to say, dependent upon mystical forces. Hence when the oracle paints a black horizon for a man he is glad to have been warned because now that he knows the dispositions of witchcraft he can get into touch with it and have the future changed to be more favourable to him.

By means of his oracles a Zande can discover the mystical forces which hang over a man and doom him in advance, and having discovered them he can counteract them or alter his plans to avoid the doom which awaits him in any particular venture. Hence it is evident that the answers he receives do not generally concern objective happenings and therefore cannot easily be contrary to experience.

None the less, I have often noticed that Azande on being informed that sickness lies ahead of them do not even proceed to discover the name of the witch whose influence is going to cause them sickness and get him to blow out water but merely wait for a few days and then consult the oracle again to find out whether their health will be good for the coming month, hoping that by the time of the second consultation the evil influence which hung over their future at the time of the first consultation will no longer be there.

It follows that present and future have not entirely the same meaning for Azande as they have for us. It is difficult to formulate the problem in our language, but it would appear from their behaviour that the present and future overlap in some way so that the present partakes of the future as it were. Hence a man's future health and happiness depend on future conditions that are already in existence and can be exposed by the oracles and altered. The future depends on the disposition of mystical forces that can be tackled here and now. Moreoever, when the oracles announce that a man will fall sick, i.e. he bewitched in the near future, his 'condition' is therefore already bad, his future is already part of him. Azande cannot explain these matters, they content themselves with believing and enacting them.

By the same token, the oracle is protected by its position in the order of events. When a Zande wishes to slay a witch who has killed one of his kinsmen or a thief who has stolen his property he does not ask the oracle to identify the witch or thief and then make magic against this known person, but he first makes magic against an unknown criminal, and when people in the neighbourhood die he asks the oracle whether one of them is the victim of his punitive magic.

But in spite of the many ways in which belief in the poison oracle is sustained it may be doubted whether it could have maintained prestige in a democratic community. In Zandeland its verdicts derive an historic sanction from the fact that its verdicts were traditionally backed by the full authority of the king. The decisions of the king's oracle were final. Had there been any appeal from this to private oracles there would have been general confusion, since everybody would have been able to produce oracular verdicts to support his own point of view and there would have been no way of deciding between them. In legal disputes, therefore, the authority of the poison oracle was formerly the authority of the king, and this in itself would tend to prevent any serious challenge to its veracity.

VI

There is a final problem to discuss. As I have recorded in earlier sections, each situation demands the particular pattern of thought appropriate to it. Hence an individual in one situation will employ a notion he excludes in a different situation. The many beliefs I have recorded are so many different tools of thought, and he selects the ones that are chiefly to his advantage. A Zande does not readily accept an oracular verdict which conflicts seriously with his interests. No one believes that the oracle is nonsense, but everyone thinks that for some particular reason in this particular case the particular poison used is in error in respect to himself. Azande are only sceptical of particular oracles and not of oracles in general, and their scepticism is always expressed in a mystical idiom that vouches for the validity of the poison oracle as an institution.

Also, apart from criminal cases, there can be no doubt that a man takes advantage of every loop-hole the oracle allows him to obtain what he wants or to refrain from doing what he does not want to do. Moreover, he uses the authority of the oracle to excuse his conduct or to compel others to accept it. The oracle is often very useful in such a question as whether a man's wife shall pay her parents a visit. It is difficult for the husband to forbid her visit, but if he can say that the oracles advise against it he can both prevent it and checkmate objections on the part of his parents-in-law.

In the actual operation of the oracle, Azande like to receive a favourable prediction in the first test and to put off the corroborative test that may contradict it for as long as possible. Tradition allows them a certain latitude in the order in which they arrange their questions to the oracle and also in the number of doses that are administered to the fowls. There is an art in questioning the oracle, for it must answer 'yes' or 'no' to a question and a man can therefore define the terms of the answer by stating them in the question. By close interpretations of the reactions of fowls to the poison it is often possible to qualify the declaration oracles give by killing or sparing them.

In all this Azande are not employing trickery. A man uses for his individual needs in certain situations those notions that most favour his desires. Azande cannot go beyond the limits set by their culture and invent notions, but within these limits human behaviour is not rigidly determined by custom and a man has some freedom of action and thought.

CHAPTER X

Other Zande Oracles

I

AZANDE esteem *dakpa*, or the termites oracle, next to the poison oracle. A man will not place a verdict of the termites oracle before the rubbing-board oracle for confirmation, and he will not place a verdict of the poison oracle to the termites for confirmation. If more than one oracle is consulted they consult always the lesser before the greater in the order of: (1) rubbing-board, (2) termites, (3) poison. *Dakpa* is the poor man's poison oracle. There are no expenses involved, for a man has only to find a termite mound and insert two branches of different trees into one of their runs and return next day to see which of the two the termites have eaten. The main drawback to the oracle from the Zande point of view is that it is lengthy and limited. It takes an entire night to answer a question, and very few questions can be asked at the same time.

On all important matters the decisions of the termites oracle must be corroborated by the poison oracle. Legal action cannot be taken without a decision from the poison oracle. But poison is expensive and it is cheaper to obtain preliminary verdicts from the termites and ask the poison oracle for a final decision. Thus a man finds out which among half a dozen sites is a suitable one for him to build his homestead in and can place the choice of the termites before the poison oracle for confirmation. Women can consult the termites oracle as well as men, and children sometimes use it. It is known to, and can be used by, everyone.

The oracle is regarded as very reliable, much more so than the rubbing-board. Azande say that the termites do not listen to all the talk which is going on outside in homesteads and only hear the questions put to them. Older men try to consult the termites oracle at the beginning of each month to discover whether they will continue in good health. A wealthy man asks the same question of the poison oracle.

The oracle is called after one of the trees, a branch of which is inserted into a termite mound in its operation. Azande may address their questions to these branches. Nevertheless, they ordinarily address the termites and in their commentaries on the oracle it is clear that they think of the termites as listening to their questions and giving answers to them. But the fact that they address both shows that no general and independent intelligence is attributed to either the termites or to the trees but only a specific intelligence in the operation of the oracle, and that it is the oracle as a whole, as something *sui generis*, which is the object of inquiry.

A man ought to observe the same taboos as for the poison oracle, but they are less strict. The termites are always approached towards evening. A man goes to one of his own termite mounds because people may object if he disturbs their termites by thrusting branches into their runs. He does not take branches of *dakpa* and *kpoyo* from his homestead because these two trees are found everywhere in the bush. With the haft of his spear he opens up one of the great shafts that lead into the mound, or one of the runs at the side of it, takes a branch of either tree in each hand, and, speaking to the termites, which rush to the seat of disturbance, says some such words as: 'O termites, I will die this year, eat *dakpa*. I will not die, eat *kpoyo*.' He may address the branches as though they were eating: '*Dakpa* I will die this year, *dakpa* you eat; I will not die this year, *kpoyo* you eat.' The words vary according to the question, but they are always spoken in one of the traditional forms. While making this speech he thrusts the two branches into the shaft, or run, and after placing a few of the lumps of earth he has excavated around them he returns home.

Early next morning the questioner goes to the mound to receive an answer. The termites may have eaten *kpoyo* and left *dakpa*, or they may have eaten *dakpa* and left *kpoyo*. They may have eaten both, or left both untouched. The answer depends therefore on the way in which the question is phrased. When it concerns the welfare of the questioner or of his kin it is asked in such a way that if the termites eat *dakpa* it is a prophecy of misfortune, and if they eat *kpoyo* it is a prophecy of good fortune. Having obtained a verdict, they can then either place it at once before the poison oracle or, if they do not want to do that, they can obtain from termites a *gingo*, or corroborative test, similar to that they demand from the poison oracle. I believe, however, that this is not generally done, for cases which demand such care are usually so important that they must go before the poison oracle which will supply all the confirmation needed.

It sometimes happens that neither branch is eaten. Then Azande simply say that the termites refuse an answer and they try another mound. Frequently they eat both branches. This is not an invalid verdict as it is when the poison kills or spares two fowls. The same unambiguous answer is not expected from termites. Doubtless we would be right in relating this acceptance of unprecise answers to the fact that the questions put to the termites oracle have not the social importance of those put to the poison oracle and do not settle legal issues. When both branches are eaten the interpretation is not a complete answer to the question but a partial answer, e.g if *dakpa* is the branch mainly eaten, the answer is a qualified verdict leaning towards a negative or affirmative according to the terms of the question.

If both branches are eaten about equally Azande may say that the ants were merely hungry and ate to satisfy their appetites, or they may say that a taboo has been broken or that witchcraft has interfered with the oracle. But they do not evoke mystical entities to account for the failure of the termites oracle to give unambiguous answers with the frequency and luxuriance of those evoked to explain discrepancies in the verdicts of the poison oracle.

II

Another Zande oracle is called *mapingo*. It can be used by everyone, but except in choosing a site for a homestead adult men do not often employ it. It is considered especially the oracle of women and children. It is by using *mapingo* that children gain their first experience in oracular consultations. Its operation is as simple as can be. Three small pieces of wood about half an inch long and rounded are cut from branches of a tree or from the stalk of the manioc. Three pieces of wood are required for each question to be asked. The material always lies ready at hand. Two pieces of stick are placed side by side on the ground and the third piece is placed on top of them and parallel to them. These little pieces of stick are generally arranged just before nightfall in a clearing at the edge of the garden where it borders the homestead or at the back of a hut. When asking about a new homestead they are arranged in a small clearing in the proposed site in the bush. The oracle gives its answers by the three sticks remaining in position all night or by the structure falling. Azande sometimes say that a person ought to observe the usual taboos for a short time before using the three sticks oracle, but I very much doubt whether anyone does so.

When the sticks have been set in position a man addresses them and tells them what he wants enlightenment about, or perhaps, we might rather say, he speaks a conditional clause over them.

When consulting about a homestead site a man usually erects two piles of sticks, one for himself and one for his wife. He addresses his pile somewhat as follows:

I will die, there is badness over this homestead site, if I build my homestead on it I will die there. *Mapingo* you scatter to show that my 'condition' is bad. I will not die on it, let me come to examine you and find you in position to show my good 'condition'.

Generally the question is so phrased that the displacement of the sticks gives an inauspicious prognostication and their remaining in position gives an auspicious prognostication.

The oracle is not considered important. Women and children ask it many questions, but they are questions about their own affairs and have little social significance. Men also use it on occasion. Its verdicts are not made public and a man cannot approach a witch on its findings alone. It is sometimes used as a preliminary to the termites or poison oracles. Notwithstanding, it is considered very reliable, especially in reference to homestead sites, and a man would not neglect its advice.

III

The most used of all Zande oracles is *iwa*, the rubbing-board. The poison oracle needs preparation. Often, especially today, it is difficult to obtain oracle poison, and a man may have to wait many days until he learns that a kinsman or blood-brother is about to consult the oracle and will allow him to bring one or two fowls to solve his problems. But a man cannot wait when he fears that he may be a victim of witchcraft or trickery. At any time a sudden problem may confront him, a sudden suspicion assail him. If he possesses a rubbing-board oracle and is qualified to use it he will carry it with him wherever he goes in his little skin or grass plaited bag so that he can take it out at a moment's notice and inquire from it what he is to do. Otherwise he may easily find a kinsman or friend who will consult their oracles on his behalf, for it is a small service and costs them nothing. And it is not only in situations requiring immediate action that the rubbing-board is more suitable an oracle than the poison, but also in dozens of situations when the issues are of minor importance and hardly worthy of being presented to the poison oracle. Azande do not place complete faith in its statements and contrast its reliability unfavourably with that of the other oracles which have been described. They put its revelations on a par with those of witch-doctors. The rubbing-board is looked upon as an inferior judge which sorts out a case so that it is reduced to preliminary issues that can then go before the poison oracle. Thus a man is ill and a great many persons occur to him as likely to be bewitching him. It would be a tedious and expensive business to place six or seven names before the poison oracle when, perhaps, the last on the list is the right one. But it will not take him longer than ten minutes to place the names before his little wooden instrument, and when it has chosen from among them the responsible witch all that need be asked of the greater poison oracle is to confirm its choice. The poison oracle is always the final authority, and if the matter is one involving relations between two persons it must be consulted. For this reason, unless the matter is urgent, they bring all important social questions directly before the poison oracle. It is only minor or preliminary questions that are asked of the rubbing-board. Azande say it answers so many questions that it is bound to be wrong sometimes. We may observe that this admission can be made because situations of use are minor and do not involve social interrelations.

The oracles consist of miniature table-like constructions. Smaller ones are carried about in bags. Larger ones are kept in homesteads. They are carved out of the wood of various trees. They have two parts, the 'female', or the flat surface of the table supported by two legs and its tail, and the 'male', or the piece which fits the surface of the table like a lid. The shape of the

table is round to oval. When not in operation a barkcloth cover-
ing is tied over the head of the instrument.

When fashioning a rubbing-board a man is subject to taboos.
He must abstain for two days from sexual relations and from
the same foods prohibited in connexion with the poison oracle
before he commences to manufacture it. He cuts it with an adze,
fashioning the bottom part before the upper part. He then
blackens it by rubbing the surface with a red-hot spear. The
carving of the board is only part of the process of manufacture.
It is still nothing but two pieces of carved wood and has to be
endowed with mystical potency, i.e. the wood has to be transformed into an oracle. This is done by two actions. In the first
place the table is anointed with medicine derived from roots
which have been boiled, their juices then mixed with oil and
boiled again and, during this second boiling, stirred and
addressed in the pot. I was told that the owner says over the
pot:

This is my rubbing-board oracle which I am going to doctor. When
I consult it on a man's behalf may it speak the truth, may it foretell
the death (threatened death) of a man. May it reveal things to me,
may it not hide things from me. May it not lose its potency. If a man
eats tabooed food, such as elephant (and comes near my oracle), may
it not lose its potency.

He then takes the mixture off the fire and, having made incisions on the table of the oracle, he rubs some of it into them.
The remainder of the oil and juices he mixes with ashes of various plants and rubs them on to the face of the table. The incisions may be partly the cause of the lid of the oracle sticking
or running smoothly on the table according to the direction
of pressure.

In the second place the oracle has to be buried. It has been
doctored, but the medicines have to be given time to sink in
and there is still 'coldness' about it which must be removed.
It is wrapped up in new barkcloth or perhaps in the skin of
a small animal like a small bushbuck and is placed in a hole
dug in the centre of a path. The earth is well trodden down
to disguise the fact that something has been buried there,
because if a man notices that the earth has been disturbed he
will go round the spot in fear of sorcery, and this will spoil the
preparation of the oracle, because it is passers-by who 'take

away all "coldness" from the rubbing-board in the centre of the path' as they pass over it. After two days the owner digs it up.

He now tests it by rubbing the wooden lid backwards and forwards on the table. He says to it: 'Rubbing-board, if you will speak the truth to people, stick.' It sticks in declaration of its potency and powers of discrimination. The owner then addresses the oracle, saying, 'Rubbing-board, I take a little wealth to redeem you with it. You speak the truth to me. I take ashes to hold your legs with them. You speak the truth to me.' He then places a knife before it as a payment. Since the knife is taken away again Azande say, 'He deceives the rubbing-board with a knife.' He then binds barkcloth round it and places it under his veranda. The rubbing-board is ready for use.

It is operated in the following manner. A man sits on the ground and steadies the board by placing his right foot on its tail, while with his right hand he jerks the lid backwards and forwards, towards and away from him, between his thumb and first finger. Before operating the oracle he squeezes juices of plants or grates wood of various trees on to the table. Generally they use the fruit of the Kaffir apple for this purpose. The operator dips the lid into a gourd of water which he keeps at his side and applies its flat surface to the surface of the table. As soon as they touch, the juices or gratings on the table become moistened and begin to froth and bubble. He jerks the lid backwards and forwards a few times and then begins to question the oracle. From time to time during the consultations he moistens the lid in the gourd of water.

When the operator jerks the lid over the table it generally either moves smoothly backwards and forwards or it sticks to the board so firmly that no jerking will further move it, and it has to be pulled upwards with considerable force to detach it from the table. These two actions—smooth sliding and firm sticking—are the two ways in which the oracle answers questions. They correspond to the slaying or sparing of fowls by the poison, the eating or refusing of the branches by the termites, and the disturbance or non-disturbance of the pile of sticks. Every question is therefore framed thus: If such is the case, 'stick', and if such is not the case, 'run smoothly'. In consultations of the rubbing-board sticking of the lid almost always gives an affirmative answer and smooth running of the lid almost always gives a negative answer.

Whatever other questions a man intends to place before the oracle he generally asks as his first question, 'Shall I die this year?' and the oracle runs smoothly, giving its answer 'No'. Sometimes instead of going smoothly backwards and forwards or sticking fast the lid runs from side to side or round and round. Sometimes it alternately sticks and runs. The oracle is here refusing to give a verdict, and this generally means that it is doubtful of the issue or sees something outside the terms of the question that would seriously qualify the unequivocal answer given by either sticking or sliding.

Strictly speaking, as with the poison and termites oracles, a second and confirmatory test should be made. If the lid has stuck in the first test, then in the second test it must slide backwards and forwards smoothly, and vice versa, if the verdict is to be valid. In fact, however, they very seldom make a second test. In important issues the question will be placed before the poison oracle, which supplies all the confirmation needed. Also Azande must be aware that the second test always confirms the first one. But they do not trouble themselves to any great extent about such matters because in serious questions a higher authority is consulted.

IV

Before consulting the rubbing-board its owner is supposed to observe the same prohibitions as those in force when using the poison oracle, though it is not required that he shall observe them for so long a period before operating it. Since the oracle may be consulted at a moment's notice the taboos would prove irksome to its owner and to those who wish him to operate it on their behalf if it were not that their observance can be rendered unnecessary by a process known as 'spoiling the rubbing-board'. A piece of an elephant's skin, or a fish-bone, and perhaps of a piece of wood on which a woman has sat (for a menstruating woman can destroy the potency of any oracle if she goes near it), are burnt and the ashes are rubbed over the table of the board. Instead of burning fish-bone they may sprinkle the table with a few drops of water in which a fish has been cooked. It will not matter after this has been done if a man eats elephant's flesh or fish or a menstruating woman approaches the oracle.

That people, in fact, do not observe taboos is well known. Azande have told me that whilst every oracle owner sleeps regularly with his wife, few have been heard to refuse to operate the oracle on that account. Nevertheless, they say that a sincere man who wished to keep his oracle potent would not use it for two or three days after having had sexual intercourse. They attribute much of the error in the oracle's judgements to slackness in this respect. In the past only a few old men owned rubbing-boards, and in those days taboos were more rigidly observed, for old men are more careful than their juniors to avoid contamination. Even today not many men own rubbing-boards.

Azande say that the accuracy of a rubbing-board depends upon its not becoming 'cold'. They say that if a man's oracle makes many mistakes he will realize that it has lost its potency. It can be rehabilitated by placing medicine on its table and wrapping it in barkcloth and burying it again in a path. I was told that they say to it as they place it in the hole, 'You are rubbing-board, why do you lie? Speak the truth.' After two days the owner digs it up and burns a little *benge* and rubs the soot on to the board, and says to it, 'Rubbing-board you speak the truth just as *benge* speaks it.' He then puts a pinch of oracle poison on the table, wraps it up in backcloth, and places it under his veranda to rest for a few days.

Operation of the rubbing-board differs from operation of the other oracles in that only certain persons can operate it. With the exception of the one or two peculiar women who have even been known to consult the poison oracle and a few female ghost-diviners, these persons are all middle-aged or old men. Women may occasionally watch the oracle being operated as it is being consulted in homesteads, and often publicly, unlike the poison and termites oracles which are consulted in the bush, but they are not encouraged to approach near to it and cannot operate it. Children do not use it, and I have never known a young man operate it. Moreover, its use is not conditioned by age and sex alone, for it is necessary for a man to have absorbed certain medicines before he can hope to operate the instrument. The poison, termites, and three sticks oracles can be operated by any man who has kept the taboos, but when the rubbing-board is operated the owner as well as the instrument itself has to be doctored. He will get a magician to doctor him. The potency of the oracle is due to the medicines which it absorbs when the board is being made, the medicines applied to its table before use, the medicines rubbed into the hand and foot of the operator and eaten by him, and its operation subject to customary conditions.

Only the owner of a rubbing-board uses it. He will not let other people operate it. He will consult it about the affairs of kinsmen and great friends without exacting a fee, but from neighbours he expects a present of a knife, or half-piastre, or ring, or some such small gift. He can courteously demand payment by pointing out that the oracle will not work properly unless it sees a gift laid on the ground before it. If you do not produce a fee when asking him to consult his oracle on your behalf he may say that he is sorry but his rubbing-board is broken or that he has not kept taboos the day before or that he has not ritually cleansed himself after assisting at a burial.

Azande are well aware that people can cheat in operating the rubbing-board oracle, and this is one of the reasons why they consider it inferior to the other oracles. However, they do not think that people often cheat, and a man only mentions that an operator may have cheated when the oracle has spoken against him or he particularly dislikes the operator. No owner of a good oracle cheats or fails to observe taboos lest it cease to be a good oracle. Some men's oracles have a wide reputation for accuracy and enjoy this reputation in contrast to others. Since the rubbing-board has no legal status, there is no reason why tradition and authority should exclude, or explain away by assertion and by the use of secondary elaborations, the possibility of improper manipulation. A man must believe, or at any rate express belief, in the poison oracle and submit to its declarations. But the statements of the rubbing-board need not inconvenience anyone except its consulter, and custom does not compel a man to use it or to submit to its verdicts.

I have little doubt that the operator improperly manipulates the oracle in most inquiries. Nevertheless, owners of rubbing-boards frequently consult them about their own affairs, and it can scarcely be imagined that they deliberately cheat on such occasions. It may also be asked why, if they cheat, they should go to the trouble of burying the board and doctoring it and themselves.

It must be difficult for a man who is considering a question to move his hand quite haphazardly when the movement is supposed to provide an answer to the question and when pressure makes all the difference between 'Yes' and 'No'. It may well be that Azande are not entirely aware that they control the oracle in accordance with conclusions reached in their minds and that between the thinking out of the questions and the movement of the hand in answer the middle clause, 'I must make the lid stick (or go smoothly)', is not consciously formulated. If this is the case 'cheating' is perhaps too strong a word to use.

v

Azande speak of dreams as oracles, for they reveal hidden things (*soroka*). In a sense all dreams foretell events, but some more clearly than others. Those dreams in which a man actually experiences witchcraft portend misfortune to the dreamer as a consequence of his having been bewitched, and dreams about ghosts, not recorded in this book, inform people about happenings among the dead. But many dreams are explained solely in terms of prophecy without reference to witchcraft, though what may at the time have appeared to have been a dream of one type may be shown by events to have been a dream of another type and to have been misinterpreted.

There are stereotyped explanations of dreams. These are generally straightforward affirmations that what happened in the dream will later take place in waking life, but sometimes dream images are regarded as symbols which require interpretation. Nevertheless, in such cases the interpretation is often traditional and it is merely necessary to find someone who knows it. Azande do not always know how to interpret dreams, though an obscure dream is always vaguely considered good or bad. On the whole, what we would call bad dreams are evidence of witchcraft, and what we would call pleasant dreams are oracular and the dreamer believes that they may happen to him in the future.

Some men eat *ngua musumo*, dream-medicines, which enable

them to dream true dreams. When the dream is oracular it will then prophesy the future truly and warn a man of impending danger and tell him of fortune to come, e.g. if he goes hunting or pays a visit to his prince to ask for a gift of spears he will kill animals or receive the gift. If the dream is a nightmare he will then be able to see the features of the witch who is attacking him so that he will know his enemy.

Azande attach great importance to the prognostication of dreams. They say that dream-prophecies are as true as those of the rubbing-board oracle. However, dreams do not often lead directly to action. Azande like to place their prognostications before one of the four main oracles, *benge*, *dakpa*, *mapingo*, and *iwa*, to make certain that they have correctly interpreted them.[1]

---

[1] For further information on dreams, cf. Appendix II.

CHAPTER XI

Magic and Medicines

I

ALREADY in the development of this book a large number of magic rites have been described, but only incidentally, and in relation to witchcraft and oracles. It is now time to consider Zande magic more closely, and in this final part it is regarded as the important variable in the ritual complex of witchcraft, oracles, and magic.

Witchcraft, oracles, and magic are like three sides to a triangle. Oracles and magic are two different ways of combating witchcraft. Oracles determine who has injured or who is about to injure another by witchcraft, and whether witchcraft looms ahead. When the name of a witch is discovered he is dealt with by the procedure described in Chapter III. Where witchcraft lies in the path of a project it can be circumvented either by abandoning the project till more favourable conditions ensue or by discovering the witch whose ill-will threatens the endeavour and persuading him to withdraw it.

Magic is the chief foe of witchcraft, and it would be useless to describe Zande magical rites and notions had their beliefs in witches not previously been recorded. Having grasped the ideas Azande have of witchcraft, we shall have no difficulty in understanding the main purpose of their magic.

The use of magic for socially approved ends, such as combating witchcraft, is sharply distinguished by Azande from its evil and anti-social use in sorcery. To them, the difference between a sorcerer and a witch is that the former uses the technique of magic and derives his power from medicines, while the latter acts without rites and spells and uses hereditary psycho-physical powers to attain his ends. Both alike are enemies of men, and Azande class them together. Witchcraft and sorcery are opposed to, and opposed by, good magic.

Good magic and sorcery alike involve magical rites using objects fashioned from trees and plants. These objects are what we have called 'medicines'. After more or less preparation they are used to attain certain ends. A Zande rite is not a formalized affair. There are certain actions a man must perform, but the sequence of these actions depends on the logic of the rite and does not otherwise condition its efficacy. Hence it is seldom that one observes a particular rite performed in exactly the same way on several occasions. There are usually variations, often large variations, in what is said and done and in the sequence of words and actions. The sequence of ritual acts is determined solely by technical needs and common sense.

The homoeopathic element is so evident in many magical rites and in much of the *materia medica* that there is no need to give examples. It is recognized by the Azande themselves. They say, 'We use such-and-such a plant because it is like such-and-such a thing,' naming the object towards which the rite is directed. Nevertheless, there need be no similarity between medicines and their purposes, or between the action of a rite and the action it is supposed to produce. The whistles and bulbs which are so often the source of magical power have no similarity to the objects they are believed to affect, and the ordinary modes of eating medicines and rubbing them into the body are rites which do not imitate the result aimed at.

Important magical rites are normally accompanied by spells. The magician addresses (*sima*) the medicines and tells them what he wants them to do. These spells are never formulae. The magician chooses his words as he utters the spell. There is no power in the address itself. All that is required is that the meaning shall be clear because the medicines have a commission to carry out and they must know exactly what the commission is. Needless to say, however, people who use the same medicines for the same purposes tend to use the same phrases, and after listening to a number of spells it is easy for anyone to construct them for himself. The virtue of a magical rite lies principally in the medicines themselves. If they are operated correctly, and the requisite taboos are observed, they must obey the magician, and if they are potent they will do as they are bid.

In asking a medicine to act on his behalf a man does not beseech it to do so. He is not entreating it to grant a favour. He tells it what it is to do, just as he would tell a boy were he dispatching him on an errend. Most spells are spoken in normal, matter-of-fact voices and the medicines are addressed in a casual manner that has often surprised me. However, more regard to them is paid when they are dangerous and when their task is one of great social importance, for example, when vengeance-magic is used great attention is paid to the medicines, which are carefully instructed by name in each clause about the action required of them.

Azande do not always address medicines. I have seen antidotes to medicines—and these are counter-medicines—administered without a word being spoken to them. I have also witnessed a long rite cancelling vengeance-magic after its purpose has been achieved and noticed that throughout the cooking, stirring, and eating of the medicines they were not addressed. When I remarked on this fact I was told that since they did not wish the medicines to accomplish any task there was nothing about which to instruct them.

Moreover, in minor magical acts, such as putting a stone in a tree to delay sunset, blowing a whistle to make rain-clouds pass over, spearing leaves of pumpkins with *bingba* grass, and so forth, a spell is often omitted in practice, though in giving me texts my informants usually inserted one. Also Azande seldom address charms worn about their persons.

Before using potent medicines and the greater oracles a man ought to observe a number of taboos. People do not inconvenience themselves by observing taboos when performing unimportant rites and when consulting the lesser oracles. There is no agreement about the length of time a taboo must be observed before magic is made. Some magicians observe them for longer periods than others, and one man observes a greater range of taboos than another. When an owner of medicines, like those for theft and vengeance, uses them on behalf of another, this other man performs the rites, or part of them, and it is he, and not the owner, who has to observe the taboos.

II

The following list of situations in which Azande use medicines comprises all the purposes of magic (other than its use in sorcery) of which I have knowledge:

Medicines connected with natural forces: to prevent rain from falling; to delay sunset.

Medicines connected with hoe culture: to ensure the fruitfulness of various food-plants.

Medicines connected with hunting, fishing, and collecting: for wet-season hunting in game-squares; for hunting by firing grass in the dry season; to make a hunter invisible; to prevent wounded animals from escaping; to doctor game-nets; to doctor game-pits; to doctor traps and nooses; for hunting dangerous beasts, elephant, lion, and leopard; to doctor spears; to doctor bows and arrows; to direct the aim of spearmen and bowmen; to give power of scent and fleetness to hunting dogs; to kill fish (fish-poison); for women's fishing; to doctor guinea-fowl nets; to ensure flight and capture of all species of edible termites.

Medicines connected with arts and crafts: for smelting; for iron-working; for beer-brewing; for warfare (to doctor body and shield and to acquire enemy spears); for singing; for dancing; for drum- and gong-beating.

Medicines connected with mystical powers: medicines against witches, sorcerers, and other evil agencies; to qualify as a witch-doctor; to qualify as an operator of the rubbing-board oracle; to produce true revelations in dreams.

Medicines connected with social activities: to attract followers; to ensure successful exchange at feasts; for sexual potency; for success in love affairs; to obtain wives; for safety and success in journeys; to procure return of stolen property; to protect widows and widowers from injury through contamination by the dead; to be at peace with all men; to be in wealth, health, and safety; to make babies grow strong; to procure abortion; to ensure that a new wife will settle happily in her husband's home; to avenge homicide, adultery, and theft; to protect oneself and family from all dangers; to protect wives and property; to make a prince favourable.

Medicines connected with sickness: every disease has special medicines for treating it.

I have constructed rough categories for Zande medicines by listing the types of activity they are supposed to promote and also by noting their purposes. The Zande himself tends to classify them also by their form and their mode of use. Thus he sometimes says of a medicine that it is a *ranga*, a bulb. One often sees bulbs growing in the centre of a Zande homestead, usually at the foot of a ghost-shrine. They have many magical uses.

Either their leaves are eaten raw or they are boiled in water with sesame and salt, and this mixture is eaten. The bulbs are transplanted from the bush. A man who knows a bulb with special magical uses either shows it in the bush to another man or points it out to him in his homestead. Once a man knows the leaf of this particular bulb he can seek it himself in the bush. Transmission of knowledge therefore does not consist in merely showing a man the plant, for he can see it any day growing in the magician's homestead. It consists rather in instructing him in its uses.

Another category is *ngbimi*. These are arboreal parasites and are the material from which the most potent whistles and charms are manufactured. Parasites of very many trees are used in one or other form as medicines. A third category are creepers (*gire*) which figure frequently in magical rites, particularly to enclose gardens and for winding round the wrist of a man as a charm. Many of these plants are rare and cannot be found without diligent search.

Azande also divide their medicines into classes based upon their modes of preparation and use. Often the species of plant employed in a rite indicates by its form its mode of use as explained in relation to *ranga*, *ngbimi*, and *gire*. The principal modes of use are:

(1) Whistles (*kura*). The wood of certain trees is fashioned in the shape of a whistle. Though the cavity hollowed out at one end is shallow it emits a shrill blast when blown. Magical whistles are used for many purposes. Before making a whistle a man ought to observe taboos. Early in the morning he leaves his homestead without washing his face or rinsing his mouth and cuts the wood and fashions it. He utters spells when cutting the wood and when boring the cavity at one end. Whistles are worn around the neck, over the shoulder, at the waist, or on the wrist. Very powerful whistles are hidden away from the owner's hut, often in the fowl-house or in a hole in a tree.

(2) Body-medicines (*ngua kpoto*). In doctoring babies a magician usually chews up medicines and spits them on their bodies. He does this to protect them from harm and to make them grow strong. In doctoring older persons he makes a paste of burnt vegetable matter and oil and rubs it into incisions made on chest and back and face.

(3) Medicines rubbed into incisions on hand and wrist (*nzati*). The medicine is made of burnt vegetable matter mixed with oil. Such medicines are those that give skill in spear-throwing and in operating the rubbing-board oracle.

(4) Drops of an infusion (*togo*). Vegetable matter is burnt and the soot mixed with water in a leaf funnel which, when squeezed, acts as a filter.

(5) Soot mixed with oil (*mbiro*). This is one of the most popular ways of preparing medicine for consumption. It may then be eaten, or used as described above in (2), (3), and (4).

(6) Cord, often a creeper, twisted as it is addressed in a spell by a magician (*kpira*). This is sometimes done in hunting-magic, but is usually a rite performed against an enemy.

Some Zande medicines actually do produce the effect aimed at, but so far as I have been able to observe the Zande does not make any qualitative distinction between these medicines and those that have no objective consequences. To him they are all alike *ngua*, medicine, and all are operated in magical rites in much the same manner. A Zande observes taboos and addresses fish-poisons before throwing them into the water just as he addresses a crocodile's tooth while he rubs the stems of his bananas with it to make them grow. And the fish-poison really does paralyse the fish while, truth to tell, the crocodile's tooth has no influence over bananas. Likewise the milky sap of the *Euphorbia candelabra* is used as arrow poison. But Azande do not merely tap the succulent. It must be given offerings, and the hunter addresses the sap in the same manner as he addresses some magic unguent which he is rubbing into his wrist to ensure swiftness and sureness in throwing his spear. Therefore, since Azande speak of, and use, medicines which really are poisonous in the same way as medicines which are harmless, I conclude that they do not distinguish between them.

III

Witch-doctors eat medicines at a communal meal, as do members of closed associations. War magic used to be made by a king in the presence of his subjects, and other rites may sometimes be performed publicly. For example, magic to prevent rain may be made in public at feasts when many people are gathered together, or close kinsmen of a dead person may witness in company certain phases of vengeance through magical operations. But generally magical actions concern only the welfare of an individual who performs them in the privacy of his hut or alone in the bush. For example, a man carries a whistle to protect himself against misfortunes, and normally he blows it when he is alone, usually in the early morning before he makes his ablutions.

All Zande ritual acts, even addresses to the ghosts, are performed with a minimum of publicity. Good magic and bad magic alike are secretly enacted. This is due in part to spatial distribution, for when a homestead is far from its neighbours its owner necessarily performs most actions alone or in the presence of his family, unless he particularly wishes publicity. Azande are, moreover, anxious that no one should see them making magic, if it is for any important purpose, lest there be among those who witness the rite a witch who will spoil the venture. Furthermore, a man does not like others to know what medicines he possesses because they will pester him to make magic on their behalf. Also they may recognize the root or leaves he is using and thenceforth be able to perform magic independently. Life in settlements has not made Azande more inclined to welcome publicity.

Secrecy in performance would not in itself have been a bar to observation of magical rites, because I knew many Azande well enough to have been invited to witness such activities. But rarity of performance was a more serious obstacle. It is true that some people perform rites more often than others, but the performance is never more than an occasional break in routine activities of daily life.

Medicines are an individual possession and, with a few exceptions, are used at the discretion of their owner and for his own ends. The lack of social compulsion behind magical rites, and of common interest in their purposes, may be related to a difference of attitude towards them between men brought up at a prince's court and men who have always led a provincial life. Princes and courtiers use medicines far less than provincials and are even contemptuous of much of the magic in Zande culture.

Furthermore, it is not advisable at court to know much about medicines, other than a few old-established ones, because a man who is found to possess a strange medicine may be suspected of sorcery.

The principal old-established medicines which are used by most commoners of high standing at court, and even by princes themselves, are: medicines to attract dependants; medicine of vengeance for homicide (it has gained in prestige since direct vengeance has been prohibited by European administrations); magic of lighting, principally employed to avenge theft; magic of invisibility, formerly used in prosecuting vengeance; medicines to protect a homestead; medicines to protect cultivations; medicines to protect the person against witches and sorcerers; virility medicines; and a few medicines for hunting, for doctoring game-nets, and for catching termites. To these must be added the many medicines used in leechcraft.

Generally there is no necessity to use even these medicines, but a few form links in social activities so that there is moral compulsion to use them. A man must employ a magician to avenge the death of a kinsman. Also, the use of some medicines, like certain hunting medicines, is so general and has been customary for so long that they are compulsory in the sense of being traditional, though not in the sense of involving social sanctions of any weight.

Outside these principal medicines there is a vast range of lesser medicines, many of recent introduction, which are employed for a variety of purposes. Courtiers are suspicious of some of these, but they have little interest in most of them.

I do not think any Zande would declare that these smaller medicines entirely lack potency, but most men regard them as unimportant and one sometimes sees a man trained at court, and now living in the provinces, conducting his affairs without employing most of the medicines his neighbours use in their pursuits.

Moreover, among men who have been brought up in similar circumstances some are more, and some are less, superstitious about magic. One does not have to live long among Azande before one is able to distinguish men who are always more anxious to acquire medicines, use them more frequently, perform rites with greater intensity, and express greater faith in magic than others. I have known many men who do not care whether they possess medicines or not, and who only use them when it is customary and then without enthusiasm.

Magicians have no great prestige in Zande society. I have not heard people speak highly of a man because he possesses medicines. People envy owners of vengeance-magic because this is magic that everyone must employ, and the owners charge heavy fees for its use. But to Azande it is a very small distinction to possess medicines to protect gardens, for hunting, for making bananas and pumpkins fruitful, etc. Also in Zande society political status overshadows all other distinctions.

Most magic is a male prerogative. Women sometimes act as witch-doctors and leeches and take part in the ritual of closed associations, but most magic is unknown to them and one does not see them wearing charms and magic whistles like the men. This is partly because a great many medicines are associated with male activities, e.g. hunting magic. But it is also due to an opinion that women ought not to practise magic, which is a field reserved for men. Magic gives power which is best in the hands of men. In so far as women need magical protection against witchcraft and sorcery they may rely on their husbands to perform rites for the welfare of the family as a whole. Women are expected to use only those medicines which are associated with purely feminine pursuits, fishing by ladling out water from dry-season pools, salt-making, beer-brewing, etc., and with purely feminine conditions, childbirth, abortion, menstruation, lactation, and suchlike processes.

Owners of medicines are usually old or middle-aged men. Here again the fact is partly to be accounted for by the greater range of social activities in which older men engage. But there is also the opinion that youths, like women, ought not to practise magic which is the privilege and concern of their elders. Moreover, youths have no wealth with which to purchase medicines, nor have they had the years in which to collect them. Nevertheless, youths possess medicines which are specially employed in youthful actions, dancing and singing, beating of drum and gong, love-making, and so forth. In recent years age qualifications of status have begun to count less and youths do not find it so difficult to acquire medicines as before.

When a man builds a new homestead or plants his staple crop of eleusine he may ask a friend to doctor the eleusine or the homestead for him. The magician buries certain medicines in the homestead or cultivation. Similarly, a man employs a magician for such purposes as exacting vengeance, to retain stolen property, to cure sickness, and to punish adultery. He pays for these services a small or large fee according to custom. In such cases the owner of a medicine makes it for another and performs himself the appropriate magical rite. He tells the medicine the name of the man on whose behalf he is acting. He remains both owner and operator. A prince would not make magic on behalf of others in this way, and it is very unusual for any member of the noble class to do so.

A man may, however, obtain actual ownership of medicines and become himself the magician who operates them. This is particularly the case with charms and magic whistles. A man wants a whistle which he can blow to protect himself against misfortunes, to enable him to drum well, to hunt elephants successfully, or for some other purpose, and he asks a magician to make him one. He pays his fee and obtains his whistle. He does not have to inquire how it is used. Everyone knows how to blow magical whistles and utter spells. But he may not know the tree from which the whistle was made; so that he becomes owner of a single whistle and not owner of the medicine in a more complete sense.

Normally, however, when a man acquires medicines he learns their botanical sources and thereby becomes a fully fledged magician in his own right. Such are the magical plants which are grown in homesteads; such are many of the whistles and charms one sees people wearing; and such are many bush plants and trees used for curing sickness, as safeguards against witchcraft and sorcery, and for hunting and hoe-culture.

Very many medicines are known to all, and anyone who wishes to use them may do so at his pleasure. Such are simple medicines used in cultivation of food-plants, simple hunting medicines, and a number of medicines for catching termites. Everyone knows that he can delay sunset by placing a stone in the fork of a tree, and prevent rain from falling by a number of simple rites. The vast majority of medicines, including the simple drugs used in leechcraft, are widely known, since knowledge of them is imparted without payment in virtue of parenthood, kinship, blood-brotherhood, affinity, or friendship.

Men who possess medicines of a specialized activity, like witch-doctors and those who practise the blacksmith's art, pass on their knowledge to one of their sons when he learns the craft. Likewise, a man who knows valuable medicine, like vengeance-magic, teaches it bit by bit to a favourite son over a long period of time, for several rare plants and other objects often furnish different elements in the magical compound. Old men sometimes hand over a treasured charm, like the whistle which gives invisibility, to a son as an heirloom.

When a magical object changes hands a small payment is generally made. This is more than a fee, for it is also the means of preserving the potency of the medicine during transfer. It may lose its power unless its owner is happy at handing it over to another man, and it will not work unless it sees it has been paid for.

For full knowledge of a few medicines, or rather collections of medicines, large payments must be made. These are medicines used in vengeance-magic, medicines of witch-doctors, and medicines of closed associations. Payment for them is usually stated by Azande to be twenty 'spears', by which is meant a few actual spears and a number of other objects, hoes, knives, piastres, pots of beer, and baskets of eleusine. Before a man acquires these medicines he asks the poison oracle whether it is advisable for him to do so.

Purchase of the use of some medicines implies becoming a member of an association, like the lodges of the closed associations, or of the loose association of witch-doctors, or the still looser grouping of singers who act as chorus to their leader at dances. Purchase of these and of important medicines unconnected with associations means the forging of a social link between the purchaser and the seller. The purchaser places himself for the time being under the tuition of the seller and each has a definite status in relation to the other. The social link remains even after the medicines have been finally paid for. The purchaser and pupil continues to respect the seller and teacher and will hand him part of the proceeds of his first magical activities. If the pupil wrongs the teacher it is said that his anger may cause the medicine to lose its potency.

Some medicines are used only by princes and commoners of

standing. Only a prince or an important prince's deputy would use medicines to attract followers, and only a householder would use *bingiya* medicine for the general prosperity of his household, and eleusine medicine for the welfare of his staple crop. Nevertheless, every Zande, except small children, whether old or young, whether man or woman, is to some extent a magician. At some time or other a man is sure to use some or other medicine. Throughout life men are constantly associated with medicines, even if some do not use them much.

If a man wishes magic to be made on his behalf or to acquire possession of medicines he has no difficulty in satisfying his desire. It is well known who possess different medicines in a district, and these people are often kinsmen of, or in some way socially linked with, the man who requires their services.

Azande insist that magic must be proved efficacious if they are to employ it. They say that some magicians have better magic than others, and when they require a magician's services they choose one whose magic is known to be efficacious. Thus the vengeance-medicines of some magicians have a reputation for quick and decisive action, whereas the medicines of others are said to be more dilatory in achieving vengeance.

Azande do not suppose that success in an empirical activity is due to use of medicines, for they know that it is often attained without their assistance. But they are inclined to attribute unusual success to magic. Indeed, just as serious failure in an activity is ascribed to the influence of witches, so great success is often ascribed to magic, though the notion of success being due to magic is less emphasized because it is not expressed in action as is the belief of failure being due to witchcraft. A man without medicines may have great success. Then Azande say that he has had good luck (*tandu*).

IV

In differentiating between good magic and sorcery, Azande do not stigmatize the latter because it destroys the health and property of others, but because it flouts moral and legal rules. Good magic may be destructive, even lethal, but it strikes only at persons who have committed a crime, whereas bad magic is used out of spite against men who have not broken any law or moral convention. Good medicines cannot be used for evil purposes.

Certain medicines are classified as good, certain medicines as bad, while about yet others there is no strong moral opinion or Azande are uncertain whether to place them in the category of good or bad.

Any type of magic may be performed privately. Privacy is a characteristic of all Zande magic, for Azande object to others witnessing their actions and are always afraid lest sorcerers and witches get to know that they are making magic and interfere with it. A man's friends and neighbours know, or think they know, what magic he possesses. He does not try to conceal his ownership. But sorcery is a secret rite in a very different sense. It is performed at dead of night, for if the act is witnessed the sorcerer will probably be slain. No one, except the fellow sorcerer who has sold him the medicines, knows that he possesses them.

Neither by virtue of privacy in performance nor of destructive qualities is good magic distinguished from sorcery. Indeed, *bagbuduma*, magic of vengeance, is the most destructive and at the same time the most honourable of all Zande medicines. Its purpose is typical of the purposes of good magic in general. When a man dies Azande consider that he is a victim of witchcraft or sorcery and they make vengeance-magic to slay the slayer of the dead man. It is regarded as a judge which seeks out the person who is responsible for the death, and as an executioner which slays him. Azande say of it that 'it decides cases' and that it 'settles cases as judiciously as princes'. Like all good magic, it acts impartially and according to the merits of the case. Hence Azande say of a medicine either that 'it judges equitably' (*si nape zunga*) or that 'it is evil medicine'.

Were a man to use a medicine like vengeance-medicine to kill out of spite a man innocent of crime it would not only prove ineffectual but would turn against the magician who employed it and destroy him. Azande speak of the medicine as searching for the criminal and eventually, being unable to find him, for he does not exist, returning to slay the man who sent it forth. At the first stroke of sickness he will try to end its activity by throwing it into cold water. Therefore before making vengeance-magic Azande are supposed to seek from the poison oracle assurance that their kinsman died at the hands of witch or sorcerer and not as a result of his own misdeeds through the action of good magic. For vengeance-magic may seek in vain for a witch or sorcerer responsible for the death and return pregnant with undelivered judgement to destroy the magician who sent it forth and who wears the girdle of mourning. Good magic with destructive functions of this kind only acts against criminals. When a crime is expiated, it is necessary to destroy the magic quickly before it does injury to the magician. A man loses some article, perhaps an axe, perhaps a bundle of marriage-spears. He hastens to erect a little shelter under which he either buries medicines in the ground or hangs them from the roof of the shelter. As he does so he utters a spell to cause them to seek for his possessions and to punish the man who has stolen them.

May misfortune come upon you, thunder roar, seize you, and kill you. May a snake bite you so that you die. May death come upon you from ulcers. May you die if you drink water. May every kind of sickness trouble you. May the magic hand you over to the Europeans so that they will imprison you and you will perish in their prison. May you not survive this year. May every kind of trouble fall upon you. If you eat cooked foods may you die. When you stand in the centre of the net, hunting animals, may your friend spear you in mistake.

I wish to emphasize that to a Zande the whole idea of *pe zunga* is equivalent to the carrying out of justice in the sense in which we use the expression in our own society. Magic used against persons can only receive the moral and legal sanction of the community if it acts regularly and impartially.

Sorcery, on the other hand, does not give judgements (*si na penga zunga te*). It is not only bad medicine but also stupid medicine, for it does not judge an issue between persons but slays one of the parties to a dispute without regard to the merits of the case. It is a personal weapon aimed at some individual whom the sorcerer dislikes.

Good magic is moral because it is used against unknown persons. For if a man knows who has committed adultery with his wife or stolen his spears or killed his kinsman he takes the matter to court. There is no need to make magic. It is only when he does not know who has committed a crime that he uses good magic against unknown persons. Bad magic, on the other hand, is made against definite persons, and for this reason it is evidently bad, because if the person against whom it is used had injured the magician in any way recognized by law the matter would have been taken to court and damages claimed. It is only because the sorcerer has no legal case against a man that he uses magic to destroy him.

v

It is very difficult to obtain information about sorcery, for Azande consider possession of bad medicines to be a serious crime. You will never meet a Zande who professes himself a sorcerer, and they do not like even to discuss the subject lest it be thought that the knowledge they have of it comes from practice. They may in strict privacy cast suspicion on someone, but it is always the vaguest of hints, qualified at the same time by expression of ignorance about the whole matter. A man can sometimes show you in the bush a plant which some people say may be used by sorcerers. He may tell you the way in which it is said that sorcerers work their rites. He may be able to tell you how certain persons have been slain by sorcery. The subject is very obscure, and the question arises whether sorcerers exist any more than witches.

The most feared of all bad medicine, and the one most often cited as cause of sickness, is *menzere*. It is probably derived from an arboreal parasite. The sorcerer goes by night, generally at full moon, to the homestead of his victim and places the medicine on his threshold, in the centre of his homestead, or in the path leading to it. As he does so he utters a spell over it. It is said that if he succeeds in slaying his enemy he will mourn for him by wearing a girdle of *bingba* grass for several days after his death. If the sorcerer neglects this rite he may fall sick. The girdle would not lead to his detection because men often mourn for a few days after the death of distant relatives.

Menzere is so potent a medicine that should any man for whom it is not intended step over it he will be ill for a while though he will not die. There are many antidotes to *menzere*, and a man who knows these is sent for immediately a man suspects he is attacked by it. *Menzere* is regarded with abhorrence by all. Azande have always told me that in the past those who killed men with witchcraft were generally allowed to pay compensation, but that those who killed men by sorcery were invariably put to death, and probably their kinsmen also.

Besides the various medicines that are eaten to counteract *menzere* an informant described the following way of protecting oneself against it:

If sorcery is made against a man, namely, the *menzere* medicine, he goes to a much-frequented cross-roads and there kneels and scratches up the earth with his hand. He addresses the centre of the path, saying:

'You, *menzere*, inside me, which a man has made against me, I scratch the centre of the path on your account. If it is *menzere* may it follow all paths; may it go as far as Wau, may it go as far as Tembura, may it go also as far as Meridi. When the medicine has followed every path which I have trod when I was small, then, when it has finished all the journeys, let it kill me. If it does not follow me everywhere I have been may it not kill me. let me live in spite of it.'

The soul (*mbisimo*) of a medicine cannot travel so long and so far and therefore is prevented from killing the man who utters this spell.

There are a few bad medicines besides *menzere*. One that dates from the time of Gbudwe is a parasitic plant called *mbimi gbara*. Today hairs of the ant-bear are said to be used to kill people. They have a spell uttered over them and are afterwards placed in a man's beer to slay him. They cause his neck and tongue to swell, and if an antidote is not administered he will quickly die.

Not only homicidal medicines are illegal but also medicines which corrupt legal procedure and which destroy a man's happiness and interfere with his family relations. Magic which influences the poison oracle in its verdicts is sorcery. Azande also condemn medicines which are used to break up a man's household, either out of malice or with the further object of obtaining his wife in marriage. After the sorcerer has made this magic at night in the homestead of his victim the contentment of its inmates is destroyed and husband and wife begin to quarrel and divorce may result.

Even powerful kings are frightened about sorcery, indeed, they more than anyone. A prince does not expect that he will be killed by a commoner witch. His enemies are other nobles, and it is not said that they bewitch one another. But they may kill by sorcery, and nobles frequently accuse one another of this intention.

Sometimes an important commoner will consult the oracle on behalf of his prince about a gift from another prince, for Azande, especially princes, are often suspicious about gifts, fearing that they may be the medium of sorcery.

VI

It should be noted that Azande know of very few medicines which come definitely under the heading of sorcery, whereas their good medicines are legion. The reason for this would seem to be that the vast majority of situations in which the interests of men are injured or threatened are associated with witchcraft and not with sorcery, and often an event attributed to sorcery may equally be attributed to witchcraft, e.g. failure of the poison oracle to function normally or family disruption. Indeed, the concept of sorcery appears to be redundant, a fact that itself invites historical explanation. We know that many of their magical techniques are recently acquired from neighbouring peoples.

After weighing the evidence, I am still doubtful whether bad medicines—or sorcerers—really exist. Notions of sorcery, like notions of witchcraft, are evoked in special situations and only by certain persons. If a man falls suddenly sick his friends may say that someone has made sorcery against him, but other people think that he has probably committed some secret crime and brought magic of vengeance on himself. A man falls suddenly ill after a beer-party. He and his kinsmen are convinced that someone put a hair of the ant-bear in his beer. The owner of the beer is convinced that the man is a witch who came in the guise of a bat to destroy his eleusine. A man starts to quarrel with his wife and thinks that it is due to *gbarawasi* medicine. Other people say that it is due to his stupidity. The owner of bad oracle poison may attribute its failure to sorcery. Others may think it more likely that the owner has broken a taboo.

My reasons for thinking that such medicines as *menzere* are imaginary are as follows: (1) No one has, to my knowledge, admitted ownership of such medicines. I cannot therefore say more than that Azande allege the use of such medicines by certain people. (2) Azande are unable to produce many instances of persons being punished for sorcery and are unable in these cases to adduce evidence of guilt other than that furnished by the poison oracle. The verdict of oracles is usually the sole proof of sorcery. (3) Sudden and violent sickness is diagnosed as sorcery and treated accordingly. The sickness is the sorcery and the proof of it. Likewise, a soft chancre, household unrest, death after beer-drinking are diagnosed as *moti*, *gbarawasi*, and *garawa*. No further proof is required, since the nature of these misfortunes demonstrates their cause, and if further proof is produced it is oracular revelation. (4) The technique of sorcery is so unlike the techniques of other forms of magic that were an informant to describe rites like those for *menzere* and *gbarawasi* as rites of good magic I would regard them as aberrant forms and would hesitate before accepting them as genuine. (5) Even when medicines are discovered, as in the case cited above, I do not consider the evidence to be conclusive because there is no means, other than by oracular verdicts, of determining their nature. Even had a man placed medicines where they were discovered for innocent purposes he would have been too frightened in such incriminating circumstances to have admitted his ownership of them. (6) The use of good magic against unknown persons makes it difficult for people to see that magic has no direct effects, but it would be very obvious to a sorcerer that his rites produced no result against a definite person, and I cannot imagine that he would persevere in his practice.

Some bad medicines may exist, but I am not convinced of their existence. I incline rather to the view that whereas subjectively there is a clear division of magic into good and bad, objectively there are only medicines which men use when they consider that they have good grounds for employing them. If this view is correct the difference between witchcraft and sorcery is the difference between an alleged act that is impossible and an alleged act that is possible.

Another reason why the problem of sorcery is difficult is the existence of a large body of magic about which opinion is divided and ill-defined. It is thus possible for a magician to say that his magic is used only for legitimate purposes, while others are sceptical about its morality.

The moral issue is also very confused, because in any quarrel both sides are convinced that they are in the right. The man who has been left behind on a hunting expedition, the man who has failed to obtain favourable exchange, the man who has had his wife taken from him, all believe that they have genuine grievances. The members of the hunting expedition, the owner of the goods, the parents of the girl, are all convinced of their rectitude. The man who has ulcers sees nothing wrong in getting rid of them on someone else. The man who gets ulcers considers that he has been improperly treated. A man getting a chancre says he has been made a cuckold, but when his neighbour gets a chancre he says he is an adulterer. Each twists the notions of his culture so that they will suit himself in a particular situation. The notions do not bind everyone to identical beliefs in a given situation, but each exploits them to his own advantage.

Besides these medicines which are regarded as criminal or legal according to the purpose for which they are used, there are many less important medicines which in no way concern moral opinion. Azande have no moral feelings about the vast majority of their medicines. They are the means of an individual obtaining success in a variety of economic and social undertakings. If you ask a Zande about them he will say that they are good medicines. Otherwise you will find that they are taken for granted, and that among Azande themselves they are not explicitly pronounced good or bad medicines, but merely medicines. This is true also of a number of magical rites which would appear to us to injure others unfairly, but since the damage they cause is slight they are not the object of social condemnation. The Zande attitude towards them is non-moral.

A further difficulty arises today owing to the importation of new magic, whose qualities are unknown. In the old days there appear to have been two clearly distinguished categories, good medicines and bad medicines. All major magic could be placed in one of these two categories. Public opinion was only ill-defined about minor rites. But a great number of medicines have been introduced into Zandeland in the last thirty years, and people knowing nothing about them are afraid of them. The old Zande medicines were culturally indicated as good or bad without ambiguity. But who can say what the qualities of Baka, Bongo, Mundu and Madi medicines may be? The moral issue has become confused because Zande culture does not prescribe a definite attitude towards them.

It may also be noted that Azande fear sorcery far more than they fear witchcraft which, as I have already pointed out, evokes anger rather than fear. This may be due partly to the serious symptoms it produces in sickness and partly to the absence of machinery for countering it as adequate as that employed against witches. Indeed, today, apart from administering an antidote or making counter-magic, nothing can be done to stop an act of sorcery. It is possible to get a witch to blow out water in sign of goodwill, interpreted as innocence by himself and as withdrawal of his influence by the bewitched party; but it would be necessary to get a sorcerer to cancel his magic by further magical operations. No one would do this because to show knowledge of the manner in which sorcery can be cancelled would be to admit to the crime of sorcery. Accusations in the old days must have been infrequent, and Azande say that sorcerers were rare.

VII

Azande attribute nearly all sickness, whatever the nature, to witchcraft or sorcery: it is these forces that must be worsted in order to cure a serious illness. This does not mean that Azande entirely disregard secondary causes but, in so far as they recognize these, they generally think of them as associated with witchcraft and magic. Nor does their reference of sickness to supernatural causes lead them to neglect treatment of symptoms any more than their reference of death on the horns of a buffalo to witchcraft causes them to await its onslaught. On the contrary, they possess an enormous pharmacopoeia (I have myself collected almost a hundred plants, used to treat diseases and lesions, along the sides of a path for about two hundred yards), and in ordinary circumstances they trust to drugs to cure their ailments and only take steps to remove the primary and supernatural causes when the disease is of a serious nature or takes an alarming turn.

Azande know diseases by their major symptoms. Hence when symptoms develop they are able to diagnose them as signs of a certain disease and to tell you its name. The very fact of naming diseases and differentiating them from one another by their symptoms shows observation and common-sense inference. Azande are often skilled in the detection of early symp-

toms, and our own doctors have told me that they seldom err
in diagnosing early leprosy. They are naturally much less sure
in diagnosing diseases affecting internal organs such as the intestines, the liver, and the spleen. They know beforehand the
normal course of a disease as soon as its symptoms are
pronounced. They often know what the later symptoms will
be, and whether the patient is likely to live or die, and how
long he is likely to live. Likewise they know what infirmities
are permanent. Besides their ability to give a prognosis, they
can also tell you the aetiology of disease; and though their
notions of causes are generally far from objective reality they
recognize different causes as participating with witchcraft to
produce different illnesses. Moreover, the participating cause
often cannot help being the true one as in cuts, scalds, burns,
bites, chiggers, etc., and they are aware of facts such as that
syphilis and gonorrhoea are preceded by sexual intercourse
with an affected person. They use their drugs by trial and error;
if one does not alleviate pain they try another. Moreover,
almost every disease is not only diagnosed, its probable course
foretold, and its relation to a cause defined, but also each disease
has its own individual treatment, which in some cases has evidently been built up on experience and in other cases, though
it is probably quite ineffectual, shows a logico-experimental element.

In spite of these empirical elements in Zande treatment of
minor ailments, my own experience has been that Zande
remedies are of an almost completely magical order. Moreover,
it must not be supposed that where part of a treatment is of
real therapeutic value it is necessarily the part which Azande
stress as vital to the cure. I had a good example of the manner
in which magical and empirical treatments are employed at
the same time when a boy who formed part of my household was bitten by a snake which was said to be very poisonous.
One of our neighbours who was known to have a vast knowledge of drugs was immediately sent for and said that he knew
exactly what was required. He brought with him a knife and
some drugs (a piece of bark and some kind of grass). He first
chewed some of the bark and gave the remainder to the boy
to chew. After swallowing the juice both spat out the wood.
They did the same with the grass. The leech told me afterwards

that he partook of the medicine himself so that were the boy to die he could not well be accused of having administered bad medicine to him. He also told me that he had addressed the bark, saying that if the boy were going to recover let him belch, that if he were to die let him refrain from belching, so that the drug had an oracular action. Having administered these drugs he made incisions on the boy's foot, where he had been bitten, by raising the skin between his fingers and drawing the blade of his knife across it with several light strokes. As soon as blood began to ooze out of the cuts he took the foot in his hands and, raising it to his mouth, sucked at the incisions forcibly and for some time. He then said that the boy was to be kept perfectly quiet and admonished him not to move about. After a while the boy began to belch on account of the drugs he had eaten, and on seeing this happy augury the leech no longer had any doubt that he would speedily recover.

When a Zande suffers from a mild ailment he doctors himself. There are always older men of his kin or vicinity who will tell him a suitable drug to take. If his ailment does not disappear he visits a witch-doctor. In more serious sickness a man's kin consult without delay first the rubbing-board oracle and then the poison oracle, or, if they are poor, the termites oracle. Generally they ask it two questions—firstly, where is a safe place for the sick man to live and, secondly, who is the witch responsible for his sickness. The results of these consultations are the procedures described in Chapter III, the removal of the invalid to a grass hut in the bush or at the edge of cultivations, unless the oracle advises that he be left in his homestead, and a public warning to the people of the neighbourhood that the witch must cease to molest the sick man, or a formal presentation of a fowl's wing to the witch himself that he may blow water on to it. Or they may summon witch-doctors to dance about the man's sickness.

At the same time they apply some remedy. If they know from the symptoms or from the declaration of the oracle that the sickness is caused by good or bad magic a specialist who knows the antidote is sent for without delay, and he administers a drug specific to the magic. If the sickness is due to witchcraft they combine efforts to persuade the witch to leave the patient in peace with the administration of drugs to treat the actual symp-

toms of the disease. Here again some old men who know the
right drugs for the particular ailment will offer their services.
It is generally known who are authorities on drugs and the relatives summon one of these men to treat their kinsman. The leech
may or may not be a witch-doctor. If he is not he will probably
attend the patient free of charge for reasons of friendship, kinship, blood-brotherhood, affinity, or of some other social link.
No treatment, however, will prove efficacious if a witch is still
attacking the sick man and, vice versa, the treatment is sure
to be successful if the witch withdraws his influence.

Azande frequently summon a witch-doctor to treat them by
massage, the extraction of 'objects of witchcraft' from the seat
of pain, and by administration of drugs. But they do not like
to send for a witch-doctor unless sickness is diagnosed as serious,
because it is necessary to pay for his services. It is usually the
presence of more or less severe pain that persuades them to take
that course. Nevertheless, we must remember in describing the
Zande classification of diseases and their treatment that the
notion of witchcraft as a participant in their origin may always
be expressed, and that if Azande do not always and immediately consult their oracles to find out the witch that is responsible it is because they consider the sickness to be of a minor
character and not worth the trouble and expense of oracle consultations.

But in serious illness there is always a tendency to identify
the disease with witchcraft or sorcery, and in less serious com-
plaints to identify it with its symptoms which are participating
with witchcraft to cause pain. In sickness which is attributed
to the activity of the disease itself and to witchcraft at the same
time, it is always the presence or absence of witchcraft which
determines the patient's death or recovery. Hence the more
serious the disease becomes the less they trouble about
administering drugs and the more they consult oracles and
make counter-magic. At death the thoughts of a dead man's
kindred are directed only towards witchcraft and revenge, to
purely mystical causation, while in minor ailments or at the
early symptoms of an illness from which a man may be expected
to recover without difficulty they think less of witchcraft and
more of the disease itself and of curing it by the use of drugs.
Supernatural causes are never excluded entirely from Zande

thought about sickness, but they are sometimes more, sometimes less, prominent. If they are not always and immediately evoked, as when the sickness is slight or the means of treating it adequate and known to be unfailingly efficacious, they are always ready at hand to be evoked when a man has need of them. When his ailment begins to cause him more trouble the Zande begins to talk about witchcraft but does not perform any rites to counteract its influence. Only when it becomes serious does he start anti-witchcraft operations.

VIII

Although Zande medicines cannot be neatly classified into mutually exclusive categories of productive, protective and punitive magic, the categories do correspond to three aspects of most Zande magic, and one of these purposes may be stressed, in the use of a certain medicine or in a certain situation, rather than the other two. A man makes magic to ensure a plentiful harvest of bananas, but though we might class the rite as productive magic, we must bear in mind that Azande would attribute serious failure of their banana harvest to witchcraft. When more important crops are being treated Azande usually utter a long spell over them, and the protective and punitive action of the medicine is clearly stated in its clauses. When a man employs a magician to bury medicines in his threshold to protect his home against sorcery and witchcraft he trusts to its protective power to destroy sorcerers and witches who intend him ill. But the medicine is also asked to ensure the peace and prosperity of the householder and his family. The spells said over such medicines are therefore couched in the form of incantations against witches. Generally speaking, Zande magic works towards its ends by preventing mystical interference, usually in the form of a threat of punishment to its authors.

I wish to make this point very clear because we shall not understand Zande magic, and the differences between ritual behaviour and empirical behaviour in the lives of Azande, unless we realize that its main purpose is to combat other mystical powers rather than to produce changes favourable to man in the objective world. Thus, medicines employed to ensure a fine harvest of eleusine are not so much thought to stimulate the eleusine as to keep witches away from it. The eleusine will be all right if witchcraft can be excluded.

How do Azande think their medicines work? They do not think very much about the matter. It is an accepted fact that the more potent medicines achieve their purposes. The best proof of this is experience, particularly the mystical evidence of oracular revelations. Nevertheless, Azande see that the action of medicines is unlike the action of empirical techniques and that there is something mysterious about it that has to be accounted for. It must be remembered that a man who is a magician is also well acquainted with the technical operations of arts and crafts. A man makes vengeance-magic and it kills a witch. What is happening between these two events? Azande say that the *mbisimo ngua*, 'the soul of the medicine', has gone out to seek its victim.

The virtue of a medicine is sometimes spoken of as its soul, and is believed to rise in steam and smoke when it is being cooked. Therefore people place their faces in the steam so that the magical virtue may enter into them. Likewise, Azande say that when they cook vengeance-medicines the soul of the medicine goes up in the smoke from the fire and from on high surveys the neighbourhood for the witch it goes forth to seek.

To what extent have Azande faith in magic? I have found that they always admit that the issue of a rite is uncertain. No one can be sure that his medicines will achieve the results aimed at. There is never the same degree of confidence as in routine empirical activities. Nevertheless, Azande are usually confident that vengeance-magic will be successful. This assurance is not due solely to the importance of the end aimed at and the influence of public opinion which forces kinsmen of a dead person to make repeated and prolonged efforts to avenge his death, but is due also to the test of experience. The test of magic is experience. Therefore the proof of magical potency is always to be found in the occurrence of those events it is designed to promote or cause.

Azande can point to the fact that people are frequently dying, that invariably an effort is made to avenge them, and that it is very rare for such efforts to fail. The confirmation of its success is here of a mystical order, being oracular declarations. When making magic against a thief they have often more direct evidence of the potency of medicines—at least, so it seems, because in reality they have proof only of general belief in the potency of theft-medicines. For most Azande can give instances of stolen property having been returned after magic was made to avenge the theft, and I have observed that this sometimes happens. But Azande think that a determined thief who has lost all sense of honour will not be awed by protective medicines. Probably he will trust to antidotes to save himself. He may remove and destroy the medicines. He may hope that the medicines will take so long in looking for him that the owner of the property will become tired of observing taboos and recall it. He may take the chance of being punished by magic since earlier thefts have not brought on him retribution. Nevertheless, they say that it is very foolish to steal and run the risk of dying from magic, and when I have asked them what proof they have that thieves are so punished they have made some such reply as, 'There have been many thefts this year. There have also been many deaths from dysentery. It would seem that many debts have been settled through dysentery.'

Magic may be an alternative to empirical means of attaining an end, but it is not so satisfactory a method. It was better in the old days, when a witch either paid compensation or was slain with a spear, than it is today when one must make magic to kill him. Magic may give a greater measure of success to an undertaking than would have been obtained without its use. Thus, as was noted earlier, natural conditions and human knowledge of them, and skill in exploiting them, ensure a harvest of termites. The use of a magical technique is secondary to the use of an empirical technique. It cannot normally replace it. It is an aid rather than a substitute.

It may be asked why Azande do not perceive the futility of their magic. It would be easy to write at great length in answer to this question, but I will content myself with suggesting as shortly as possible a number of reasons.

(1) Magic is very largely employed against mystical powers, witchcraft, and sorcery. Since its action transcends experience it cannot easily be contradicted by experience.

(2) Witchcraft, oracles, and magic form an intellectually coherent system. Each explains and proves the others. Death is proof of witchcraft. It is avenged by magic. The achievement

of vengeance-magic is proved by the poison oracle. The accuracy of the poison oracle is determined by the king's oracle, which is above suspicion.

(3) Azande often observe that a medicine is unsuccessful, but they do not generalize their observations. Therefore the failure of a single medicine does not teach them that all medicines of this type are foolish. Far less does it teach them that all magic is useless.

(4) Scepticism, far from being smothered, is recognized, even inculcated. But it is only about certain medicines and certain magicians. By contrast it tends to support other medicines and magicians.

(5) The results which magic is supposed to produce actually happen after rites are performed. Vengeance-magic is made and a man dies. Hunting-magic is made and animals are speared.

(6) Contradictions between their beliefs are not noticed by Azande because the beliefs are not all present at the same time but function in different situations. They are therefore not brought into opposition.

(7) Each man and kinship group acts without cognizance of the actions of others. People do not pool their ritual experiences. For one family a death is the starting-point of vengeance, while for another family the same death is the conclusion of vengeance. In the one case the dead man is believed to have been slain by a witch. In the other case he is himself a witch who has fallen a victim to vengeance-magic.

(8) A Zande is born into a culture with ready-made patterns of belief which have the weight of tradition behind them. Many of his beliefs being axiomatic, a Zande finds it difficult to understand that other peoples do not share them.

(9) The experience of an individual counts for little against accepted opinion. If it contradicts a belief this does not show that the belief is unfounded, but that the experience is peculiar or inadequate.

(10) The failure of any rite is accounted for in advance by a variety of mystical notions—e.g. witchcraft, sorcery, and taboo. Hence the perception of error in one mystical notion in a particular situation merely proves the correctness of another and equally mystical notion.

(11) Magic is only made to produce events which are likely

to happen in any case—e.g. rain is produced in the rainy season and held up in the dry season; pumpkins and bananas are likely to flourish—they usually do so.

(12) Not too much is claimed for magic. Generally, in the use of productive magic it is only claimed that success will be greater by the use of magic than it would have been if no magic had been used. It is not claimed that without the aid of magic a man must fail—e.g. a man will catch many termites, even though he does not use termite-medicines.

(13) Magic is seldom asked to produce a result by itself, but is associated with empirical action that does in fact produce it—e.g. a prince gives food to attract followers and does not rely on magic alone.

(14) Men are sometimes compelled to perform magic as part of their social obligations—e.g. to use vengeance-magic on the death of a kinsman.

(15) Success is often expressed in terms of magic—e.g. a successful hunter gets a reputation for magic. People therefore attribute his success to his magic whether he possesses medicines or not.

(16) Political authority supports vengeance-magic.

(17) Azande do not possess sufficient knowledge to understand the real causes of things—e.g. germination of crops, disease, etc. Having no clocks, they cannot perceive that placing a stone in a tree in no way retards sunset. Moreover, they are not experimentally inclined.

(18) Not being experimentally inclined, they do not test the efficacy of their medicines.

(19) There are always stories circulating which tell of the achievement of magic. A man's belief is backed by other people's experience contained in these stories.

(20) Most Zande medicines come to them from foreign peoples, and Azande believe that foreigners know much more about magic than they do.

(21) The place occupied by the more important medicines in a sequence of events protects them from exposure as frauds. Magic is made against unknown witches, adulterers, and thieves. On the death of a man the poison oracle determines whether he died as a victim to the magic. If the oracles were first consulted to discover the criminal, and then magic were

made against him, the magic would soon be seen to be un-successful.

(22) Zande beliefs are generally vaguely formulated. A belief to be easily contradicted by experience and to be easily shown to be out of harmony with other beliefs must be clearly stated and intellectually developed—e.g. the Zande concept of a soul of medicine is so vague that it cannot clash with experience.

CHAPTER XII

An Association for the Practice of Magic

I

Most of the magical practices which I have so far mentioned are individual rites performed by individual practitioners, either singly and for private purposes or on behalf of, and in the presence of, a client. Such is one of the characteristics of Zande magic. But during the first two decades of the present century a number of associations have arisen for the practice of magic in assemblies. They show all the qualities of associations: organization, leadership, grades, fees, rites of initiation, esoteric vocabulary and greetings, and so forth. Their purpose is the performance of magical rites, and their actions conform to patterns of magic in Zandeland: plant-medicines, rambling spells, mild taboos, blowing of whistles, cooking of medicines, etc.

Whilst caution is desirable in trying to account for the introduction of closed associations into Zandeland, we may commit ourselves to the statement that they were not only introduced after European conquest of the country, but also are functions of European rule and a sign of break-down of tradition.

All the associations are of foreign origin and none formed part of Zande culture in the Sudan forty years ago. Even today they are not incorporated into Zande social organization and may be regarded as subterranean and subversive. They are indicative of wide and deep social change.

I shall describe only of these closed associations, and I have chosen *Mani* because it is the one about which I know most. I can say without hesitation that *Mani* is typical of these associations and that the others differ from it only in the medicines they use, in the stress they lay on a particular purpose out of a number of common purposes, and in peculiarities of initiatory rites. In their organization and actions they conform monotonously to a single pattern.

My knowledge of the *Mani* association was acquired in circumstances unfavourable to observation and record. It is slight, but I do not think that there is much to record that I have not noted. There were three sources of information at my disposal. Firstly, laymen gave me their opinions about the morality of the association and told me something about its history and organization. Secondly, members described to me its rites. I refrain from mentioning their names as membership is illegal. Thirdly, I joined a lodge myself and attended a few assemblies. Since the Government of the Anglo-Egyptian Sudan has declared the association illegal and punishes its members, I was not able to make full use of these sources in a thorough investigation. I had to dig beneath the surface for most of the facts recorded in this section. Suppression has, moreover, changed the social character of the association.

I want to make it quite clear that direct observations and inquiries through informants were inadequate and not of the same quantity and quality as those on which the rest of the book is based, and also that the ritual of the association does not play nearly so important a part in the life of the people as the customs I have so far described. I have several times emphasized that witchcraft, magic, witch-doctors, and oracles form a system of reciprocally dependent ideas and practices. None could be left out of my account without seriously distorting the others. But were I to omit a description of the closed associations it would not be of great consequence. If they had not been penalized the associations might have become stable institutions. As it is, they strike one as foreign and abnormal modes of behaviour.

II

When *Mani* first entered the Sudan its members used to meet in lodges in the bush, but these are no longer built. They met in the bush because in a homestead the medicines might have been polluted, and not because they wished to hide the lodge from the notice of their prince. A lodge consisted of a miniature hut and a cleared circular space in front of it. The hut was erected to shelter the medicines, which were kept in a pot resting on three short thick stakes driven into the ground. Here the pot remained between assemblies and became filled with spiders' webs which were boiled with the medicines to increase their potency. Sometimes they built a small shrine like the shrines erected in honour of the ghosts and placed the medicine-pot on it, but members of the association say that their rites do not concern the ghosts. Members sat on the cleared circular space during the rites and afterwards danced there the *Mani* dances. The lodge was situated near a stream, as immersion in water was part of a novice's initiation.

Today meetings take place in homesteads late at night in a hut, or, where there is a palisade, under the shelter of a veranda. The small space at their disposal compels the members to sit huddled together, and when the other rites are finished they dance softly in the centre of the homestead. The medicine-pot is placed on three thin stakes which are removed after each assembly and hidden till the next meeting.

At the head of every lodge is a man called *boro basa* or *gbia ngua*, 'Man of the Lodge' or 'Master of the Medicines'. I will refer to him as lodge-leader. He obtains his title by purchase of medicines from another lodge-leader. He pays him spears, knives, piastres, pots of beer, and so forth. As is the case with transference of other Zande medicines, it is desirable that the owner shall be well pleased with the gifts made him lest his ill-will should cause the medicines to lose their power. The medicines are not bought and sold all at once, but are transferred one by one over a considerable period and each in return for a payment. The owner shows the purchaser magical plants and trees in the bush, shows him the correct type of bulb to plant near his ghost-shrine in his homestead, and supplies him with a magic whistle. When he knows all the necessary medicines the purchaser pays the owner to build a little hut to house them in his lodge. He now starts a lodge of his own, but is expected to make occasional gifts to the owner of the medicines from the proceeds of his lodge activities. Magic of this type cannot be handed over simply as a gift from relative to relative or from friend to friend because unless the medicines see that they have been bought they will lose their power. Their owner must have a title by purchase.

A lodge-leader receives wealth by selling knowledge of his medicines to others in the manner described. He also gets fees from laymen who wish to become members of the association, though he is expected to share these with their sponsors and with his lodge officials. He is made small presents by junior members of the association when they wish to stir and address the medicines about their affairs, for this is a privilege that must be paid for. Members who wish to enter a higher grade buy their seniority from the lodge-leader who, in return, shows them new medicines. He has also a large rubbing-board oracle called *yanda* which he uses, on receipt of a small present, on behalf of members who have reached the highest grade in the association.

A leader has very little authority. His position is due solely to his knowledge of magic and is maintained by fear of his medicines, by the rules of the association, and by the Zande's invariable devotion to discipline and authority in social life on the pattern of his political institutions. Organizing ability, character, and prestige in the locality also count for something. Public opinion in the lodge insists on decorum and obedience to authority in matters pertaining to the association.

Besides the leader, each lodge has a few minor officials: the *kenge*, the *uze*, and the *furushi*. The *kenge*, so called after the thin stakes on which the medicine-pot rests, is next senior to the leader, and, as he often knows the medicines, he is sent into the bush by the leader to gather them. It is his duty to erect the thin stakes, to place the medicines in a pot on the fire, and to cook them. I shall speak of him as the cook. The *uze* is so called after the stick with which the medicines are stirred in the pot, and he alone may eat them on the end of the stick. It is his duty to assist in stirring the medicines, to hand them round to other members in the lodge, and to see that everyone observes the rules and pays attention to the proceedings. I shall speak of him as the stirrer. There is also sometimes an official called *furushi*, from the Arabic word for policeman. He is told to guard the lodge from interruption and spying, and to assist the stirrer in maintaining order. I shall speak of him as the sentry. None of these officials is important. The functions of each are not rigidly restricted to the holder, and in his absence any other person can perform them. The offices are no more than slightly privileged positions in the lodge held by senior members. Members of the association are usually called *Aboro Mani*, 'People of Mani', to distinguish them from *fio*, laymen. They eat the medicines off the tips of their little fingers. You can discover whether a man is a member of the association by an exchange of secret formulae. Members also have their special greetings, but it is rare for these to be used outside the lodge. There are various grades in the association. A man enters new grades by purchase of new magic. A member of Water *Mani* can be initiated into the grade of Blue-bead *Mani* and then into the grade of Night *Mani*, or Cut-throat *Mani* as it is also called because it breaks the neck of a person who injures anyone who has partaken of the medicines. There is another grade called Thunder *Mani* because the sanction behind the medicine is thunder. Though I speak of the types of *Mani* as grades they have little hierarchical organization and are not much more than different medicines which a man acquires from time to time. Since, however, the acquisition of new medicines by purchase is often accompanied by further rites of initiation, and since a man's position in the lodge depends on the number and potency of the medicines he has eaten, we may speak of grades in the association.

What happens is that people now and again bring new *Mani* medicines from either Azande of the Congo or directly from some foreign people. A man introduces a new medicine into his lodge, and, being new, it attracts the members, some of whom are prepared to purchase it. Those who have purchased it thus become graded from those who have not partaken of it. The medicine is then diffused from the lodge of the man who introduced it to other lodges and a grade in the association comes into being. Purchase of new medicine in this way is often accompanied by a simple rite of initiation. Thus a man who purchases Fire *mani* has to wriggle like a snake under hoops placed close to the ground towards the medicines in a pot on the fire, and when a man purchases Dysentery *mani*, so called because anyone who injures the partakers of it will suffer from dysentery, he has to crawl through high hoops. Azande say that these grades have come into being through love of gain, for a man who brings a new *Mani* medicine from a foreign country is likely to make a little wealth while its novelty persists, and he sells it cheaply to tempt purchasers. Consequently many people acquire it, and the more widely owned it becomes the less people value it. This flux is typical of the changes taking place the whole time in Zande magic. Often a closed association loses its popularity, its members join a new association with the attraction of novelty, and the old one remains only a memory. This has not yet happened to *Mani*.

III

I will now summarize what happens at an assembly of a lodge when a novice is introduced to the association. I shall first describe the present-day procedure and afterwards show how the old ritual differs from it.

It is arranged that a man shall be initiated at the next meeting. Medicines are collected in advance by the lodge-leader or by one of his subordinates and the magical apparatus of stakes, withies, and creepers are gathered and set in position.

When all is ready his sponsor takes the novice by the hand and leads him from where they have been awaiting orders, some distance away, to the lodge, which today is generally a space under the veranda of a hut in an ordinary homestead, used temporarily for the rites of the association. As the novice is led forward he holds a long oval leaf over his eyes. Sometimes the old custom is still maintained of dropping a little liquid into his eyes which causes the novice a certain amount of pain and prevents him from seeing clearly for a while. On his way to the lodge his future comrades hide behind trees on the route and imitate the cries of lions and leopards, and he is told that there is a snake in the hut to which he is going. When they reach the place of the ceremony the leaf is removed from his eyes and he is greeted in the special language of the association.

The novice sees a fire in the background and between him and the fire two wooden hoops joined by a branch tied from the top of one to the top of the other, the hoops and this horizontal bough being twined with various creepers. He goes down on hands and knees and crawls under this structure from one end to the other and then back again. He repeats this performance four times, and each time as he emerges at one end the people seated there turn him round in the opposite direction. The reason given for this rite is that it fixes the medicine in the novice and prevents him from receiving its virtues superficially. He then goes and sits in front of the fire, which is separated from him by a pile of leaves, and is warned not to divulge the secrets of the association. He is admonished to obey the leader of the lodge, to behave with decorum during the meetings, and not to use the lodge for fornication or adultery. He is told what taboos he must observe and is given other instructions partly by direct admonition and partly in rambling spells.

On the fire are the *Mani* medicines and water in a pot, which rests on the heads of three stakes driven into the ground. The fire is fed by sticks thrust in between the stakes. While it is cooking, first the lodge-leader, then the higher officials and senior members, and lastly, those who lay a present before the magic take a wooden stirrer in their hands and stir the medicines in the pot and utter long spells over them, asking protection for the novice, for themselves, and for all members of the lodge against a variety of evils. Each requests special protection and success for himself. Whilst a man or woman is addressing the magic those who are sitting on the ground at the far end of the veranda space will often repeat a terminal phrase of the address like a litany. Thus, when the stirrer finishes a section of his spell by saying, 'May I be at peace,' the others will repeat in a low chorus, 'May I be at peace.'

When the various roots which compose the medicines have boiled for some time they are removed from the pot, and oil and salt are added to the water and juices. This mixture is placed on the fire and during its heating further spells are uttered over it. Members watch to see whether the oil will rise well to the surface as this is considered a good omen. When it has boiled the oil at the top is poured off into a gourd, leaving a sediment. They pour some of this oil into the novice's mouth and eyes and rub it on his skin. Senior members drink what is left or anoint themselves with it.

After the paste has cooled at the bottom of the pot lumps of it are placed on leaves and handed round to members who eat them or take bits of them home. Senior members eat out of the pot. The novice is fed by the hand of his sponsor. While the paste is still cooling in the pot members place the pot on their heads and against their breasts and hold their faces in its mouth, all the while uttering spells.

When the meal is finished the novice is given his first *Mani* name and his waist-band is removed and replaced by a length of creeper. He is given one or two magical whistles by the lodge-leader who instructs him in their use. Then his sponsor leads

him by the hand away from the veranda and the meeting closes
with the dances and songs of the association.

For several days afterwards the novice must wear his creeper-
girdle and observe certain taboos. He will then pay his sponsor
to be relieved from the more onerous taboos and his sponsor
will remove the creeper from his waist and give him his final
Mani name. He is now an initiate of *Mani*.

Before the association was prohibited procedure was different. After a spell had been said over the novice he was led
from the lodge to a nearby stream, which had been previously
blocked up to bring the water to the level of a man's waist or
knees. On his way to the stream the novice was frightened by
members of the association hiding behind trees and imitating
the cries of lions and leopards. Appearing just above the surface
of the pool were one or two hoops, and the novice had to duck
three or four times under these, each time returning whence
he came. He was said to have struck the water with his club,
meaning that he struck it with his head. He was then taken
out of the water and given his first *Mani* name. Afterwards all
returned to the lodge where magic juices were poured into the
novice's eyes, causing tears, so that he was said to be weeping
for Zabagu (Zaba), the founder of the association in the Sudan.
The medicine was then cooked and addressed as described
above. Later the novice was invested with his creeper-girdle
and was instructed in the rules and customs of the association.
Dancing then began, but was interrupted now and again to
discuss business. All returned home at dawn.

The ordinary *Mani* medicines are known as Water *Mani*
because a novice passes through water to obtain the privilege
of using them. When a man wishes to acquire the further privilege of using Blue-bead medicines he pays a fee and goes
through an additional initiation in a section of the hut shut off
by a screen of banana leaves so that ordinary members of the
association cannot see what is going on. His initiation consists
of passing under hoops and picking up blue beads between his
lips. From the tops of the hoops hang more blue beads and often
a ring fastened to a whistle. The ring, the whistle,
and one of the blue beads are presented to the novice at the end
of the ceremony. One of the rites is to tie the blue bead to the
end of a stick and hold it, while uttering spells, in the smoke and

steam arising from fire and boiling medicines. By paying another fee a member can see the rubbing-board oracle of the association and get the leader to use it on his behalf. The use of other medicines can similarly be bought, though I am not certain whether there are separate rites of initiation for each. From this précis, one important fact emerges that may be missed if it is not separately indicated. Though all members of *Mani* partake of Water *Mani* medicines, and all members of grades partake of their different medicines, only the leaders know the plants and herbs from which the medicines are taken. Any man who buys that knowledge from a leader becomes himself a leader. Otherwise his payments only enable him to make magic with the leader's medicines. Hence he can only use *Mani* medicines in the lodge in the company of other members. He cannot use them in his own home.

Nevertheless, each member acquires at initiation certain magical weapons in full ownership. Each has a whistle which he can blow, uttering spells, in the early morning before washing his face. He is warned that to blow it for illegitimate purposes is dangerous.

The blue bead also has magical power. Some people attach it to their whistles, and others keep it in oil in a tiny bottle-gourd and in difficult times anoint themselves with the oil. Its owner may also hold the bead in the smoke of a fire and utter spells over it. If the oracles tell you that a certain man is doing you an injury you may enter his homestead at night and bounce the bead on the threshold of his hut. When the man has died from your magic it must be recalled lest it harm you also. You recall it by tapping yourself on your legs, arms, head, and other parts of your body with your *Mani* whistle and by blowing water from your mouth to the ground. Finally, each member of the association is given a bulb which he plants in the centre of his homestead near his ghost-shrine. If he is depressed or frightened he can eat a piece of its leaf.

Nevertheless, in spite of private ownership of medicines and individual usage of magical weapons, there is a group action that we do not find elsewhere in the practice of Zande magic, save among witch-doctors. The rites are organized and are not merely a number of individual actions performed in rotation. Moreover, when a member is uttering a spell he speaks on behalf of the whole society as well as for himself and the other members present repeat many phrases in his spell as a litany. I have also sometimes observed heightened emotional expression at *Mani* ceremonies which I did not note at most other magical performances.

IV

Mani is spread over the whole of Zandeland. Its membership must number thousands, though it is impossible to take any kind of census. Each locality has its lodge, and a man does not know many members of the association outside his own lodge. In the past members wore a blue bead as a badge, but they are too frightened to display it today. I was told that there would often be as many as forty or fifty members present at a lodge assembly, but I have myself never observed an attendance of more than fifteen persons. Though children and old persons do not as a rule belong to the association, there are no restrictions of age or sex to enrolment. Anyone can join on payment of two or three piastres at the most [5 piastres = 1 shilling]. A piastre or two are given by the initiate to his sponsor and his sponsor hands them over to his lodge-leader. Later the novice will pay a piastre to his sponsor when he asks him to remove the waist-cord he wears when subject to food and sex taboos during initiation. The old barkcloth which a novice wears at his initiation also goes to his sponsor. A sponsor may be of either sex and a woman may sponsor a man, though this is said to be unusual. If a man sponsors a woman he ought to be either her husband or a kinsman, for otherwise serious trouble is likely to be caused by her husband and her family. One of my informants said that the same man must not sponsor both husband and wife, but he gave no reason for the prohibition.

As far as I was able to observe, men and women join the association in about equal numbers. This does not lead to improprieties in the lodge itself, but husbands are doubtless right when they say that wives attend meetings with the object of starting clandestine relations with other men and that, such is female inconstancy, no woman is able to resist adultery if an opportunity presents itself. For even if a man has no opportunity to speak to a woman at an assembly, there is, Azande

say, a language of the eyes that is as effective as language of
the lips, and if a man has no opportunities for dalliance on the
way to and from an assembly he can at least start an acquaint-
anceship which may subsequently be advanced. Hence men
strongly object to their wives joining a lodge if they are not
themselves members. Nevertheless, it sometimes happens that
a woman joins without her husband's knowledge.

Women are, indeed, keen on joining the association to obtain
magic and escape from the boredom of family life and the drud-
gery of household labour. The inclusion of women is a revolu-
tionary breakaway from custom in a society where segregation
of the sexes is rigidly enforced. Even at *Mani* assemblies women
sit apart from men and there are separate paths for the sexes
to and from the lodge. But they come into closer contact than
on most other occasions, and it is in itself remarkable that
women should be allowed to take part in the ritual at all, for
they are, with few exceptions, excluded from any part in magical performances in which men participate, and there is strict
sexual division of labour in other social activities. That women
should take equal part with men and sometimes sponsor men
and hold offices, even that of leader, in the associations, shows
that *Mani* (and the same is true of the other closed associations)
is not only a new social grouping but a social grouping which
conflicts with established rules of conduct. It is a function of
the new order of things.

Aged persons of both sexes do not as a rule join the association, and when an occasional old man joins it he prefers that
the fact shall not be widely known as it is not becoming for
a senior man to associate on equal terms with youngsters. Quite
small children are occasionally present, as they come with their
mothers and are initiated. The mass of members are youths and
maidens and young married couples. Here again we see that
the association runs counter to most Zande institutions for
among commoners the older men have everywhere control and
the younger are socially and economically dependent on them.
Mani and similar associations are a challenge to their superior
status, and they realize this and oppose them.

Mani challenges traditional patterns of behaviour not only
in relation to sex and age but also in relation to status. In almost
every activity of Zande life in which nobles take part they act

as leaders. Even in the activities in which nobles usually refrain from participating, e.g. in dancing, they assume, when they do take part in them, either the role of leader or an independent role which places them outside commoner authority. In *Mani*, though the nobles do not as a rule enter into full and regular participation in the ceremonies, and probably ruling princes never attend assemblies, when a noble becomes a member and visits a lodge he cannot act as a leader unless he happens to own the medicines. Hence, even if he is treated with the respect due to his class, he must be subordinate to a commoner in the ritual. *Mani* was introduced without the backing of the nobles and has remained a commoner grouping which derives its power and independence from its medicines. Therefore it lies outside ordinary social life where the authority of the nobles is supreme, personal, and direct. It even contradicts their authority.

v

When I asked Azande why princes should be hostile to *Mani* they gave me one or more of several reasons. They said that princes are always conservative and against the introduction of a new custom simply because it is not traditional. They were able to quote as other evidences of conservatism King Gbudwe's opposition to circumcision and to the introduction of habits of Arabic-speaking peoples. They said that princes were especially opposed to closed associations because their members built lodges far away in the bush, and because they performed rites which were only partly known to the nobles. Nobles are often ignorant of what is familiar to commoners. In boyhood they seldom depart from the courts of their kinsmen to visit the homesteads of commoners. When they grow up they are given provinces to administer and rarely travel beyond their courts and gardens. Consequently they rely mainly on information they receive from a few confidential courtiers about happenings in their provinces. These courtiers are generally old men with polygamous households and of conservative spirit. They are strongly opposed to the closed associations which, they tell their princes, lead to disloyalty and immorality. It is truly remarkable how close a watch Zande nobles and wealthy commoners keep on their wives. They spy on their every movement. It is therefore easy to understand their opposition to closed associations which allow female as well as male membership and which provide a meeting-place for the sexes.

Azande also attribute the antipathy shown by princes to their associations to jealousy. For lodge-leaders settle minor disputes between members concerning incidents in the lodge itself. Slight though their judicial functions are—for Azande have contempt for magical sanctions when engaged in serious litigation—they are thought to challenge the despotic prerogative of the princes. Because, however minor the disputes settled by lodge-leaders, they settle them in their own right; whereas in ordinary social life disputes settled by commoners are settled in virtue of authority delegated by a prince.

But perhaps the most weighty reason for noble opposition has always been fear of sorcery, for their is no certainty whether newly imported medicines are good or bad. Members of the association claim that they practise good magic, but outsiders sometimes accuse them of sorcery. The secrecy of rites and spells and the mystery surrounding initiation naturally give support to suspicions of sorcery.

None the less, according to my own observations, and from what initiates have told me, *Mani* medicines have the attributes of all good magic, for a man can ask of them only favours that will not cause loss or injury to innocent persons. He can only use the medicines against a man who has committed, or has the intent to commit, an offence recognized as such by Zande law and not against a man merely because he dislikes him. It is true that occasionally *Mani* magic is used as a weapon of offence and a man mentions the name of an enemy in the spell spoken to the medicines. Nevertheless, members declare that by the rules of the association they may only take this step after they have attempted unsuccessfully to obtain redress through the usual legal channels. They say it is only when a prince has awarded damages to a member and he cannot extract them from the defendant that the member is allowed to employ magical sanctions—e.g. when a wife leaves her husband and leads a licentious life away from him or marries another man and the husband is unable to obtain return of her bride-wealth; or when a man is injured by witchcraft or sorcery, or has been assaulted. These situations could not easily have occurred in old times, when redress for injury could generally have been obtained at a prince's court, and they may be regarded as symptomatic of social disintegration.

I do not know whether members only use magic against others when they are justified by the occasion, but such is their assertion. Laymen are sceptical of their claims because they have no proof that they are true. Hence laymen are often hostile to *Mani* and other closed associations, and commoners who attend a prince's court regularly, and regard themselves as men of higher social position than ordinary folk, seldom join them. Many laymen who are not hostile express doubt about the morality of *Mani* magic. There is no way by which an observer can reach a satisfactory conclusion about such a matter because he is never in possession of all the facts relative to it. Members say that if they were to use magic against any person who had not wronged them the magic would turn round and strike those who had sent it on its errand. But what one man considers to be a reprisal another considers to be an unprovoked attack, so that while the one says the magical weapon he is using is moral the other protests against criminal usage. Opponents of *Mani* also declare that the medicines enable members to influence court decisions, and this accusation seems justified by the spells they utter. But Azande know how to escape any criticism by verbal twistings and turnings. So members say that their medicines do not enable criminals to escape punishment for their offences but merely that if a member blows a *Mani* whistle on his way to court and asks the magic to assist him he will be able to state his case well and if condemned will receive lighter punishment than he would otherwise have suffered.

So *Mani* not only cuts across custom in relation to sex, age, and class, but confuses also the accepted division of magic into good and bad, for here some approve and some condemn instead of all being of one mind as we saw was elsewhere the case in reference to important medicines.

Finally, I wish to draw attention to the fact that *Mani* lodges are local groupings. This means that members of a lodge have already numerous social interrelations: ties of kinship, political ties, ties of blood-brotherhood, ties of initiation, and so forth; and bring a history of neighbourly friendships, enmities, and common experience with them to assemblies. I have not observed that a lodge-leader is otherwise a man of social importance in the community, though he gains some importance in virtue of his magical powers.

Each lodge is an independent unit consisting of a man who knows the medicines and those who collect to eat them in a small locality. A lodge has no relations with other lodges, but a man who has joined the association in one lodge will be recognized as a member by other lodges if he visits them. The grades are similar in the different lodges.

As a lodge is dependent on the knowledge of one or two men, and as its insignia are a few objects which are easily removed, it has little stability and permanence. The leader may leave the district and there may be no one in his particular lodge who can prepare the medicines and initiate members into the higher grades. Then people go to eat medicines at the hands of other leaders, i.e. they join a new lodge. There is nothing to prevent a man who knows the rites and medicines from starting a lodge in a district where other leaders are well established.

Conditions which may have been favourable to the spread of *Mani* have been the break-down of political authority following European conquest; the fact that some of the younger nobles have joined the association and have influenced their more powerful kinsmen in its favour or have themselves succeeded to political office; and direct conversion of a few princes. An important prince would sometimes make inquiries about the new magic and order a trusted courtier to report to him about its purpose and uses. If he were favourably impressed by the report he would send for the lodge-leader to learn more about the medicines and might even partake of them in private. Nevertheless, in questioning princes about *Mani* I found that they were even less prepared to give information than their subjects because they feared lest they might be punished by the Government if they were to show any knowledge of its ritual.

Europeans, without, it is feared, having understood the organization and purpose of these closed associations, condemned them. In the Sudan 'The Unlawful Societies Ordinance' of 1919 made them illegal, and similar measures appear to have been taken earlier in the Belgian Congo. Missionaries of every sect agree that closed associations are a menace. I do not think that *Mani* members were imprisoned by the Government of the Anglo-Egyptian Sudan during my residence in

Zandeland, but if participation in the rites of the association was tolerated Azande were unaware of their liberties, and this is not surprising, because members of other associations were often punished. Azande believed that the Government was equally hostile to all their magical associations.

The consequences of Government opposition are not easy to assess. Certainly the associations continue to flourish, but they are not easy to observe. They have now become secret, instead of merely closed, associations. Before European intervention everyone knew who were members, where lodges were situated, and when meetings took place. It was only certain rites and medicines that were kept secret from outsiders. Nowadays everything is kept as secret as possible.

CHAPTER XIII

Witchcraft, Oracles, and Magic, in the Situation of Death

I

I AM aware that my account of Zande magic suffers from lack of co-ordination. So does Zande magic. Magical rites do not form an interrelated system, and there is no nexus between one rite and another. Each is an isolated activity, so that they cannot all be described in an ordered account. Any description of them must appear somewhat haphazard. Indeed, by treating them all together I have given them a unity by abstraction that they do not possess in reality.

This lack of co-ordination between magical rites contrasts with the general coherence and interdependence of Zande beliefs in other fields. Those I have described in this book are difficult for Europeans to understand. Witchcraft is a notion so foreign to us that it is hard for us to appreciate Zande convictions about its reality. Let it be remembered that it is no less hard for Azande to appreciate our ignorance and disbelief about the subject. I once heard a Zande say about us: 'Perhaps in their country people are not murdered by witches, but here they are.'

Throughout I have emphasized the coherency of Zande beliefs when they are considered together and are interpreted in terms of situations and social relationships. I have tried to show also the plasticity of beliefs as functions of situations. They are not indivisible ideational structures but are loose associations of notions. When a writer brings them together in a book and presents them as a conceptual system their insufficiencies and contradictions are at once apparent. In real life they do not function as a whole but in bits. A man in one situation utilizes what in the beliefs are convenient to him and pays no attention to other elements which he might use in different situations. Hence a single event may evoke a number of different and contradictory beliefs among different persons.

I hope that I have persuaded the reader of one thing, namely, the intellectual consistency of Zande notions. They only appear inconsistent when ranged like lifeless museum objects. When we see how an individual uses them we may say that they are mystical but we cannot say that his use of them is illogical or even that it is uncritical. I had no difficulty in using Zande notions as Azande themselves use them. Once the idiom is learnt the rest is easy, for in Zandeland one mystical idea follows on another as reasonably as one common-sense idea follows on another in our own society.

It is in connexion with death that Zande belief in witchcraft, oracles, and magic is most coherent and is most intelligible to us. Therefore, though I have before briefly described the interplay of these notions at death it is fitting to give a slightly fuller account in conclusion, for it is death that answers the riddle of mystical beliefs.

It is not my intention to give a detailed description of Zande funeral ceremonies and vengeance. I shall not even attempt to recount the elaborate magical rites by which vengeance is accomplished, but only give the barest outline of what happens from the time a man falls sick to the time his death is avenged.

It is with death and its premonitions that Azande most frequently and feelingly associate witchcraft, and it is only with regard to death that witchcraft evokes violent retaliation. It is likewise in connexion with death that greatest attention is paid to oracles and magical rites. Witchcraft, oracles, and magic attain their height of significance, as procedures and ideologies, at death.

When a man falls sick his kinsmen direct their activities along two lines. They attack witchcraft by oracles, public warnings, approaches to the witch, making of magic, removal of the invalid to the bush, and dances of witch-doctors. They attack the disease by administration of drugs, usually summoning a leech who is also a witch-doctor, in serious sickness.

A leech attends a man till all hope of his recovery is abandoned. His relations gather and weep around him. As soon as he is dead they wail, and the relatives-in-law dig the grave. Before burial the dead man's kin cut off a piece of barkcloth and wipe his lips with it and cut off a piece of his finger-nail. These substances are necessary to make vengeance-magic.

ſometimes earth from the first sod dug when the grave is being ɔrepared is added to them.

On the day following burial steps are taken towards ven-ʒeance. The elder kinsmen of the dead man consult the poison ɔracle. In theory they ask it first whether the dead man has died as a result of some crime he has committed. But in practice, except on rare occasions when his kinsmen know that he has committed adultery or some other crime, and that the injured man has made lethal magic, this step is omitted. Not that a Zande would admit its omission. He would say that if this ques-tion were not directly put to the oracle it is contained in those questions that follow, for the oracle would not announce that their magic would be successful unless the dead man were inno-cent of crime and were a victim of witchcraft.

In practice, therefore, they first ask it to choose the man who will undertake to act as avenger. His duties are to dispatch magic on the tracks of the witch under the direction of a magi-cian who owns it, and to observe the onerous taboos that enable it to achieve its purpose. If the kin of the dead man wish to make certain of avenging him they insist on placing only the names of adults as candidates for this office, but usually senior men are anxious to avoid the ascetic routine it imposes and propose the name of a lad who is too young to feel the hardship of sex taboos and yet old enough to realize the seriousness of food taboos, and of sufficient character to observe them. They ask the oracle whether the magic will be successful in its quest if a certain boy observes the taboos. If the oracle says that it will be unsuccessful they place before it the name of another man or boy. When it has chosen a name they ask as a corrobora-tive verdict whether the boy will die during his observance of the taboos. He might die as a result of breaking a taboo or because the man they wish to avenge was slain in expiation of a crime. If the oracle declares that the boy will survive ven-geance is assured.

They then ask the poison oracle to choose a magician to provide vengeance-magic. They put before it the name of a magician and ask it whether vengeance will be accomplished if his medicine is used. If the oracle rejects one name they propose to it another.

Having chosen a boy to observe the taboos and a magician

to provide the medicines, they proceed to prosecute vengeance. I will not describe the various types of medicines employed nor the rites that dispatch them on their errand. It is not expected that they will immediately accomplish their purpose. Indeed, if people in the vicinity die shortly after the rites have been performed the kinsmen do not suppose that they are victims of their magic.

From time to time the kinsmen make presents of beer to the magician to stir up the medicines, because Azande think that they go out on their mission and, not having discovered the guilty man, return to their hiding-place. They have to be sent forth afresh on their quest by further rites. This may happen many times before vengeance has been accomplished, perhaps two years after magic has first been made, and usually not before six months afterwards. Although the taboos are only incumbent on a single boy in so far as the virtue of the magic is concerned, all near kinsmen and the spouse of the dead must respect irksome prohibitions to a greater or lesser degree, for a variety of reasons, and all are anxious to end their fast. Nevertheless, everything must be done in good order and without haste. From time to time they ask the poison oracle whether the medicines are being diligent in their search and for further assurance of ultimate success.

In the past medicine of vengeance was placed on the dead man's grave, but it is said that people interfered with it there, either removing it and plunging it into a marsh to deprive it of power, or spoiling it by bringing it into a marsh to deprive it of power, or spoiling it by bringing it into contact with some impure substance, like elephant's flesh. Today they often continue to place some medicines on the grave but they also hide others in the bush, generally in the cavity of a tree. There they are safe from contamination by ill-disposed persons.

Several months after magic has been made someone dies in the vicinity and they inquire of the poison oracle whether this man is their victim. They do not, as a rule, inquire about persons who have died several miles away from the homestead of the deceased. If the oracle tells them that the magic has not yet struck they wait till another neighbour dies and consult it again. In course of time the oracle declares that the death of a man in the neighbourhood is due to their magic and that this man is the victim whom they have slain to avenge their kins-man.

They then ask the oracle whether the slain man is the only witch who killed their kinsman or whether there is another witch who assisted in the murder. If there is another witch they wait till he also is slain, but if the oracle tells them that the man who recently died was alone responsible they go to their prince and present him with the wings of the fowl that died in declaration of the witch's guilt. The prince consults his own poison oracle, and if it states that the oracle of his subjects has deceived them they will have to await other deaths in their neighbourhood and seek to establish that one of them was caused by their magic.

When the oracle of the prince agrees with the oracle of the kinsmen vengeance is accomplished. The wings of the fowls that have died in acknowledgement of their victory are hung up, with the barkcloth and sleeping-mat of the boy who has observed taboos, on a tree at the side of a frequented path in public notification that the kinsmen have done their duty.

The owner of the medicine is now summoned and is asked to recall it. When his fee has been paid he cooks an antidote for the boy who has borne the burden of taboos, the kinsmen of the dead, and the widow; and he destroys the medicine, for it has accomplished its task. He destroys it so that it can do no further harm. Those who are close kinsmen of the dead man may now live unrestricted lives.

Thus death evokes the notion of witchcraft; oracles are con-sulted to determine the course of vengeance; magic is made to attain it; oracles decide when magic has executed vengeance; and its magical task being ended, the medicine is destroyed.

Azande say that in the past, before Europeans conquered their country, their customs were different. Provincials used the methods I have just described, but men who regularly attended court did not make magic. On the death of a kinsman they con-sulted their poison oracles and presented to their prince the name of a witch accused by them. If the prince's oracle agreed with their oracles they exacted compensation of a woman and twenty spears from the witch or slew him. In those days death evoked the notion of witchcraft; oracles denounced the witch; compensation was exacted or vengeance executed.

A List of Terms Employed
in describing Zande Customs and Beliefs

I N my use of anthropological terms I am mainly concerned with following Zande thought. I have classed under a single heading what Azande call by a single word, and I have distinguished between types of behaviour that they consider different. I am not anxious to define witchcraft, oracles, and magic as ideal types of thought, but desire to describe what Azande understand by *mangu*, *soroka*, and *ngua*. I am therefore not greatly concerned with the question whether oracles should be classed as magic; nor whether the belief that children are unlucky who cut their upper teeth before their lower teeth is a form of witchcraft; nor yet whether taboo is negative magic. My aim has been to make a number of English words stand for Zande notions and to use the same term only and always when the same notion is being discussed. For example, the Zande does not speak of oracles or taboos as *ngua*, and therefore I do not call them 'magic'. I do not here raise the question whether Azande are aware of a classification of all forms of behaviour denoted by the same term or whether the unity is merely our abstraction.

In the first column are the Zande words that stand for certain notions. In the second column are the English words that I use whenever I speak of these notions. The meaning of the terms is developed in the text, and the object of giving formal and condensed definitions is to facilitate reading, since description of some notions and actions must precede description of others. I do not want to quarrel about words, and if anyone cares to designate these notions and actions by terms other than those I have used I should raise no objection.

Mangu	(1) WITCHCRAFT-SUBSTANCE: a material substance in the bodies of certain persons. It is discovered by autopsy in the dead and is supposed to be diagnosed by oracles in the living.
	(2) WITCHCRAFT: a supposed psychic emanation from witchcraft-substance which is believed to cause injury to health and property.
	(3) WITCHCRAFT-PHLEGM: among witch-doctors *mangu* occasionally refers to a supposed substance in their bodies which they say is pro-

duced by medicines. In their opinion it is entirely different to the witchcraft-substance mentioned above. They are able to expectorate phlegm which they claim to be derived from this substance.

Boro (ira) mangu WITCH: a person whose body contains, or is declared by oracles or diviners to contain, witchcraft-substance and who is supposed to practise witchcraft.

Ngua (1) MAGIC: a technique that is supposed to achieve its purpose by the use of medicines. The operation of these medicines is a magic rite and is usually accompanied by a spell.

(2) MEDICINES: any object in which mystical power is supposed to reside and which is used in magic rites. They are usually of vegetable nature.

(3) LEECHCRAFT: the treatment of pathological conditions, whether by empirical or by magical means, through physic or surgery. Physic is treatment by administration of drugs (empirical) or medicines (magical). Surgery is manual treatment. Normally leechcraft is simple magic, but the term is given separately because it is a special department of magic and because it leaves open the question whether treatment contains an empirical element.

(4) CLOSED ASSOCIATIONS: the Azande have a number of associations for the practise of communal magic rites. Their ritual is restricted to members. In this book only the *Mani* association is described.

Sima SPELL: an address accompanying rites and forming an integral part of them. When the address is made to medicines I call it a spell. When it is made to oracles I call it an oracular address. An address to the ghosts or to the Supreme Being I call a prayer.

Boro ngua (ira ngua) (1) MAGICIAN: any person who possesses medicines and uses them in magic rites.

(2) LEECH: a person who practises leechcraft.

Gbegbere (gbigbita) ngua, kitikiti ngua (1) SORCERY (BAD MAGIC): magic that is illicit or is considered immoral.

(2) BAD MEDICINES: medicines that are used in sorcery.

Wene ngua (1) GOOD MAGIC: magic that is socially approved. Unless it is stated to the contrary, all references to magic refer to good magic.

(2) GOOD MEDICINES: medicines that are used in good magic.

Ira gbegbere (kitikiti) ngua

SORCERER: anyone who possesses bad medicines and uses them in rites of sorcery.

Gira

TABOO: the refraining from some action on account of a mystical belief that its performance will cause an undesired event or interfere with a desired event.

Soroka

ORACLES: techniques which are supposed to reveal what cannot be discovered at all, or cannot be discovered for certain, by experiment and logical inferences therefrom. The principal Zande oracles are:

(*a*) *benge*, poison oracle, which operates through the administration of strychnine to fowls, and formerly to human beings also.

(*b*) *iwa*, rubbing-board oracle, which operates by means of a wooden instrument.

(*c*) *dakpa*, termites oracle, which operates by the insertion of branches of two trees into runs of certain species of termites.

(*d*) *mapingo*, three sticks oracle, which operates by means of a pile of three small sticks.

Pa ngua (pa atoro)

DIVINATION: a method of discovering what is unknown, and often cannot be known, by experiment and logic. The instrument is here a human being who is inspired by medicines (*ngua*), or by ghosts (*atoro*), or by both.

Abinza (Avule)

WITCH-DOCTORS: a corporation of diviners who are believed to diagnose and combat witchcraft in virtue of medicines which they have eaten, by certain dances, and by leechcraft.

Mbisimo

SOUL: a supposed psychic property in persons and things that at times is separated from them.

Atoro

GHOSTS: souls of persons when finally separated from their bodies at death.

Mbori

SUPREME BEING: a ghostly being to whom the creation of the world is attributed.

In addition to terms directly derived from Zande notions, and purporting to translate them, I have found it necessary to use a number of further categories to classify both the notions themselves and the behaviour associated with them. I now list these additional terms, together with the meanings I attach to them. It should be noted that this is purely an *ad hoc* classification for descriptive purposes. If anyone should object to these terms, or wish to attach different meanings to them or to class the facts under different headings he is at liberty to do so. Terms are only labels which help us to sort out facts of the same kind from facts which are different, or are in some respects different. If the labels do not prove helpful we can discard them. The facts will be the same without their labels.

MYSTICAL NOTIONS. These are patterns of thought that attribute to phenomena supra-sensible qualities which, or part of which, are not derived from observation or cannot be logically inferred from it, and which they do not possess.

COMMON-SENSE NOTIONS. These are patterns of thought that attribute to phenomena only what men observe in them or what can logically be inferred from observation. So long as a notion does not assert something which has not been observed, it is not classed as mystical even though it is mistaken on account of incomplete observation. It still differs from mystical notions in which supra-sensible forces are always posited.

SCIENTIFIC NOTIONS. Science has developed out of common sense but is far more methodical and has better techniques of observation and reasoning. Common sense uses experience and rules of thumb. Science uses experiment and rules of Logic. Common sense observes only some links in a chain of causation. Science observes all, or many more of, the links. In this place we need not define scientific notions more clearly because Azande have none, or very few, according to where we draw the line between common sense and science. The term is introduced because we need a judge to whom we can appeal for a decision when the question arises whether a notion shall be classed as mystical or common sense. Our body of scientific knowledge and Logic are the sole arbiters of what are mystical, common-sense, and scientific notions. Their judgements are never absolute.

RITUAL BEHAVIOUR. Any behaviour that is accounted for by mystical notions. There is no objective nexus between the behaviour and the event it is intended to cause. Such behaviour is usually intelligible to us only when we know the mystical notions associated with it.

EMPIRICAL BEHAVIOUR. Any behaviour that is accounted for by common-sense notions. Such behaviour is usually intelligible to us without explanation if we see the whole of it and its effects.

Witchcraft and Dreams

AZANDE distinguish between witchcraft-dreams and oracular dreams; usually, a bad dream, i.e. a nightmare, is a witchcraft-dream and a pleasant one an oracular dream. Nevertheless, all dreams are in a sense oracular: a bad dream is regarded as both an actual experience of witchcraft and a prognostication of misfortune, for if a man is being bewitched it is obviously likely that some misfortune will follow. Also, Azande associate witchcraft with an oracular dream that foretells a misfortune, the dream and the misfortune being linked products of witchcraft. The dream is a shadow cast by witchcraft before the event it is about to produce—in a sense has already produced, though at the time the dreamer does not know what it is.

Here I give only dreams of the kind that are regarded by Azande as experiences of witchcraft. I did not find it easy to record Zande dreams, and it was yet more difficult to obtain the context in which they were experienced. Part of the information contained in this Appendix was obtained by consulting many Azande on different occasions about the sort of dreams people dream and their meanings. More intimate informants gave me detailed accounts of actual dreams, but it was very seldom that I was able to obtain an account at the time of the experience. Most of the dreams were told me a long time after they were dreamt. Owing to their dramatic character and their relation to events of importance to the dreamer they had been remembered. They thus represent highly selected samples; but their interest is not thereby diminished as they clearly show what Azande regard as typical dreams and the interpretations, both general and particular, offered by their culture. For it will be perceived that dreams have accepted interpretations, but that, here as elsewhere, a man selects from stock interpretations what suits his individual circumstances and twists accepted interpretations to meet special requirements.

It must be remembered that a bad dream is not a symbol of witchcraft but an actual experience of it. In waking life a man knows that he has been bewitched only by experiencing a subsequent misfortune or by oracular revelation, but in dreams he actually sees witches and may even converse with them. We may say that Azande see witchcraft in a dream rather than that they dream of witchcraft. Therefore a man who dreams that he is being chased by a human-headed beast for example, does not think that he has been attacked by witches during the night: he is quite certain of the matter. He has experienced it, and the only question that troubles him is who has bewitched him. In fact it would be more in accordance with Zande thought to say that it is the soul of the sleeper which has these experiences. Azande, while perceiving that the sensations of dream-happenings are not like those of daily life, are certain that in sleep the soul is released from the body and can roam about at will and meet other spirits and have adventures. Likewise they believe that a witch who is sleeping can send the soul of his witchcraft to eat the soul of the flesh of his victim. The hours of sleep are hence an appropriate setting for the psychical battle that witchcraft means to a Zande, a struggle between his soul and the soul of witchcraft when both are free to roam about at will while he and the witch are asleep.

A witch may attack a person in any form, the form being in fact of little importance, since all bad dreams are alike attacks by witchcraft. The commonest bad dreams are dreams of being chased by lions, leopards or elephants, being attacked by men with animals' heads, being seized by enemies and being unable to call for assistance, and falling from a great height without ever reaching the ground. One man told me that he fell from a high tree to the ground, where he saw a homestead occupied by strange men with white faces like Europeans. He knew it was an evil dream but could not say what misfortune it presaged. Sometimes a man is attacked by snakes. He runs away from one to find another in front of him, and they twist themselves around his arms and legs. In dreams men also see strange beasts such as *wangu*, the rainbow-snake, and *moma ime*, the water-leopard. From all such dreams men generally awake in sudden terror.

Generally in these dreams a man cannot see the face of his assailant, and often there is no circumstantial evidence which enables him to establish beyond all doubt the responsibility of any particular person. He may fall sick on waking, but even if he feels well it is advisable to consult the oracles to inquire into the meaning of a dream so that what it portends may be known in advance and warded off in good time. Azande do not always, or even usually, consult oracles about a bad dream. In most cases they ponder a while on its contents and then forget all about it unless anything untoward happens, when it is immediately linked with the dream. More than once I have heard a Zande explain in reference to some misfortune, 'Ah! that is why I dreamt a bad dream the other night. Truly dreams foretell the future!'

Sometimes a dreamer of a bad dream goes next morning to a blood-brother or relative or friend and asks him to consult the rubbing-board oracle to determine whether witchcraft has done him any harm, and who sent it to him at night. When he has discovered the name of the witch he acts in the usual way by first consulting the poison oracle for corroboration and then asking a chief's deputy to notify the witch of its findings. Men consult the oracles about dreams if they are repeated. Princes consult them if they are visited in dreams by their dead fathers and grandfathers.

Sometimes, however, a man actually recognizes the face of a witch in his dream. Kisanga was attacked by two witches, Basingbatara and his son, during sleep. They climbed on the roof of his hut and sat looking down upon him through a hole in the roof as he lay upon the ground. There was no hole in the real roof, only in the roof of the dream image. The two men had all the characters of dog-faced baboons except for their faces, which were human. Kisanga said that Basingbatara's appearance changed, now the head and belly being Basingbatara's head and belly, and now the head and belly of a baboon. After a while Basingbatara said to his son, 'You strike him,' and the youth struck him on top of the head with his spear. At this point Kisanga awoke and saw them running down the roof of his hut towards their home. Kisanga declared that he had been very ill for some weeks after this experience. He was, moreover, able to explain the motives which led to the attack. He and Basingbatara were openly on good terms, though they disliked one another. The young man who had struck Kisanga with his spear was engaged to his daughter, but there was no love lost between the two families, and a fair time after he had experienced his dream Kisanga was prosecuting them in the chief's court because the young man's brother had made advances to his wife. This was more than adultery, since the woman counted as his mother-in-law.

Sometimes a man who has not seen the face of a witch during a dream surmises that it was a certain man from previous events. Kamanga told me of a dream he had dreamt a long time ago in which, while he was lying on his bed, a creature approached who was human from shoulders to feet but with an elephant's head and tusks and trunk in the place of human head and face. Kamanga was very frightened and pretended to be asleep while squinting through his eyelashes to see what the creature was doing. The witch moved his elephant's head as though looking for him and then, after a while, went out of the hut. Kamanga immediately leapt from his bed and rushed wildly out of the hut, and, lifting his arms like a bird, flew through the air towards a nearby tree, round which he curled his legs and arms. The witch saw him fly past but was unable to locate his hiding-place. Kamanga told me without hesitation who the witch was who had come to attack him. When I asked him how he knew the man he replied that he recognized him by his body and that this man, who was surely a witch, was vowing vengeance on him because of a marriage dispute in which Kamanga had acted against his interests. When Kamanga was a boy his mother had died leaving his sister a little child who could walk but who still needed the breast. His father's sister wanted to take the child and give it milk. As she was going home with the child she met this man who had attacked Kamanga in the dream. He had been for a long time desirous of marrying her and took this opportunity to press his suit. On being refused he seized the baby and ran away with her to his homestead. At the time Kamanga was serving as a page at the court of Prince Ngere and complained to him about this man's conduct. Ngere told Kamanga that his elder brothers were to recover the child. Four of them went together and, meeting with the man and his two sons on the road, his brothers gave him a hiding while Kamanga seized the baby and ran away with her. Because he had informed the prince of the affair the man bore a grudge against him and attacked him when he was asleep. Kamanga added that the man was well known in the neighbourhood as a witch because the gardens of his neighbours did not prosper. Kamanga was uncertain what exactly would have happened had the elephant-man caught him, but he was sure that he would have been very ill.

It is interesting to compare Kamanga's account of his dream with a second account he gave me some months afterwards and which I took down in his own words:

I slept soundly and dreams came to me and I dreamt a dream. A man came in the guise of an elephant and began to attack me. This elephant stood outside my hut and put its trunk through the side of the roof and hauled me outside.

The bottom part of its body was like a man, and its head was the head of an elephant. It had hair like grass on its head, so that its head resembled the head of an aged man. I sprang in haste before it from where it threw me and began to run and run. It pursued me and I climbed a tree. It continued to pursue me and rubbed its head up against the tree and I was perched just above its back. It walked about looking for me and threw its trunk this way and that, and I was on the tree. It searched after me in vain and it moved away from this tree and went and stood some way behind it and gazed round after me. I remained there for a long time where I was and then jumped down from the tree. As it was looking round it saw me and charged furiously at me to try once again to kill me. It had only just started on its path when I awoke from the dream.

Another dream by the same youth further illustrates how events preceding, or subsequent to, a dream are related to its images, and also the manner in which dreams are interpreted by selection of happenings and persons by the affective bias of a dreamer. On the afternoon preceding the dream I had suggested to members of my household that they might lend a hand in building Kamanga's hut. This suggestion did not meet with their approval, for I afterwards learnt that they had abused him in the kitchen-hut and, so Kamanga said, would have delighted in striking him. On the following morning Kamanga told me that he was in pain down his left side. He said that in the middle of the night the souls of his companions had attacked him and beaten his left side with their fists, thus doing what they had feared to do in the daytime. When I questioned him further he said that he did not see their faces but that he knew it must be his fellow-servants. He added that though a man's body might be asleep his soul was awake.

It is difficult to know whether it is the soul of a witch who bewitches a man at night or whether this soul is different from a soul of witchcraft which does the deed independently. I think Azande have no clear beliefs on this point.

It is not uncommon to dream of composite animals (*kodikodi anya*) like the human body surmounted with an elephant's head seen by Kamanga and the man with a dog-faced baboon's head seen by Kisanga. I was told that the following creatures are seen in dreams: a creature with the face of a man, the head, beak, and body of a bird, and the tail of a snake; a creature with the face of a man, the tusks and ears of an elephant, the body of a dog, and the legs of an old man; and a creature with the face of a man, the body of a swallow, and the wings of a bat. Kisanga's wife was attacked by a man called Böli with a human face and a leopard's body. This man had made advances to her which she had rebuffed. Later she had a deep-seated abscess in the place where the leopard-man had clawed her in her dream.

It is very common for a witch to assume some of the attributes of an elephant or buffalo or water-buck, and a man who has absorbed body-medicines against witchcraft may often see a witch in human guise before he changes into an animal shape. I was told that it is not only witches who appear in dreams in animal shapes, but that a man may see a friend thus transformed and will later say to him: 'I saw you in a dream last night and you had a buffalo's head. Some witch must have presented you to me in this way,' to which his friend replies, 'Is that so? Alas, it is a bad affair if it was a witch.' In this case the notion of witchcraft is excluded by feelings of friendship, for if the man with a buffalo's head had not been a friend the dreamer would undoubtedly have dubbed him a witch.

The dreams I have recounted show us from a different angle how the notion of witchcraft is a function of misfortunes and of enmities. When a misfortune occurs that can be related to a previous dream both are alike evidences of witchcraft. The dream is an actual experience of witchcraft as is demonstrated by the misfortune that follows it. A witchcraft-dream is therefore known to presage disaster. The man is already bewitched, already doomed to some misadventure. A bad dream is like an unpropitious declaration of an oracle. In both cases the man is at the time well and happy, but he has a premonition of disaster. Indeed, the dream and the oracular indication are more than harbingers of misfortune, for they are a sign that the misfortune has already taken place, as it were, in the future. It is necessary therefore to proceed as though the misadventure had an inevitable future occurrence and to lift the doom from over the head of the victim by approaching its author in the manner already described.

We have also seen how a Zande seeks to interpret dream-experiences in the same manner as he interprets other misfortune by attributing them to machinations of his enemies. He may actually perceive these enemies in dreams; or he may know that persons who have appeared in them must be his detractors, although he has not recognized their faces, because previous events so clearly indicate these persons; or he may be in doubt about their identity and place the names of enemies before the oracles to discover among them who is the guilty party.

Other Evil Agents associated with Witchcraft

WITCHCRAFT is sometimes found in dogs and is associated with various other animals and birds. The dog has a malicious way of looking at people and is so greedy that it resembles human beings, and on account of these and other deficiencies Azande think that dogs are often witches. Their opinion is said to have been sustained by a few cases in which dogs have been proved guilty of witchcraft by judgements of the poison oracle. Azande told me that sometimes relatives of a dead man have in vain consulted the oracle about their neighbours and have at last asked it whether a dog was responsible for his death and have received an affirmative answer. No actual case of this happening was recorded.

It is difficult to say to what extent Azande take seriously the tradition that other animals are witches. In ordinary situations of daily life I have generally found that Azande treat the subject with humour, though I have seen them express alarm at the appearance or cry of an animal associated with witchcraft. This is especially so with nocturnal birds and animals which are very definitely associated with witchcraft and are even thought to be the servants of witches. Bats are universally disliked, and owls are considered very unlucky if they hoot around a homestead during the night. There is an owl called *gbuku* that cries *he he he he* at night, and when a man hears its cry he knows that a witch is abroad and blows his magic whistle and seats himself by the medicines that grow in the centre of his homestead. A jackal howling near a homestead is considered a harbinger of death.

But Azande also speak jokingly of animals as witches when nothing more is meant than that they are clever and possess powers which appear strange to man. Thus they say of a domesticated cock which crows to welcome the dawn before men can see the first signs of its approach: 'It sees the daylight within itself, it is a witch.' Azande were not surprised to find witchcraft-substance in my goat and recalled that it had tried to butt people during its lifetime and was a grumpy, ill-natured creature.

One never knows what animals in the bush have witchcraft, especially the cunning ones which appear to know everything the hunter is doing. Azande will say of an animal that eludes their nets and pits,

'It is a witch.' Though I believe that this expression ought generally to be rather translated 'As clever as a witch,' it suggests an association between great intelligence or skill and the possession of witchcraft such as we find clearly enunciated by several peoples in the Congo who, like the Azande, regard witchcraft as an organic substance.

The most feared of all these evil creatures that are classed by analogy with witchcraft is a species of wild cat called *adandara*. They live in the bush and are said to have bright bodies and gleaming eyes and to utter shrill cries in the night. Azande often say of these cats, 'It is witchcraft, they are the same as witchcraft.' The male cats have sexual relations with women who give birth to kittens and suckle them like human infants. Everyone agrees that these cats exist and that it is fatal to see them. It is unlucky even to hear their cries. I heard a cat cry one night and shortly afterwards one of my servants came to my hut to borrow a magic whistle which I had bought and which was made especially for warding off the influence of these cats. He uttered a spell and blew on the whistle and went back to his hut seemingly satisfied that he had warded off danger from our home.

A text about the cats runs thus:

A woman who bears cats has sexual congress with a male cat and then with a man. She becomes gravid with child and with cats. She is pregnant with child and with cats. When she approaches the time of labour she goes to a woman who makes a practice of delivering cats and says to her that she is in pangs of childbirth and that she wishes her to act as midwife. She rises and they go together, and having arrived at a termite mound which she has sighted they seat themselves beside it. She gives birth to cats and the midwife places them on the ground and washes them. They hide them in the termite mound and return home. The midwife says to the woman who bore the cats that she is going to grind *kurukpu* and sesame to anoint the cats with it. The woman who bore the cats assents. She grinds *kurukpu* and takes oil and brings it with her and anoints the cats with *kurukpu* and oil. The midwife returns home.

The following day she bears a child and no one knows that she has borne cats. The cats grow big and take to eating fowls. In his homestead the owner cries out on account of his fowls and says 'Who has brought cats to eat my fowls', for he does not know that his wife has given birth to the cats.

These animals are terrible, and if a man sees them he is not likely to recover but will die. There are not many women who give birth to cats, only a few. An ordinary woman cannot bear cats but only a woman whose mother has borne cats can bear them after the manner of her mother.

My personal contacts included only two cases of persons who had actually seen *adandara*; but there are a number of cases in Zande tradition. It is said of some great kings of the past that they died from sight of these cats, and I think that this is a tribute to their royal position since it took more than ordinary witchcraft, such as is responsible for the death of their subjects, to kill such famous people. It is to celebrated cases of this kind that Azande appeal if you question the authenticity of their cats. All believe firmly in their existence, and many carry magic whistles as a protection against them.

Azande often refer to Lesbian practices between women as *adandara*. They say, 'It is the same as cats.' This comparison is based upon the like inauspiciousness of both phenomena and on the fact that both are female actions which may cause the death of any man who witnesses them. In this place only a few words need to be written about Lesbianism and certain kindred practices considered unlucky by Azande. Zande women, especially in the homesteads of princes, indulge in homosexual relations by means of a phallus fashioned from roots. It is said that in the past a prince did not hesitate to execute a wife whose homosexual activities were discovered, and even today I have known a prince to expel wives from his household for the same reason. Among lesser folk, if a man discovers that his wife has Lesbian relations with other women he flogs her and there is a scandal. The husband's anger is due to his fear of the unlucky consequences that may ensue from such practices. Azande therefore speak of them as evil in the same way as they speak of witchcraft and cats as evil, and they say, moreover, that homosexual women are the sort who may well give birth to cats and be witches also. In giving birth to cats and in Lesbianism the evil is associated with the sexual functions of women, and it is to be noted that any unusual action of the female genitalia is considered unlucky. It is injurious to a man if a woman provokingly exposes her vagina to him, and it is yet more serious if she exposes her anus in the presence of men. A woman will sometimes end a family argument by exposing a part of her body in this way to her husband's eyes. These customs are mentioned here in order that the reader may appreciate that witchcraft is not the sole agent of misfortune, but that there are a number of other agencies which are thought to have an inauspicious influence over human beings, and they are also mentioned because, when Azande talk about them, they compare their inauspiciousness to that of witchcraft which is the prototype of all evil. Other unlucky agencies, such as menstruating women, could be enumerated also, but have no particular association with witchcraft.

There is one unlucky agent, however, who bears so close a resemblance to witches that he must be described here. This is the person who cuts his upper teeth first. Such a man is called an *irakörinde*; *ira*, possessor of, *kö* (a contraction of *kere*), bad, and *rinde*, teeth. He is considered unlucky but not a serious menace, like witches, since he never kills people. I have not seen a person who was known to be a possessor of bad teeth; but then, as Azande ask, how can you know whether a man is one or not? Nevertheless, people say that it is sometimes known if a baby has shown upper teeth before lower ones, and I was told that such a child would be considered a danger to the crops of neighbours, and that if its evil influence were not counteracted by magic it would run a risk of falling a victim to protective medicines. They say of such a child:

Oh, what a child to have his teeth appearing above. It is a witch. Oh protect my first-fruits lest that possessor of evil teeth goes to eat them.

For at sowing time men protect their crops against witchcraft and possessors of bad teeth. There are probably special medicines which injure possessors of bad teeth if they partake of the first-fruits of a food crop, for it is the eating of first-fruits that does the greatest harm. A man digs up some of his ground-nuts, leaving the main crop un-garnered. With these his wife makes a pasty flavouring to accompany porridge and he invites a few neighbours to partake of the meal. Should a possessor of bad teeth partake of it the whole ground-nut crop in the gardens may be ruined. Since there is no means of knowing who are possessors of bad teeth people trust in protection of magic, from fear of which possessors of bad teeth will abstain from partaking of the first-fruits of their neighbours' crops. These medicines are con-sidered at the same time to have a productive action, causing ground-nuts, eleusine, and maize to give forth abundantly.

Azande say also that a possessor of bad teeth may injure anything new besides first-fruits. If a man makes a fine new stool or bowl or pot and one of these people comes and admires it and fingers it, it will crack. I gathered that a possessor of bad teeth injures people's possessions without malice and perhaps also without intent, though Zande opinion was not very decided on this point. Nevertheless, he is responsible, since he knows of his evil influence and should avoid eating first-fruits and handling new utensils. Moreover, his father should have used magic to have rendered him innocuous as soon as he discovered the abnormality. He has therefore only himself to blame if he suffers injury from protective magic. I have never heard that people consult oracles to find out which possessor of bad teeth has injured their possessions, and consequently they are not identified. When a Zande has suffered an injury he asks about witchcraft, not about bad teeth. Moreover, except for making protective magic against possessors of bad teeth, there is no special social behaviour associated with them. Azande do not treat them very seriously, and it is very seldom that one hears them mentioned.

Some Reminiscences and Reflections
on Fieldwork

I HAVE often been asked how one goes about fieldwork, and how we fared in what must seem to them those distant days. It had not occurred to me as clearly as it should have done that the information we gathered and published might some time or other be scrutinized and evaluated to some extent by the circumstances of one kind or another in which we conducted our research. So I have jotted down these notes as a fragment of anthropological history.[1]

I

That charming and intelligent Austrian-American anthropologist Paul Radin has said that no one quite knows how one goes about fieldwork. Perhaps we should leave the question with that sort of answer. But when I was a serious young student in London I thought I would try to get a few tips from experienced fieldworkers before setting out for Central Africa. I first sought advice from Westermarck. All I got from him was 'don't converse with an informant for more than twenty minutes because if you aren't bored by that time he will be'. Very good advice, even if somewhat inadequate. I sought instruction from Haddon, a man foremost in field-research. He told me that it was really all quite simple; one should always behave as a gentleman. Also very good advice. My teacher, Seligman, told me to take ten grains of quinine every night and to keep off women. The famous Egyptologist, Sir Flinders Petrie, just told me not to bother about drinking dirty water as one soon became immune to it. Finally, I asked Malinowski and was told not to be a bloody fool. So there is no clear answer, much will depend on the man, on the society he is to study, and the conditions in which he is to make it.

Sometimes people say that anybody can make observations and write a book about a primitive people. Perhaps anybody can, but it may not be a contribution to anthropology. In science, as in life, one finds only what one seeks. One cannot have the answers without knowing what the questions are. Consequently the first imperative is a rigorous training in general theory before attempting field-research so that one may know how and what to observe, what is signifi-

[1]. This paper is based on talks given in the Universities of Cambridge and Cardiff.

cant in the light of theory. It is essential to realize that facts are in themselves meaningless. To be meaningful they must have a degree of generality. It is useless going into the field blind. One must know precisely what one wants to know and that can only be acquired by a systematic training in academic social anthropology.

For instance, I am sure that I could not have written my book on Zande witchcraft in the way I did or even made the observations on which it is based had I not read the books written by that noble man Lévy-Bruhl, and I doubt whether I could ever have convinced myself that I was not deluding myself in my description and interpretation of the lineage system of the Nuer had I not, almost suddenly, realized that Robertson Smith had presented, in almost the same words as I was to use, a similar system among the Ancient Arabians. I do not think I could have made a contribution to an understanding of the political structure of the Shilluk and Anuak if I had not been deep in mediaeval studies. And I could not have written as I did about the Sanusi had I not had in my mind the model of the history of other religious movements. These last examples illustrate a further point. Strictly speaking, mediaeval Europe and religious movements might be held to lie outside social anthropological studies, but on reflection it might be accepted that this is not really so, that all knowledge is relevant to our researches and may, though not taught as anthropology, influence the direction of our interests and through them our observations and the manner in which we finally present them. Moreover, one may say that since what we study are human beings the study involves the whole personality, heart as well as mind; and therefore what has shaped that personality, and not just academic background: sex, age, class, nationality, family and home, school, church, companions—one could enumerate any number of such influences. All I want to emphasize is that what one brings out of a field-study largely depends on what one brings to it. That has certainly been my experience, both in my own researches and in what I have concluded from those of my colleagues.

It used to be said, and perhaps still is, that the anthropologist goes into the field with preconceived ideas about the nature of primitive societies and that his observations are directed by theoretical bias, as though this were a vice and not a virtue. Everybody goes to a primitive people with preconceived ideas but, as Malinowski used to point out, whereas the layman's are uninformed, usually prejudiced, the anthropologist's are scientific, at any rate in the sense that they are based on a very considerable body of accumulated and sifted knowledge. If he did not go with preconceptions he would not know what and how to observe. And of course the anthropologist's observations are biased by his theoretical dispositions, which merely means that he is aware of various hypotheses derived from existing knowledge and deductions from it and, if his field data permit, he tests these hypotheses. How could it be otherwise? One cannot study anything without a theory about its nature.

On the other hand, the anthropologist must follow what he finds in the society he has selected for study: the social organization of its people, their values and sentiments and so forth. I illustrate this fact from what happened in my own case. I had no interest in witchcraft when I went to Zandeland, but the Azande had; so I had to let myself by guided by them. I had no particular interest in cows when I went to Nuerland, but the Nuer had, so willy-nilly I had to become cattle-minded too.

It will have been evident from what has already been said that it is desirable that a student should make a study of more than one society, though this is not always, for one reason or another, possible. If he makes only a single study it is inevitable that he will view its people's institutions in contrast to his own and their ideas and values in contrast to those of his own culture; and this in spite of the corrective given by his previous reading of anthropological literature. When he makes a study of a second alien society he will approach it and see its people's culture in the light of his experience of the first—as it were through different lenses, in different perspectives—and this is likely to make his study more objective, or at any rate give him fruitful lines of inquiry which might possibly not otherwise have occurred to him. For instance, Azande have kings and princes and a fairly elaborate political organization and bureaucracy. When I went to live among the Nuer after many months among the Azande, I found that although they had quite substantial political groups there appeared to be no political authority of any significance; so naturally I asked myself what gave a sense of unity within these tribal groups, and in the course of my inquiries I was led to unravel their lineage system. Then, while the Azande were deeply concerned with witchcraft, the Nuer appeared to be almost totally uninterested in the notion or in any similar notion, so I asked myself to what they attributed any misfortune or untoward event. This led to a study of their concept of *kwoth*, spirit, and eventually to my book on their religion.

The study of a second society has the advantage also that one has learnt by experience what mistakes to avoid and how from the start to go about making observations, how to make short-cuts in the investigation, and how to exercise economy in what one finds it relevant to relate, since one sees the fundamental problems more quickly. It has its disadvantage that the writing-up period is greatly extended— I have still published only a portion of my Zande notes taken down during a study begun in 1927! It is the British intense emphasis of field-research which certainly in part accounts for the demise of the once much-extolled comparative method. Everyone is so busy writing up his own field-notes that no one has much time to read books written by others.

The importance of a thorough grounding in general theory begins to reveal itself when the fieldworker returns home to write a book about the people he has studied. I have had much, too much, field-experience, and I have long ago discovered that the decisive battle is not fought in the field but in the study afterwards. Anyone who is not a complete idiot can do fieldwork, and if the people he is working among have not been studied before he cannot help making an original contribution to knowledge. But will it be to theoretical, or just to factual, knowledge? Anyone can produce a new fact; the thing is to produce a new idea. It has been my woeful experience that many a student comes home from the field to write just another book about just another people, hardly knowing what to do with the grain he has been at such pains to garner. Can it be too often said that in science empirical observation to be of value must be guided and inspired by some general view of the nature of the phenomena being studied? The theoretical conclusions will then be found to be implicit in an exact and detailed description.

II

This brings me to what anthropologists sometimes speak of as participant-observation. By this they mean that in so far as it is both possible and convenient they live the life of the people among whom they are doing their research. This is a somewhat complicated matter and I shall only touch on the material side of it. I found it useful if I wanted to understand how and why Africans are doing certain things to do them myself: I had a hut and byre like theirs; I went hunting with them with spear and bow and arrow; I learnt to make pots; I consulted oracles; and so forth. But clearly one has to recognize that there is a certain pretence in such attempts at participation, and people do not always appreciate them. One enters into another culture and withdraws from it at the same time. One cannot really become a Zande or a Nuer or a Bedouin Arab, and the best compliment one can pay them is to remain apart from them in essentials. In any case one always remains oneself, inwardly a member of one's own society and a sojourner in a strange land. Perhaps it would be better to say that one lives in two different worlds of thought at the same time, in categories and concepts and values which often cannot easily be reconciled. One becomes, at least temporarily, a sort of double marginal man, alienated from both worlds.

The problem is most obvious and acute when one is confronted with notions not found in our own present-day culture and therefore unfamiliar to us. Such ideas as God and soul are familiar and with some adjustment transference can readily be made, but what about beliefs in witchcraft, magic, and oracles? I have often been asked whether, when I was among the Azande, I got to accept their ideas about witchcraft. This is a difficult question to answer. I suppose you can say I accepted them; I had no choice. In my own culture, in the climate of thought I was born into and brought up in and have been conditioned by, I rejected, and reject, Zande notions of witchcraft. In their culture, in the set of ideas I then lived in, I accepted them; in a kind of way I believed them. Azande were talking about witchcraft daily, both among themselves and to me; any communication was well-nigh impossible unless one took witchcraft for granted. You cannot have a remunerative, even intelligent, conversation with people about something they take as self-evident if you give them the impression that you regard their belief as an illusion or a delusion. Mutual understanding, and with it sympathy, would soon be ended, if it ever got started. Anyhow, I had to act as though I trusted the Zande oracles and therefore to give assent to their dogma of witchcraft, whatever reservations I might have. If I wanted to go hunting or on a journey, for instance, no one would willingly accompany me unless I was able to produce a verdict of the poison oracle that all would be well, that witchcraft did not threaten our project; and if one goes on arranging one's affairs, organizing one's life in harmony with the lives of one's hosts, whose companionship one seeks and without which one would sink into disorientated craziness, one must eventually give way, or at any rate partially give way. If one must act as though one believed, one ends in believing, or half-believing as one acts.

Here arises a question with regard to which my colleagues have not always seen eye to eye with me. In writing about the beliefs of primitive peoples does it matter one way or the other whether one accords them validity or regards them as fallacious? Take witchcraft again. Does it make any difference whether one believes in it or not, or can one just describe how a people who believe in it, think and act about it, and how the belief affects relations between persons? I think it does make a difference, for if one does not think that the psychic assumptions on which witchcraft-beliefs are based are tenable, one has to account for what is common-sense to others but is incomprehensible to oneself. One is in a different position with regard to belief in God, or at any rate I was. We do not think that witchcraft exists, but we have been taught that God does, so we do not here feel that we have to account for an illusion. We have only to describe how a people think of what we both regard as a reality and how in various ways the belief influences their lives. The atheist, however, is faced with the same problem as with witchcraft and feels the need to account for an illusion by various psychological or sociological hypotheses. I admit that this is a very difficult philosophical question, for it might reasonably be asked why, other than in faith, should one accept God and not witchcraft, since it could be held, as many anthropologists do, that the evidence for the one is no greater than for the other. The point is, I suppose, that in our culture (leaving out past history and modern scepticism) the one makes sense and the other not. I raise the question even if I cannot give a very satisfactory answer to it. After all, it does make a difference whether one thinks that a cow exists or is an illusion!

Since this question of entering into the thought of another people has been raised, I might touch on a further implication. I wonder whether anthropologists always realize that in the course of their fieldwork they can be, and sometimes are, transformed by the people they are making a study of, that in a subtle kind of way and possibly unknown to themselves they have what used to be called 'gone native'. If an anthropologist is a sensitive person it could hardly be otherwise. This is a highly personal matter and I will only say that I learnt from African 'primitives' much more than they learnt from me, much that I was never taught at school, something more of courage, endurance, patience, resignation, and forebearance that I had no great understanding of before. Just to give one example: I would say that I learnt more about the nature of God and our human predicament from the Nuer than I ever learnt at home.

III

It is an academic issue of some importance and one which is often confused and sometimes leads to rancour: what is the difference between sociology and social anthropology? I have discussed this question elsewhere and will not go into it again here, especially as it is only peripheral to my topic. But I would like to touch on a query put to me from time to time by sociology students: why do anthropologists in their fieldwork not employ some of the techniques used by sociologists in theirs, such as questionnaires, sampling, interviews, statistics and so forth. The answer is that, though I suppose the situation is now somewhat different, in my day the use of such techniques among a primitive people would not have been to any extent worthwhile, or even possible at all. The peoples I worked among were totally illiterate, so the distribution of questionnaires would have been a waste of time. With a homogeneous rural or semi-nomadic people sampling, such as is required in a socially heterogeneous urban community in our own country, is not only unnecessary but more or less meaningless. Set interviews in the anthropologist's hut or tent, as distinct from informal conversations are generally impossible because natives would not co-operate; and in any case they are undesirable because they are held outside of the context of a people's activities. I made it a rule never to take a notebook with me in public, not that people would have had any idea of what I was doing but because I felt that somehow a notebook came in between them and me and broke our contact. I memorized what I saw and heard and wrote it down when I got back to the privacy of my abode. Statistics have a very limited value even when the required numerical data can be obtained—had I asked a Nuer woman how many children she had borne she simply would not have told me, and had I asked a Nuer man how many cattle he possessed he would have, unless he knew me very well indeed, all too likely have withdrawn into an unbroken taciturnity, or perhaps have been violent.

When I say that in my time set interviews were out of the question, private conversations with a few individuals, those whom anthropologists call informants (an unfortunate word) must be excluded. There are certain matters which cannot be discussed in public; there are explanations which cannot be asked for on the spot (as for instance during a funeral or a religious ceremony) without intruding and causing embarrassment; and there are texts to be taken down, which can only be done in seclusion. It is necessary, therefore, to have confidential informants who are prepared to attend regular sessions, maybe daily; and it is evident that they must be men of integrity, truthful, intelligent, knowledgeable, and genuinely interested in your endeavours to understand the way of life of their people. They will become your friends. Among the Azande I relied mostly on my two personal servants and on two paid informants, but as usual in Africa, there were always people connected with them coming in and out of my home. The one young man whom I came across who was capable of writing Zande was for a time my clerk, having been sacked from the C.M.S. Mission for having married a divorced woman. Among the Nuer and Anuak and Bedouin I never found anyone who could, or would, become an informant in the sense I have set forth above, and so I had to do the best I could, gathering information from all and sundry. One has to be very careful in one's selection of informants, if one has the opportunity to be selective, for it may be found that it is only a particular sort of person who is prepared to act in this capacity, possibly a person who is ready to serve a European as the best way of escaping from family and other social obligations. Such a man may give a slant to one's way of looking at thing a perspective one might not get from others.

Sometimes it is said that the anthropologist is often hoodwinked
and lied to. Not if he is a good anthropologist and a good judge of
character. Why should anyone lie to you if there is trust between you?
And if there is not, you might as well go home. If you are in the hands
of an interpreter it is true that it can be a hazard, but if you speak
the native language you can check and re-check. It would be improbable in these circumstances, unless everybody is telling the same story,
for a man to get away with an untruth. There may be, and very often
is, a difference, sometimes a considerable difference of opinion
between one informant and another about a fact, or its interpretation,
but this does not mean that either is telling a lie. Natives are not all of
the same opinion any more than we are; and some are better informed
than others. There may, of course, be secret matters about which an
informant does not wish to speak and he may then prevaricate and
put you off from pursuing a line of inquiry for one reason or another.
Till towards the end of my stay among the Azande my inquiries, even
among those I knew and trusted most, about their secret societies
met with lack of response. Informants, who were members of these
societies, pretended to know nothing about them. As they were sworn
to secrecy they could scarcely have done otherwise. However, to an
observant anthropologist a lie may be more revealing than a truth,
for if he suspects, or knows, that he is not being told the truth he asks
himself what is the motive of concealment and this may lead him into
hidden depths.

Perhaps here is the place to discuss another question which has frequently been put to me. Does one get the native view about life (and
about women) from men only or can one get to know the women as well
and see things from their viewpoint? Much depends on the people
one is studying and the status of women among them. During an abor-
tive (war broke out) field-study in an Upper Egyptian (Quft) village
I never spoke to a woman or even had more than a flitting sight of
one at night. Bedouin women in Cyrenaica did not veil and could
be conversed with if not with intimacy, at least without embarrassment. The Zande women were almost an inferior castle, and unless elderly matrons, shy and tongue-tied. In Nuerland, where women
have high status and assert their independence, they would come and
talk to me whenever they chose, often at times most inconvenient to
me. It seemed to be an endless flirtation. Certainly it was they and
not I, who made the going. On the whole I would say that the male
anthropologist, not fitting into native categories of male and female
and not therefore being likely to behave as a male in certain circumstances might be expected to behave, does not come within their range
of suspicions, judgements and codes. In a sense he is, since he lies outside their social life, however much he may try to identify himself

with it, sexless. For example, nobody in Zandeland objected to my chatting to their womenfolk, but had an unrelated Zande done so there would have been serious trouble; in pre-European days indemnity would have been demanded or emasculation would have ensued.

It is asking a rather different question, whether a woman anthropologist can obtain more, or better, information about women's habits and ideas than a man can. Here again much depends on the kind of society. Obviously in an urban Moslem society, where women are secluded in hareems only a woman has access to them. But I would say that elsewhere I have seen little evidence that female anthropologists have done more research into woman's position in society and in general their way of life than have male anthropologists. I would add that I doubt whether it is even an advantage for an anthropologist to be accompanied by his wife in the field. They then form a little closed community of their own, making it difficult for both to learn the native language quickly and correctly and to make the required transference which only the feeling of need for close company and friendship can force a man to make. However, I would imagine that the man with a wife in the field gets at least better fed; but since I was not married when I did my research this hardly comes within my reminiscences. But I cannot resist the observation that, as I see it, what eventually ruined our relations with the peoples of the Southern Sudan were motor-cars and British wives.

Another matter which has some bearing on the subject of informants is the anthropologist's relations with other Europeans in the areas in which he is working. In the Southern Sudan in my day this presented no great problem. There were only a handful of administrative officials, a few missionaries and an occasional doctor. With one or two exceptions, I found them kindly, hospitable, and willing to be helpful. Sometimes they were able to give me information which, though it was not always accurate or from an anthropological point of view adequate, saved me time and enabled me at least to make a start. This was particularly the case with the American Presbyterian missionaries in Nuerland, with Mr. Elliot Smith among the Anuak, and Archdeacon Owen among the Luo of Kenya. In this matter the anthropologist has to be wise. After all he is, so to speak, an intruder into their territory, a territory about which they have often and for a long time been considered, and considered themselves to be, the main or even sole authority. There is no need or purpose in his being condescending, and if he has got the sense not to be, they will not in my experience hold back a willing hand. Let him therefore always remember that, at any rate at the beginning of his research, though he may know more general anthropology than they, they possibly know more about the local ethnographical facts than he. Also let him remind himself that if he cannot get on with his own people he is unlikely to get on with anyone. And, furthermore, they are part of what he is supposed to be studying.

But I must caution students not to accept, above all in religious matters, what they may find in mission literature. The missionary generally only knows a language outside of the context of native life and therefore may well miss the full meaning of words which only that context can give him. The fact that he has been among a people for a long time proves nothing: what counts is the manner and mode of his residence among them and whether God has given him, among other blessings, the gift of intelligence. I have advised caution above all in religious matters. It is, or should be, obvious that since the natives do not understand English the missionary in his propaganda has no option but to look in the native language for words which might serve for such concepts as 'God', 'soul', 'sin' and so forth. He is not translating native words into his own tongue but trying to translate European words, which he possibly does not understand, into words in a native tongue, which he may understand even less. The result of this exercise can be confusing, even chaotic. I have published a note on the near idiocy of English hymns translated into Zande. Missionaries, for instance, have used the word *mbori* in Zande for 'God', without any clear understanding of what the word means to the Azande themselves. Even worse things have happened in the Nilotic languages, or some of them. I am not going to pursue this matter further now beyond saying that in the end we are involved in total entanglement, for having chosen in a native language a word to stand for 'God' in their own, the missionaries endow the native word with the sense and qualities the word 'God' has for them. I suppose they could hardly have done otherwise. I have not in the past made this criticism of missionaries because I did not wish to give offence and because I thought any intelligent person could make it for himself.

Here might be a suitable place to discuss a related topic. How much help can the anthropologist get from technical experts who have worked in his area of research—agronomists, hydrologists, botanists, doctors, vets and others? The answer is that he can gain information he cannot himself obtain and that some of it may be relevant to his own problems and lines of inquiry. Only he can judge what has relevance and what has not. Succinctly stated, a physical fact becomes a social one when it becomes important for a community and therefore for the student of it. That the Azande are unable, whether they would wish to or not, to keep domesticated animals, other than dog and fowl, on account of *tsetse morsitans* is obviously a fact important to know, but knowledge of the pathology of the trypanasomes is not going to shed much light on the social effects of what they do. But one must beware of accepting what anyone tells you about native life, whatever his special qualifications may be. An awful example would be de Schlippe's book on Zande agriculture, for what he describes in it are less Zande modes of cultivation than those imposed on the Azande by the Government of the Anglo-Egyptian Sudan. Had de Schlippe been able to speak and understand the Zande language he might have realized this. Also beware of a joint team of research. It can only lead to waste of time and irritation. Meyer Fortes told me that when he was in such a team in Ghana he spent much of his time and energy in trying to explain to other members of the team the significance of their observations, and when I became a member of a team for study in Kenya I was the only member of it who turned up and did anything. When I did my research in the Sudan there were no agronomists, entomologists, and so on, so I had to do the best I could to be my own expert. Perhaps it was just as well.

All that was required in one's dealings with Europeans in a country ruled by the British were tact and humility. Things have changed. In the first place, it has become increasingly difficult, often impossible, to conduct anthropological research in many parts of the world. Clearly, at present, one would be unlikely to be encouraged to do so in Soviet Russia, and at any rate some of its satellites, or in China. In present circumstances I would not, though I speak Arabic, care to try to do research in most of the Arab lands. Even were I given permission to do so, there would be constant supervision and interference. In such countries the anthropologist is regarded as a spy, his knowledge likely to be used in certain circumstances by the Intelligence of his country; and he is also resented as a busybody prying into other people's affairs.

Even when this is not the case and in countries where no acute political issues are involved, there may be, and I think generally is, a hostile attitude to anthropological inquiries. There is the feeling that they suggest that the people of the country where they are made are uncivilized, savages. Anthropology smells to them as cultural colonialism, an arrogant assertion of European superiority—the white man studying the inferior black man; and they have some justification for their suspicions and resentment, for anthropologists have in the past only too readily lent and sold themselves in the service of colonial interests. The late Dr. Nkrumah once complained to me that anthropologists tried to make the African look as primitive as possible: photographing people in the nude and writing about witchcraft and fetishes and other superstitions and ignoring roads, harbours, schools, factories, etc. Indeed, anthropology has, I think rather unfairly, and without its intentions and achievements being really understood, become a bad word for the peoples of new and independent states, perhaps especially in Africa. So I have for many years advised students about to embark on fieldwork to claim that they are historians or linguists, subjects which no one can take offence at; or they can talk vaguely about sociology.

On the question of the length of fieldwork, I would say that a first study of a people takes, if it is to be thorough, up to two years. (My stay among the Azande was twenty months.) I do not think it can be much less (in spite of the American way of doing research). Ideally, the programme would be something like a year in the field and then a break of some months to chew the cud on what one has gathered, discussing with friends problems that have arisen in the course of one's work, and sorting out what has been omitted and overlooked during it. Then back to the field for another year. This has not always, or even often, proved to be possible. Furthermore, a student must, if anything is to become of his research, have at least another year for writing-up. This, again, is not always, or even often, possible, and the fieldworker may be compelled to accept a post in which he is plunged into teaching, and the results of his research become stale. How often has this not happened?

IV

Obviously the most essential of all things the anthropologist must have in the conduct of his inquiries is a thorough knowledge of the language of the people about whom he is going to tell us. By no other path can their thought (which is what I have myself chiefly been interested in and why I have spent a lifetime in anthropology) be understood and presented. So in the researches I have made, other than the ethnographical surveys (through the medium of Arabic) to oblige Prof. Seligman, I have struggled with and mastered the native language— Zande, Nuer, Anuak, Bedouin, Arabic, and even Luo and Galla to some extent. All English anthropologists today, unlike their predecessors, Rivers, Haddon, Seligman and others, would pay at any rate lip-service to this requirement and would claim that they have spoken native tongue well. They may have done so, but they seldom display evidence of their ability. Even when I have little doubt that they understood languages, a critic may, and probably will, at some time in the future ask what their credentials are. In the past these could be presented in the form of texts (with translations), but today this cannot be accepted as certain evidence, for as most 'primitive' societies become literate it is possible for the anthropologist, as it was seldom, often never, possible in my day, to find people to write his texts for him and to translate them. I met only one Zande who could write at all coherently, while among the Nuer, Anuak, Bedouin Arabs and other peoples there was no one; so I had to take down texts myself, and in the hard way, there being at that time no tape-recorders, an instrument not always an advantage. Being brought up on Greek and Latin, texts were for me a necessary accomplishment and my passion for them was inflamed by Malinowski who in his turn had been inspired in this matter by the Egyptologist Sir Alan Gardiner. The trouble, however, is to get vernacular texts published—who can or wants to read them? I have done my best for Zande. It has cost me much time and money; and I have given up all hope of publishing others in that language or in other languages.

One of the things I have often been asked is how does an anthropologist make even a start in his study of a primitive society. I must answer the question in the light of my own experience, which may not be quite the same as that of others working in different conditions.[2] It helped of course that most of my research was carried out in a country, the Sudan, at that time ruled by the British and with a government and its officers friendly disposed to anthropological research. What helped also, I think, and even more, was that the British were few and far between, that in other words one could be liked or disliked, accepted or rejected, as a person and not as a member of a class of persons (which was very unlike Kenya, where it was hard to decide who were the more unpleasant, the officials or the settlers, both of whom were so loathed by the Africans that it was difficult for a white anthropologist to gain their confidence). But given favourable conditions, such as generally obtained in the Sudan, it has always seemed to me to be perfectly simple to walk into a so-called primitive society and sojourn there. Why should anybody object since one does no harm and is a guest? Would not I feel the same if one of them came to live near me? I did not expect, as some American anthropologists appear to, to be loved. I wanted to give and not to be given to; but I was always received with a kindly welcome—except among the Nuer, but they were bitterly hostile to the Government at the time. I suppose that if one knows one is going to be so received one just turns up and hopes to get to know people, and in my experience they are happy to be known. It may happen that an anthropologist who has encountered difficulties among one people might not have done so among another. To this extent it could be said that there is an element of chance.

There are really no directions that can be imparted about how one

---

[2] *Notes and Queries* was certainly of little help to me. I carried my books in my head, but for the record I will say this: before I went to Nuerland I talked over with Max Gluckman the problem of books and we decided that if I could take only one to guide me it should be Lowie's *Primitive Society*. It was a very good choice.

gets to know people. Somehow or another one finds a couple of servants, or more likely they find you, and one or two men who are prepared for a reward to teach you the language; and these people tend to identify themselves with you so that nothing you possess is 'yours' any more, it is 'ours'. Then they get some kudos for having—I was going to say owning—their white man, and are happy to introduce him to their families and friends, and so it goes on. There is an initial period of bewilderment, one can even say of despair, but if one perseveres one eventually breaks through. I have always found that the best way, largely unintentional on my part, of overcoming my shyness and sometimes my hosts' suspicion has been through the children, who do not have the same reserve towards a stranger, nor if it comes to that, did I on my side towards them. So I started among the Azande by getting the boys to teach me games and among the Nuer by going fishing every morning with the boys. I found that when their children accepted me their elders accepted me too. Another tip I venture to give is not to start trying to make inquiries into social matters—family, kin, chieftainship, religion or whatever it may be before the language has to some extent been mastered and personal relationships have been established, otherwise misunderstandings and confusions may result which it may be difficult to overcome. Anyhow if you do what I did, refuse, or are unable, to make use of an interpreter you cannot in the early stages of research inquire into such matters. The way to begin is to work steadily for twelve hours a day at learning the language, making use of everybody you meet for the purpose. That means that you are their pupil, an infant to be taught and guided. Also people easily understand that you want to speak their language, and in my experience in your initial gropings they are sympathetic and try to help you. The strictest teachers were the Nuer, who would correct me, politely but firmly, if I pronounced a word wrongly or was mistaken in its meaning. They were quite proud of their pupil when he began to talk more or less intelligibly. Then, being mute to begin with, one learns each day through the eye as well as by the ear. Here again it seems to people both innocent and reasonable, if sometimes a bit amusing, that you should, since you have sprung up from nowhere, to join them, take an interest in what is going on around you and learn to do what they do: cultivating, pot-making, herding, saddling camels, dancing, or whatever it may be.

I will only add to these random remarks that I have always advised students going into the field to begin by learning a few new words each day, and by noting material things. Every social process, every relationship, every idea has its representation in words and objects, and if one can master words and things, nothing can eventually escape one. A final hint: get away from servants and regular informants from time to time, and meet people who do not know you; then you will know how badly you are speaking their tongue!

V

It may well be asked, and it sooner or later has to be, what should one record about a people one makes a study of and how much of the record should one publish. I have always held, and still hold, that one should record in one's notebooks as much as possible, everything one observes. I know that this is an impossible task, but long after, maybe many years after one has left the field and one's memory has faded, one will be glad that one has recorded the most familiar and everyday things—what, how, and when people cook, for example. I have now lived to regret that I did not always do so. And how much that goes into the notebooks should go into print? Ideally, I suppose, everything, because what is not published may be, and generally is, forever lost—the picture of a people's way of life at a point of time goes down into the dark unfathomed caves. And one cannot know how valuable what may appear to one at the time to be a trifle may be to a student in the future who may be asking questions which one did not ask oneself. I feel it therefore to be a duty to publish all one knows, though this is a burden hard to be borne—and publishers think so too. One is burdened for the rest of one's life with what one has recorded, imprisoned in the prison one has built for oneself, but one owes a debt to posterity.

It may be here that I should make a protest about anthropologists' books about peoples. A certain degree of abstraction is of course required, otherwise we would get nowhere, but is it really necessary to just make a book out of human beings? I find the usual account of field-research so boring as often to be unreadable—kinship systems, political systems, ritual systems, every sort of system, structure and function, but little flesh and blood. One seldom gets the impression that the anthropologist felt at one with the people about whom he writes. If this is romanticism and sentimentality I accept those terms.

E. E. Evans-Pritchard

Suggestions for Further Reading

THE first and most obvious advice to the student whose appetite has been whetted by this abridgement is to go on and read the full, original version of E. E. Evans-Pritchard's *Witchcraft, Oracles, and Magic among the Azande.* An abridgement, necessarily, leaves out a great deal; in this instance I have had, very regretfully, to exclude a vast number of case-histories and examples, which are not only interesting and delightful in themselves but made up much of the value and rich intrinsic character of the original book. So the first suggestion for further reading must be:

EVANS-PRITCHARD E. E.: *Witchcraft, Oracles, and Magic among the Azande.* Oxford, The Clarendon Press, 1937.

Other suggestions may be grouped under the following headings:

(A) *Further material about the Azande*

EVANS-PRITCHARD E. E.: *The Azande: History and Political Institutions.* Oxford, The Clarendon Press, 1971.

Contains the author's earlier writings on aspects of Zande history, culture and political institutions, preceded by a new Preface and followed by a good Bibliography of the early travellers and explorers who visited the area.

SINGER A. and STREET B. V. (eds.): *Zande Themes.* Oxford: Basil Blackwell, 1972.

Essays presented to Evans-Pritchard by a number of his pupils, dealing with different aspects of Zande society.

REINING C. C.: The Zande Scheme. Evanston, Illinois: Northwestern University Press, 1966.

An informative book on the later history of the Sudanese Azande.

(B) *Comparative material about neighbouring peoples*

Only one other people has been thoroughly studied in this area: the Nzakara of the République Centrafricaine, under their Bandiya royal dynasty. Their French ethnographers regard them as a people quite distinct from the Azande, though with similar culture and institutions; Evans-Pritchard (1971, pp. 27–8) is less certain. In any case they exhibit interesting material for comparative studies, both as regards resemblances and differences.

DE DAMPIERRE E.: *Un ancien royaume Bandia du Haut Oubangui.* Paris: Plon, 1967.

Demography, history, political institutions.

RETEL-LAURENTIN A.: *Oracles et ordalies chez les Nzakara.* Paris: Mouton, 1969.

A well-documented study of the practice of oracle divination among a people in many respects similar to the Azande.

(C) *Theoretical and comparative material about witchcraft, sorcery and the interpretation of misfortune*

An abundant literature has sprung up on these topics, most of it based on theoretical considerations first made explicit in *Witchcraft, Oracles, and Magic among the Azande.* Only a few publications are indicated here, and the ethnographic material is confined to Africa. The student will find additional bibliography in the works cited.

DOUGLAS M.: Witch Beliefs in Central Africa. *Africa*, XXXVII, 1 (Jan. 1967), pp. 72–80.

DOUGLAS M. (ed.): *Witchcraft Confessions, and Accusations*, London: Tavistock, 1970. A.S.A. 9.

Papers presented at the 1968 Conference of the Association of Social Anthropologists of the Commonwealth, held at King's College, Cambridge.

EVANS-PRITCHARD E. E.: *Theories of Primitive Religion.* London: O.U.P. 1965.

Though not perhaps strictly germane to the subject of witchcraft, this book usefully reviews the main early theories concerning the nature of 'mystical' beliefs, ending with a chapter of Lévy-Bruhl.

FORTES M. and DIETERLEN G. (eds.): *African Systems of Thought.* London: O.U.P. For the International African Institute, 1965.

Papers and discussion presented at the Third International African Institute Seminar, held at the then University College of Rhodesia and Nyasaland in 1960. Includes several papers on witchcraft and sorcery beliefs.

HORTON R.: African Traditional Thought and Western Science. *Africa*, XXXVII (1967); I; No. 1 (January), pp. 50–71; II: No. 2 (April), pp. 155–87.

Excellent, wider-range discussion of African ideas of causation, bringing out both resemblances and differences with the ideas underlying Western scientific beliefs.

WARWICK M. G.: *Sorcery in its Social Setting*. Manchester University Press, 1965.

Reviews the sociological range of sorcery accusations among the Ceŵa of Central Africa.

MIDDLETON J. and WINTER E. H. (eds): *Witchcraft and Sorcery in East Africa*. London: Routledge & Kegan Paul, 1963.

Essays by various hands apply Evans-Pritchard's concepts to the beliefs and practices of a number of East and Central African peoples.

MITCHELL J. C.: *The Yao Village*. Manchester University Press, 1956.

Contains interesting hypothesis on the sociological function of witchcraft and sorcery accusations in a lineage-based society.

Index